Music Performance in Ancient Societies

Books by David Whitwell

The Sousa Oral History Project
The Art of Musical Conducting
The Longy Club: 1900–1917
La Téléphonie and the Universal Musical Language
Extraordinary Women
A Concise History of the Wind Band
Essays on the Modern Wind Band
Essays on Performance Practice
A New History of Wind Music
The College and University Band
The Early Symphonies of Mozart
Music of the French Revolution
Stories from the Podium

On Composers
Wagner on Bands
Berlioz on Bands
Chopin: A Self-Portrait
Liszt: A Self-Portrait
Schumann: A Self-Portrait in His Own Words
Mendelssohn: A Self-Portrait in His Own Words

On Education
Philosophic Foundations of Education
Foundations of Music Education
Music Education of the Future

Aesthetics of Music
Aesthetics of Music in Ancient Civilizations
Aesthetics of Music in the Middle Ages
Aesthetics of Music in the Early Renaissance
Aesthetics of Music in Sixteenth-Century Italy, France and Spain
Aesthetics of Music in Sixteenth-Century Germany, the Low Countries and England
Aesthetics of Baroque Music in Italy, Spain, the German-Speaking Countries and the Low Countries
Aesthetics of Baroque Music in France
Aesthetics of Baroque Music in England

The History and Literature of the Wind Band and Wind Ensemble Series

Volume 1 The Wind Band and Wind Ensemble Before 1500
Volume 2 The Renaissance Wind Band and Wind Ensemble
Volume 3 The Baroque Wind Band and Wind Ensemble
Volume 4 The Wind Band and Wind Ensemble of the Classical Period (1750–1800)
Volume 5 The Nineteenth-Century Wind Band and Wind Ensemble
Volume 6 A Catalog of Multi-Part Repertoire for Wind Instruments or for Undesignated Instrumentation before 1600
Volume 7 Baroque Wind Band and Wind Ensemble Repertoire
Volume 8 Classical Period Wind Band and Wind Ensemble Repertoire
Volume 9 Nineteenth-Century Wind Band and Wind Ensemble Repertoire
Volume 10 A Supplementary Catalog of Wind Band and Wind Ensemble Repertoire
Volume 11 A Catalog of Wind Repertoire before the Twentieth Century for One to Five Players
Volume 12 A Second Supplementary Catalog of Early Wind Band and Wind Ensemble Repertoire
Volume 13 Name Index, Volumes 1–12, The History and Literature of the Wind Band and Wind Ensemble

Ancient Voices

Ancient Views on Music and Religion
Ancient Views on the Natural World
Ancient Views on What Is Music
Contemporary Descriptions of Early Musicians
Early Views of Music and Ethics
Early Thoughts on Performance Practice
Music Performance in Ancient Societies

Renaissance Voices

Essays on Renaissance Philosophies of Music
Renaissance Men on Music

www.whitwellbooks.com

David Whitwell

Ancient Voices
Views on Music by Ancient and
Medieval Writers

Music Performance in Ancient Societies

Edited by Craig Dabelstein

WHITWELL PUBLISHING • AUSTIN, TEXAS, USA

Ancient Voices: Views on music by ancient and medieval writers
Music Performance in Ancient Societies
Dr. David Whitwell

WHITWELL PUBLISHING
AUSTIN, TX 78701
WWW.WHITWELLPUBLISHING.COM

Based on essays originally written between 2000 and 2005.
© 2013 by David Whitwell
All rights reserved. First edition 2013

Composed in Bembo Book.
Published in the United States of America.
All images used in this book are in the public domain except where otherwise noted.

ISBN-13: 9781936512782

Cover design by Daniel Ferla.

Contents

	Acknowledgement	ix
PART 1:	MUSIC PERFORMANCE IN ANCIENT SOCIEITIES	
1	On Secular Music in Ancient Societies	3
2	On Secular Festivals in Ancient Greece and Rome	17
3	On Ancient Concert Halls	33
4	On Memories of Ancient Concerts	39
5	On the Ancient Greek Chorus	55
6	On the Ancient Roman Chorus	69
7	On Music in Ancient Courts	75
8	Theater Music in the Ancient World	87
9	On Music Competition in the Ancient World	107
PART 2:	FUNCTIONAL MUSIC IN ANCIENT SOCIETIES	
10	Entertainment Music in the Ancient World	123
11	Banquet Music in the Ancient World	137
12	Wedding Music in the Ancient World	149
13	Funeral Music in the Ancient World	157
14	Military Music in the Ancient World	161
PART 3:	SECULAR MUSIC PERFORMANCE IN THE MIDDLE AGES	
15	Medieval Military Music	175
16	Music of the Medieval Courts	183
17	Medieval Civic Music	195
18	On the Medieval Chorus	203
	Bibliography	213
	About the Author	229
	About the Editor	231

Acknowledgments

I am indebted to my friend and colleague, Craig Dabelstein, for his help in preparing this book for publication.

David Whitwell
Austin, Texas

PART I
MUSIC PERFORMANCE IN ANCIENT SOCIETIES

On Secular Music in Ancient Societies

THE SURVIVING LITERATURE OF GREECE, Italy and the Old Testament offers us a comprehensive view of the uses of music in ancient societies. The fact that the kinds of employment of music, and the descriptions of the instruments themselves, already seem of an international character suggests that these traditions are much older than literature itself. In this book the reader will find a broad sampling of the music people heard other than in religious ceremonies, a subject covered in another book.

One occasion when ancient peoples of all classes could hear music must have been the great processions through the towns. Indeed, we know of an actual form of a processional song sung with the aulos in ancient Greece, called the 'Prosodia.' Plutarch claims that this same inventor-musician, Clonas, 'an elegiac and epic poet,' is also credited as beginning the tradition of singing with the aulos, although he adds that some writers give credit, instead, to Ardalus the Troezenian.[1]

A fragment by one of the best known of the ancient Greek lyric poets, Sappho (ca. 640–550 BC), mentions a procession with songs and instrumental music.

> A long parade sings its way from the sea.
> The auloi are keen and the drums tight.[2]

By the time of ancient Rome, processions had become civic affairs of great size, such as one in the time of Ptolemaeus Philadelphus (283–246 BC), for example, which included no fewer than six hundred singers and three hundred kithara players.[3]

We should also mention a reference in the Old Testament to bridal processions, 'in the streets of Jerusalem,' which the Lord threatens to eliminate 'for the land shall become a waste.'[4] An even more extraordinary account which mentions such a procession is found in the first Book of Maccabees, one of the books left out of the Old Testament used by the modern Christian Church.

> The bridegroom came forth, and his friends and brethren, to meet them with drums, and instruments of music ...,[5]

---

[1] Plutarch, 'Concerning Music.'

[2] Guy Davenport, *Archilochos, Sappho, Alkman* (Berkeley: University of California Press, 1980).

[3] Alfred Sendrey, in *Music in the Social and Religious Life of Antiquity* (Rutherford: Fairleigh Dickinson University Press, 1974), 411.

[4] Jeremiah 7:17, 34

[5] Jeremiah 7:34.

only to be slaughtered by Jonathan.

> Thus was the marriage turned into mourning, and the noise of their melody into lamentation.[6]

Another occasion for broad public viewing must have been the original Olympics. These included a category for trumpet playing, beginning with the 96th Olympiad of 396 BC. These seem to have been more physical contests, rather than musical, and perhaps the modern Olympic motto, *citius, altius, fortius* (faster, higher, stronger) describes them well. We know the names of a few of the famous winners and the information about them reads like a description of sumo wrestlers. We are told, for example, that Heradorus of Megara consumed, in a typical meal, six pints of wheat bread, twenty pounds of meat and six quarts of wine![7]

The broad public must have also heard music in the outdoor theater productions. For the reader's interest, we quote here the history of Roman theater by the famous early historian, Livy. He provides a remarkable and logical summary of the birth of art song and theater, which he dates from the middle of the fourth century BC, as part of ceremonies meant to reconcile the people to the gods following a plague.

> Amongst their other ceremonies intended to placate divine wrath, they are said to have introduced scenic entertainments, something quite novel for a warlike people whose only previous public spectacle had been that of the circus. These began only in a modest way, as most things do, and were in fact imported from abroad. Players were brought from Etruria to dance to the strains of the aulos without any singing or miming of song, and made quite graceful movements in the Etruscan style. Then the young Romans began to copy them, exchanging jokes at the same time in crude improvised verse, with gestures to fit the words. Thus the entertainment was adopted and became established by frequent repetition. The native actors were called *histriones*, because the Etruscan word for an actor is *ister*; they stopped bandying ribald improvised lines, like Fescennine verses, and began to perform *saturae* or medleys amplified with music, the singing properly arranged to fit the aulos and movement in harmony with it.
>
> Some years later, Livius first ventured to give up the *satura* and compose a play with a plot. Like everyone else at the time, he also acted in his own dramas; and the tale is told that when he lost his voice after repeated recalls, he was given permission to place a boy in front of the aulos player to sing the songs while he acted them himself, and did so with a good deal more vigor when not hampered by having to use his voice. From then on began the actors' practice of employing singers while they confined themselves to gesture and used their voices only for dialog. This style of performance began to detach the play from impromptu joking to raise a laugh, and drama gradually developed into an art.[8]

Some of the music heard in the theater, such as described above, must have been music familiar to the public. Indeed Suetonius describes an occasion in the first century AD when the audience joins in singing a song performed as part of a play.

---

6   1 Maccabees 9:39ff.

7   Athenaeus, *Deipnosophistae*, X, 414.

8   Livy, *A History of Rome*, VII, 2.

[The emperor] Galba's accession was not entirely popular, as became obvious at the first theatrical show he attended. This was an Atellan farce, in which occurred the well-known song, 'Here comes Onesimus, down from the farm ...' The whole audience took up the chorus with fervor, repeating that particular line over and over again.[9]

Suetonius also,[10] for the earlier period of Julius Caesar, mentions 'and the following popular song was sung everywhere:

> Caesar led the Gauls in triumph,
> Led them uphill, led them down,
> To the Senate House he took them,
> Once the glory of our town.
> 'Pull those breeches off,' he shouted,
> 'Change into a purple gown!'

This use of music by the civic authorities to 'reconcile the people to the gods following a plague' is an early example what we might call political music. A very similar report speaks of music and plays offered the general public by the Etruscan leaders, Tyrrhenus and Lydus, to appease public opinion during a famine.[11] We might also mention here that an early writer observed that the Etruscans 'knead bread, practice boxing, and flog their slaves to the accompaniment of the aulos.'[12]

Another example of specific functional use of music by the civic authorities was 'watch' music, something the reader will be more familiar with from the Middle Ages in Northern Europe. We see such a civic musician in the Old Testament where it is said he, 'blows the trumpet and warns the people.'[13] Another example, from the Augustian Age of ancient Rome (27 BC–14 AD) is found in a poem. Here the civic watchman-musician serves as a surrogate clock. This is a common feature in descriptions of medieval civic life, but in this reference we can see that the tradition is much older. In this instance it is the instrumental signal given to announce impending dawn, which in the Middle Ages became the type of music known as the *aubade*.

> Now the fourth horn sings coming light,
> & the stars glide down seaward,
> I will search for sleep,
> search for you in dreams ...[14]

---

9   Suetonius, *The Twelve Caesars* (New York: Penguin, 1989), 254.

10 Ibid., 48.

11 Cited by Sendrey, *Music in the Social and Religious Life of Antiquity*, 377.

12 Alcimus, quoted in Athenaeus, *Deipnosophistae*, XII, 518. The British Museum has a beautiful pot [B 64] from the sixth century BC which shows two boxing figures and a man playing the aulos. In a wall painting on the tomb of Golini I, Orvieto, one can see a fourth century BC aulos player playing in the kitchen while servants work.

13 Ezekiel 33:2ff. Jeremiah 20:16 speaks of 'an alarm at noon.'

14 Propertius, *The Poems*, IV, 4.

Another example of specific functional music to serve a civic purpose, and one we are again surprised to find had roots so early, was the use of musicians to participate in public punishments. We even find an example of this in the Old Testament:

> And every stroke of the staff of punishment which the Lord lays upon them will be to the sound of timbrels and lyres.[15]

Plutarch gives another illustration of this practice, adding the very interesting explanation that when it was necessary to punish one, the guilty one had to parade around the city singing a satire of his own composition which reflected on the folly of his crime.[16]

Evidence of private music making in the home is difficult to find, even though one would assume the practice was not rare. A typical reference in early literature is contained in a letter of Pliny the Younger (63–113 AD).

> At supper, if I have only my wife or a few friends with me, some author is read to us; and after supper we are entertained either with music or an interlude.[17]

Sendry mentions a fresco which depicts music in the home.

> In a fresco of Herculaneum (now in the Naples Museum) a concert is depicted in the home of a wealthy man. It shows a female aulos player … and accompanied by a kithara player. That it is a real house concert and not merely a private musical entertainment is evident from the large audience depicted in this fresco.[18]

Finally, it is our understanding that there are also Egyptian tomb paintings, some even dating from the end of the Old Kingdom, which show a similar tradition of music making by the family, in the home, although we have not seen them.

One species of civic music in ancient societies for which there is much documentation is what we call 'occupational music.' The range is broad and examples can be found in all lands. A stone slab from Assur, dating ca. 800 BC, includes actual songs for craftsmen, shepherds, and festival songs intended to encourage crops to grow.[19]

An Egyptian tomb painting shows a scene from ca. 1,365 BC of a group of women, accompanying a hunter, scaring birds in a forest by beating drums. From a relief in the tomb of Kahif at Giza we see an aulos player making music for the workers in the field.

While again no music survives, the texts for some songs of workers is extant, among them songs for shepherds, the thrasher, and the sedan-chair bearer. One of these, sung by thrashers to the oxen treading on the corn, goes,

---

[15] Isaiah 30:32.

[16] 'Customs of the Lacedaemonians.'

[17] Letter CVIII, to Fuscus.

[18] Sendrey, *Music in the Social and Religious Life of Antiquity*, 387ff.

[19] Ibid., 54.

> Thrash ye for yourselves,
> Thrash ye for yourselves, O oxen,
> Thrash ye for yourselves,
> Thrash ye for yourselves,
> The straw which is yours,
> The corn which is your master's.

We find only two such references to occupational music in the Old Testament. The first is a reference to the shepherds 'piping to flocks'[20] and the second is merely an inference, 'and in the vineyards no songs are sung.'[21]

There are many references to occupational music in ancient Greek literature. In the most ancient, that of the epic poets, two are interesting. Hesiod mentions workers in the vineyards working to music supplied by an aulos player.[22] Homer tells of two herdsmen (who were soon unfortunately killed!) playing their traditional panpipes.[23]

Since this kind of music must have been a common part of every day life, it is no surprise to find such comments in the plays of the great Greek dramatists. In Aristophanes' *The Acharnians*, for example, the character, Dicaeopolis, says,

> We hear nothing but the sound of whistles, of flutes [aulos] and fifes to encourage the workers.[24]

In *The Frogs*, the same playwright speaks of music used to provide the beat for rowers.

> You'll row all right; as soon as you fall to,
> You'll hear a first-rate tune that *makes* you row.[25]

The occupation of the shepherd is mentioned twice in the plays and both times, of course, he appears with his traditional panpipe instrument. First, in Sophocles', *Philoctetes*,

> Like the shepherd with his rural pipe
> And cheerful song …[26]

and in Euripides' *Electra*,

> How on a day Pan, the steward of husbandry, came breathing dulcet music on his jointed pipe …[27]

---

[20] Judges 5:16.

[21] Isaiah 16:10. Perhaps another inference is found in Isaiah 5, 'Let me sing for my beloved a love song concerning his vineyard.'

[22] Apostolos N. Athanassakis, *The Homeric Hymns* (Baltimore: Johns Hopkins University Press, 1976), 299.

[23] *The Iliad*, XVIII, 526.

[24] 555.

[25] 204.

[26] 239.

[27] 703.

Finally, the early Greek historian, Athenaeus, gives an extensive list of kinds of music employed by workers, with specific kinds of music sung by those grinding grain, working the loom, the wool-spinners and wool-carders, nurses, reapers, farmers, bath-tenders, shepherds, millers, etc.[28]

The shepherd, together with a number of other examples of occupational music, are mentioned in a poem by the Roman poet, Ovid (43 BC–17 AD).

> Remember I'm in exile,
>   writing not for fame but solace, to work
>   my woe into an artifact, that change in its nature
>   a kind of distraction better even than comfort.
>   So does the shackled slave, digging his ditch, sing
>   as he swings his pick: the task remains the same,
>   but he is free and becomes his song, as the bargee does
>   performing a mule's work on the cindered towpath,
>   tugging and singing. And galley oarsmen contrive to float
>   on the purl of the very flute that sets their rhythm.
>   The shepherd perched on his rock passes the boring hours
>   with this pipes of Pan. The household slave girl spins
>   singing along with her wheel. The art is anodyne,
>   as Achilles discovered, playing upon his lyre
>   after Briseis was gone. And Orpheus sang his dirges
>   to which rocks and rivers rang in chorus
>   after he'd lost Eurydice to Hades a second time.
>   The same mercy the Muse has shown to me,
>   penitent here in the Pontus. She has been my friend,
>   undeterred by Sintians, undismayed
>   by raging seas, howling winds, or the leaden skies
>   of this vast waste.[29]

To this list Virgil (70–19 BC) adds the music of the housewife.

> One farmer stays awake and splits up wood
> For torches with his knife. And all the while
> His wife relieves her lengthy task with song.[30]

Among the poems of the Roman lyric poets there are two references to farmer's singing. Tibullus (54–18 BC) has the farmer singing as he is walking.

> Diana would blush as she met him moving through fields and farms
>   like any mortal farmer, a stray lamb in his arms;
>   and when his music sounded from valleys he walked along,
>   the bellow of the oxen would break on his song.[31]

---

[28] Athenaeus, *Deipnosophistae*, XIV, 618.

[29] Ovid, *Tristia*, IV, 1.

[30] Virgil, *Georgics*, 291.

[31] Tibullus, *The Poems*, II, iii.

Propertius (50–16 BC) mentions farmer songs in connection with a strange, primitive and unnamed cult ceremony in which 'a pale virgin descends to lurid rites.'

> If she be chaste, she returns to her parents' arms
> & the farmers sing that it will be a prosperous year.[32]

In a second-century poem, 'Daphnis and Chloe,' we read of the shepherd's use of the three kinds of instruments still found today, the transverse flute, the panpipe and the reed-pipe.[33] This same poet describes the construction of the panpipe.

> Daphnis, after cutting some slender reeds, piercing them at the joints, and fastening them together with soft wax, would practice playing the panpipe until it was dark.[34]

We read here also of a more 'modern' panpipe construction, 'nine reeds fastened together with bronze instead of wax.'[35] This same poem also mentions the singing of seamen[36] and the agricultural songs of reapers, of a 'rustic nature.'[37]

Regarding occupational music, Quintilian (35–95 AD) points to the ability of music to lighten labor as one of its important characteristics.

> Indeed nature itself seems to have given music as a boon to men to lighten the strain of labor: even the rower in the galleys is cheered to effort by song. Nor is this function of music confined to cases where the efforts of a number are given union by the sound of some sweet voice that sets the tune, but even solitary workers find solace at their toil in artless song.[38]

One of the poems of Seneca mentions the use of music not only to make the work of loom workers more pleasant, but to make them work faster.

> Now plucking the strings, now happily passing the wool.
> He keeps them to work with his song, beguiling their labor,
> No praise too much for his lyre, his brotherly songs.
> Their hands spin more than they used; and the work he salutes
> Surpasses the lot of man.[39]

---

[32] Propertius, *The Poems*, IV, 8.

[33] Longus, 'Daphnis & Chloe,' trans. Paul Turner (London: Penguin Books, 1956), I, 4.

[34] Ibid., I, 10.

[35] Ibid., I, 15.

[36] Ibid., III, 21.

[37] Ibid., IV, 38.

[38] Quintilian, *The Education of an Orator*, I, x, 16.

[39] Seneca, *Apocolocyntosis* 4.2, 15. Tacitus, *Annals*, XIV, 52, says Seneca 'composed poetry more assiduously, [only] as soon as a passion for it had seized Nero.'

Among the ancient Roman poets there is a substantial amount of pastoral repertoire which deals with an almost nostalgic look back at the simple, if remote, life of rural people. We feel the sincerity of this dream-like reflection in the first-century poet, Cyrus:

> Would that my father had taught me to shepherd fleecy flocks, so that, sitting under the elms or piping under a rock, I might cheer my sorrows with music.[40]

In another retrospective idyll, the poet Bion (ca. 105 BC) asks one of these rustic musicians to take Love to school to teach him pastoral music.

> Before me mighty Cypris took her stand;
> And silly Eros hanging of his head
> She guided onward with a shapely hand,
> And in my dream these words the goddess said:
>
> 'Master of rustic song, take Love to school;
> Teach him the pastoral music.' So she spake,
> And so departed. I, like any fool,
> Taught him as though he cared these songs to make;
>
> How Pan the panpipes invented, fair and well;
> How by Athena first the aulos was made;
> How Hermes wrought the lyre from tortoise shell;
> How sweetly Apollo on the harp played.
>
> To all my words he gave but little heed;
> Instead the amorous tunes of light love
> He taught to me, his mother's every deed,
> And passion shared by men and gods above.
>
> All I have taught to Eros slipped my mind;
> But everything that Eros taught to me,
> Of lyric love I evermore shall find
> Reverberating in my memory.[41]

The musical instrument at the center of the pastoral literature was the panpipe. While nearly all this literature is mythical in nature, we believed it important to include it in the possibility that some reader may find a trace of ancient truth, or history, in them. Several poems deal with the invention of the panpipe, among them one by Ovid (43 BC–17 AD), in his *Metamorphoses*, which has the god Mercury tell the story of the instrument always associated with Pan and known to the ancients as the *Syrinx*.

> And Mercury came flying
> On winged sandals, wearing the magic helmet,
> Bearing the sleep-producing wand, and lighted
> On earth, and put aside the wings and helmet

---

40 *The Greek Anthology*, IX, 136.
41 Henry H. Chamberlin, *Last Flowers* (Cambridge: Harvard University Press, 1937), 50.

Keeping the wand. With this he plays the shepherd
Across the pathless countryside, a driver
Of goats, collected somewhere, and he goes
Playing a little tune on a pipe of reeds,
And this new sound is wonderful to Argus.
'Whoever you are, come here and sit beside me,'
He says, 'This rock is in the shade; the grass
Is nowhere any better.' And Mercury joins him,
Whiling the time away with conversation
And soothing little melodies, and Argus
Has a hard fight with drowsiness; his eyes,
Some of them, close, but some of them stay open.
To keep himself awake by listening,
He asks about the pipe of reeds, how was it
This new invention came about?
    The god
Began the story: 'On the mountain slopes
Of cool Arcadia, a woodland nymph
Once lived, with many suitors, and her name
Was Syrinx. More than once the satyrs chased her,
And so did other gods of field or woodland,
But always she escaped them, virgin always
As she aspired to be, one like Diana,
Like her in dress and calling, though her bow
Was made of horn, not gold, but even so,
She might, sometimes, be taken for the goddess.
Pan, with a wreath of pine around his temples,
Once saw her coming back from Mount Lycaeus,
And said—' and Mercury broke off the story
And then went on to tell what Pan had told her,
How she said *No*, and fled, through pathless places,
Until she came to Ladon's river, flowing
Peaceful along the sandy banks, whose water
Halted her flight, and she implored her sisters
To change her form, and so, when Pan had caught her
And thought he held a nymph, it was only reeds
That yielded in his arms, and while he sighed,
The soft air stirring in the reeds made also
The echo of a sigh. Touched by this marvel,
Charmed by the sweetness of the tone, he murmured
This much I have! and took the reeds, and bound them
With wax, a tall and shorter one together,
And called them Syrinx, still.[42]

---

[42] Ovid, *Metamorphoses*, I, 671ff.

The most important poem which is extant from the first three centuries of the Christian Era is the 'Daphnis and Chloe' by Longus. This is a poem entirely in the spirit of the ancient poems of Greece and it is therefore no surprise to find the principal musical instrument is the rural panpipe. We read here, once again, the myth of the invention of this instrument.

> This panpipe of ours was originally not a musical instrument but a beautiful girl who had a lovely voice. She used to graze goats and play with the Nymphs and sing—just as she does now. While she was grazing and playing and singing, Pan came up to her and tried to talk her into doing what he wanted by promising to make all her she-goats have twins. But she laughed at his love and said she didn't want a lover who was neither one thing nor the other—neither a goat nor a man. So Pan started chasing her with the intention of offering her violence. She started running away, and when she was tired of running away from Pan and his violence she hid among some reeds and disappeared into a marsh. Pan angrily cut the reeds—but he didn't find the girl. So profiting by this experience he fastened some of the reeds together with wax—using reeds of unequal length since even Love had proved unequal to them—and thus invented the musical instrument.[43]

We learn in this same poem of a shepherd who broke his panpipes, because 'they charmed my cows,' but didn't have an effect on the girl.[44] And in another passage we find an erotic employment of the panpipe.

> And he used to give her lessons in playing the panpipe, and the moment she had begun to blow into it he would snatch it away and run his own lips over the reeds. This was supposed to show her where she had gone wrong, but actually it was a good excuse to kiss Chloe *via* the pipe.[45]

We also read of the shepherd's goats being charmed by the panpipes[46] and, indeed, during a description of a 'concert' for fifty-two goats, it would appear that the animals had been trained to respond to a number of specific goat tunes.

> Daphnis made [the goats] sit down like the audience at a theater, and standing under the oak he produced his panpipe from his knapsack and began by blowing on it softly—and the goats raised their heads and stood still. Then he blew the grazing tune—and the goats put their heads down and started to graze. He played another tune, very sweet and clear—and they all lay down. He also piped a shrill sort of tune—and they ran away into the wood as though a wolf was approaching.[47] A little later he sounded a recall—and they came running out of the wood and collected round his feet. You would not have found even human slaves being so obedient to their master's orders.[48]

A poem by Tibullus (55–19 BC) confirms, by its description, that the panpipe known by the ancient Romans was shaped as the one we know today.

---

43 Longus, 'Daphnis and Chloe,' II, 34.

44 Ibid., II, 7.

45 Ibid., I, 24.

46 Ibid., I, 22.

47 In another place, II, 26, Longus mentions that the panpipe could be as frightening as a trumpet.

48 Ibid., IV, 15. In Book I, 29, we also read of cows being trained to respond to the panpipe.

> A milk-drenched Pan stood in the ash-tree's shelter,
> and Pales graced a rough-carved wooden shrine;
> a pipe, its thin voice stilled, from a branch might dangle,
> the shepherd's pledge for favors a god would show—
> with its range of reeds from the largest to the lesser,
> joined by way in an ever-dwindling row.[49]

We might also mention Ovid's introduction of the giant, Cyclops, as playing a great panpipes consisting of one hundred pipes. The sound it made was proportionally large:

> All the mountains felt the sound of his rustic pipings; the waves felt it too.[50]

There are a few extant poems which offer glimpses of insight into the technique of playing the panpipe. In the second-century poem, 'Daphnis and Chloe,' there is a description of a rural flute player who not only describes technique a bit but also a reference which implies separate repertoire for various animals.

> So Philetas roused himself, and got up and sat on a chair. First of all he tested the reeds to see if they were in proper condition for playing. Then, having made sure that the air could pass freely through them, he began to play with a loud and powerful tone. You would have thought you were listening to several flutes playing in unison, so great a volume of sound did he produce. Then with a gradual *diminuendo* he changed to a sweeter tune, and showing his skill in every form of pastoral melody he played music that would be suitable for a herd of cattle, music that would be appropriate for goats, and music that would appeal to a flock of sheep. The tune for sheep was sweet, the tune for cattle was loud, and the tune for goats was shrill. In short, with that one pipe he imitated all the pipes in the world.[51]

Another contemporary description of panpipe technique appears in the dress of a metaphor for God's work in a work by Paulinus, Bishop of Nola (354–431 AD).

> Think of a man playing a harp, plucking strings producing different sounds by striking them with the one quill. Or again the man who rubs his lips by blowing on woven reeds; he plays one tune from his one mouth, but there is more than one note, and he marshals the different sounds with controlling skill. He governs the shrill-echoing apertures with his breathing and his nimble fingers, closing and opening them, and thus a tuneful wind with haste of airy movement successively passes and returns along the hollow of the reed, so that the wind instrument becomes alive and issues forth a tune unbroken. This is how God works. He is the Musician who controls that universal-sounding harmony which he exercises through all the physical world.[52]

---

[49] Tibullus, *The Poems*, II, v.

[50] Ovid, *Metamorphoses*, XIII, 780.

[51] Longus, 'Daphnis and Chloe,' II, 35.

[52] Ibid., Poem 27, 72.

One of the most frequent themes of the ancient Roman pastoral literature is musical contests. The setting is always rural, there is always a judge and nearly always a winner and sometimes they contain rare nuggets of important musical or instrumental information. Theocritus (ca. 315–264 BC) has written three of these descriptions of musical contests. In 'Idyll Nr. VIII' we find the shepherd, Menalcas, challenging the cattle boy, Daphnis, to a musical duel. Daphnis responds,

> Herdsman of wool-bearing sheep and performer on Panpipes, Menalcas,
> You'll never beat me, although you may injure yourself in the effort.

They both agree to the contest and Daphnis proposes they wager an animal from each of their care. Menalcas says he cannot wager a lamb, but instead will put at risk his instrument.

> I have a pipe that I fashioned myself,[53] it's a fine one of nine notes,
> Fastened together with white wax, even on top and on bottom,
> That I am willing to wager, but what is my father's I will not.

Daphnis responds that he, too, has a panpipe he made himself, although he injured himself in the process!

> Well, as it happens, I too have a beautiful panpipe of nine notes
> Fastened together with white wax, even on top and on bottom,
> Which I confected the day before yesterday—and even yet my
> Finger is terribly sore from a reed I was splitting which cut me.

Every contest must have an adjudicator and in this case they saw a goatherd whom they enlisted for this purpose. The contest itself consisted of each poet-musician singing alternate stanzas. They began as follows.

> Both of the children then shouted; the goatherd approached when he heard them.
> Since they were willing to sing, he was equally willing to judge them.
> First, and according to lot, the soprano Menalcas began to
> Sing, and then Daphnis in answer resumed the responsive bucolic
> Song. It is thus that Menalcas as senior began the performance.
>
> *Menalcas*
>
> Valleys and rivers, divine generation, if ever Menalcas
> Played on his panpipe or sang melody pleasing to you,
> Pasture my flocks with sincere generosity; if ever Daphnis
> Come to this place with his cows, may he obtain nothing less.

---

[53] A relatively easy instrument to construct, Bion, in an extant fragment, tells a young person not to depend on expert craftsmen for everything, but to make the instrument himself.

> Dear child, it is not right that you should bring
> Orders to specialists for everything;
> Nor give away what work you have to do.
> Make your own pipes—an easy task for you.

Daphnis
>Fountains and pasturage, sweet vegetation, if ever your Daphnis
>Made any music that might rival the nightingales', please
>Fatten his flock; if Menalcas bring anything, may he discover
>Everything generous here, grazing and welcome as well.

The contest continued in this manner until the end, when the judge decided on Daphnis.

>Daphnis, your diction is pleasant, your voice is extremely attractive.
>I'd sooner listen to you making music than sup upon honey.
>Take as your guerdon the panpipe, for you are the victor in singing.

Daphnis, we are told, celebrated by 'clapping his hands and jumping for joy, as a fawn might have jumped all around its own mother.' But, since one of the problems of all musical contests is that there must of necessity be a 'loser,' Menalcas, 'smoldered and worried his heart with his sorrow.'

One of the more frequently told myths of Greece involved a musical contest between Pan with his panpipes and Apollo with his lyre. Apollo, as a god of music, of course wins in every retelling. But in the view of some this is a metaphor for the growing sophistication of ancient music, developing from rural music (panpipes) to art music of the lyric poets, who were often accompanied by the lyre.

The adjudicator, in this version by Ovid, is a mountain god, Tmolus. Midas is the famous king who came to hate gold by having too much of it.

>But Midas, hating wealth, haunted the woods and fields, worshiping Pan, who has his dwelling in the mountain caves. But stupid his wits still remained, and his foolish mind was destined again as once before to harm its master. For Tmolus, looking far out upon the sea, stands stiff and high, with steep sides extending with one slope to Sardis, and on the other reaches down to little Hypaepae. There, while Pan was singing his songs to the soft nymphs and playing airy interludes upon his reeds close joined with wax, he dared speak slightingly of Apollo's music in comparison with his own, and came into an ill-matched contest with Tmolus as the judge.
>
>The old judge took his seat upon his own mountain-top, and shook his ears free from the trees. His dark locks were encircled by an oak-wreath only, and acorns hung around his hollow temples. He, looking at the shepherd-god, exclaimed: 'There is no delay on the judge's part.' Then Pan made music on his rustic pipes, and with his rude notes quite charmed King Midas, for he chanced to hear the strains. After Pan was done, venerable Tmolus turned his face toward Phoebus [Apollo]; and his forest turned with his face. Phoebus' golden head was wreathed with laurel of Parnasus, and his mantle, dipped in Tyrian dye, swept the ground. His lyre, inlaid with gems and Indian ivory, he held in his left hand, while his right hand held the plectrum. His very pose was that of an artist. Then with trained thumb he plucked the strings and, charmed by those sweet strains, Tmolus ordered Pan to lower his reeds before the lyre.[54]

---

[54] 'Daphnis and Chloe,' XI, 147ff.

Longus also has left a nice retelling of one of these mythical contests and in his version the cows are the judges.

> Once upon a time there was a beautiful girl who used to graze a great many cows in a wood. Now she was also very musical, and in her day cows enjoyed music. So she was able to control them without either hitting them with a staff or pricking them with a goad. She would simply sit down under a pine, and after crowning herself with pine-twigs would sing the story of Pan and the Pine, and the cows would stay close enough to hear her voice. A boy who grazed cows not far away, and who was also good-looking and musical, challenged her to a singing contest. Because of his sex, he was able to produce more volume than she could, and yet because he was only a boy, his voice had a very sweet tone. So he charmed away her eight best cows and enticed them into his own herd. The girl was annoyed at the damage done to her herd, and at being beaten at singing, and she prayed to the gods to turn her into a bird before she arrived home. The gods granted her prayer and turned her into this mountain bird, which is as musical as she was. And even now she still goes on singing, telling her sad story, and saying that she's looking for her missing cows.[55]

A final story told in this poem is a very lovely, if filled with gore, myth concerning the origin of the echo.

> There are several kinds of Nymphs. There are the Nymphs of the Ash, the Nymphs of the Oak, and the Nymphs of the Meadow. All of them are beautiful and all are musical. Well, one of these Nymphs had a daughter called Echo, who was mortal because her father was mortal, but beautiful because her mother was beautiful. She was brought up by the Nymphs and taught by the Muses to play the panpipe and the aulos, to perform upon the lute and the lyre, and to sing songs of every kind. So when she grew up and reached the flower of girlhood, she used to dance with the Nymphs and sing with the Muses. But she avoided all males, whether human or divine, for she loved virginity. Pan grew angry with the girl, partly because he envied her gift for music, and partly because he had failed to enjoy her beauty. So he sent the shepherds and goatherds mad, and they like dogs or wolves tore her to pieces and scattered her limbs about the whole earth—or rather scattered her hymns, for she still went on singing. As a favor to the Nymphs, the Earth concealed these singing limbs and preserved their music; and they, by order of the Muses, are still able to sing and imitate sounds of every kind, just as the girl did once—sounds made by gods, by men, by musical instruments, and by wild beasts. They even imitate Pan when he plays his panpipe, and he, when he hears them, jumps up and goes rushing over the mountains in pursuit. But the only love that he pursues is Knowledge—he would love to know who his invisible imitator is.[56]

---

[55] Ibid., I, 37. In Book I, 9, we read of birds teaching Nymphs to sing.

[56] Ibid., III, 23.

On the Secular Festivals of Ancient Greece and Rome

As we know from the scenes found in the prehistoric cave paintings, cult festivals with music and dance are among the oldest of man's activities. Even in the somber Old Testament a few hints of secular festivals can be found, such as,

> He will exult over you with loud singing as on a day of festival.[1]

And since the ancient Greek festivals were mostly held in the Spring, perhaps the following from the Old Testament is also a reference to such festivals.

> The flowers appear on the earth,
> the time of singing has come.[2]

Due to the absence of literature it is difficult to know much about the celebration scenes one finds among the ancient tomb paintings of Egypt. A much later account by Pliny the Elder (23–79 AD) does mention a festival in Egypt which includes a chorus of boys singing praises of the ox.[3]

From ancient Greece, most of the extant ancient lyric poetry is from the festivals held in connection with the Olympiad. These particular festivals began in 582 BC when the traditional Python festival in honor of Apollo was transformed into one given in the third year of each Olympiad. Two years later the Isthmian festival of Poseidon, in celebration of Spring, began to be held in the second and fourth year of each Olympiad. During these years the festival of the Neiman Zeus was also held. The fourth of these festivals, and the most ancient, dating from 776 BC, was the Olympian festival of Zeus, held each four years according to a lunar cycle.[4] The honoring of the athletes through the music of these lyric poets seems to have preceded somewhat the tradition of their being honored by statues, the earliest sculptors being documented from about 520 BC.[5]

One can assume the most ancient non-religious festivals of Greece were held in celebration of various rural themes. Our accounts of these are much more modern, such as Strabo's reference to the wine festival:

---

[1] Zephaniah 3:18

[2] Song of Solomon 2:12.

[3] *Natural History*, VIII, lxx, 185.

[4] Additional information on these festivals can be found in Richard C. Jebb, *Bacchylides* (Hildesheim, Georg Olms Verlagsbuchhandlung, 1967), 35, and Gregory Nagy, *Pindar's Homer* (Baltimore: Johns Hopkins University Press, 1982), 116ff.

[5] Jebb, Ibid., 37.

> Bacchic revelry with the high-pitched, sweet-sounding breath of Phrygian auloi ... and joined it to the choral dances of the Trieterides, in whom Dionysus takes delight.[6]

Athenaeus describes some of the music heard during the much more elaborate three-day celebration by the Spartans of their 'Feast of Hycinthia,'

> Boys with tunics girded high play the lyre or sing to aulos accompaniment while they run the entire gamut of the strings with the plectrum; they sing the praises of the god in anapaestic rhythm and in a high pitch. Others march through the theater mounted on gaily adorned horses; full choirs of young men singing some of their national songs, and dancers mingling among them go through the figures in the ancient style, accompanied by the aulos and the voice of the singers.[7]

A production of this scale probably represents the kind of festival objected to by the famous orator, Demosthenes (385–322 BC). He regrets the large amount of money spent on choral performances 'which affords those of us who are in the theater gratification for a fraction of a day.'[8] In another place he reports that the annual Spring Festivals were still being given on a lavish scale.

> Larger sums are lavished upon them than upon any one of your [military] expeditions [and] they are celebrated with bigger crowds and greater splendor than anything else of the kind in the world.[9]

Our main interest with respect to the discussion of festivals in ancient Greece has to be the extensive discussion by Socrates (470–399 BC), as reported by Plato in his *Laws*.[10] The ideal festivals which Socrates describes are not the rural sort, but very highly organized civic ones. He begins with a survey of a variety of possible festivals appealing to a variety of tastes. A single festival which incorporated many such tastes could not result in a single winner, for reasons he explains. He also begins his discussion of the qualifications of the judges and explains why, under no circumstances, can you leave the judging to the audience.

> AN ATHENIAN STRANGER. Our young men break forth into dancing and singing, and we who are their elders deem that we are fulfilling our part in life when we look on at them. Having lost our agility, we delight in their sports and merry-making, because we love to think of our former selves; and gladly institute contests for those who are able to awaken in us the memory of our youth.
> CLEINIAS. Very true.
> AN ATHENIAN STRANGER. Is it altogether unmeaning to say, as the common people do about festivals, that he should be adjudged the wisest of men, and the winner of the palm, who gives us the greatest amount of pleasure and mirth? For on such occasions, and when mirth is the order of the day, ought not he to be honored most, and, as I was saying, bear the palm, who gives most mirth to the greatest number? Now is this a true way of speaking or of acting?

---

6   *The Geography of Strabo*, trans. Horace L. Jones (Cambridge: Harvard University Press, 1960), X.3.11 and 13.
7   Athenaeus, *Deipnosophistae*, IV, 139.
8   'Against Leptines,' trans. J. H. Vince (Cambridge: Harvard University Press, 1954), 509.
9   'The First Philippic,' Ibid., 89.
10 Beginning 657d.

CLEINIAS. Possibly.

AN ATHENIAN STRANGER. But, my dear friend, let us distinguish between different cases, and not be hasty in forming a judgment: One way of considering the question will be to imagine a festival at which there are entertainments of all sorts, including gymnastic, musical, and equestrian contests: the citizens assembled; prizes are offered, and proclamation is made that anyone who likes may enter the lists, and that he is to bear the palm who gives the most pleasure to the spectators—there is to be no regulation about the manner how; but he who is most successful in giving pleasure is to be crowned victor, and deemed to be the pleasantest of the candidates. What is likely to be the result of such a proclamation?

CLEINIAS. In what respect?

AN ATHENIAN STRANGER. There would be various exhibitions: one man, like Homer, will exhibit a rhapsody, another a performance on the lute; one will have a tragedy, and another a comedy. Nor would there be anything astonishing in someone imagining that he could gain the prize by exhibiting a puppet-show. Suppose these competitors to meet, and not these only, but innumerable others as well—can you tell me who ought to be the victor?

CLEINIAS. I do not see how anyone can answer you, or pretend to know, unless he has heard with his own ears the several competitors; the question is absurd.

AN ATHENIAN STRANGER. Well, then, if neither of you can answer, shall I answer this question which you deem so absurd?

CLEINIAS. By all means.

AN ATHENIAN STRANGER. If very small children are to determine the question, they will decide for the puppet-show.

CLEINIAS. Of course.

AN ATHENIAN STRANGER. The older children will be advocates of comedy; educated women, and young men, and people in general, will favor tragedy.

CLEINIAS. Very likely.

AN ATHENIAN STRANGER. And I believe that we old men would have the greatest pleasure in hearing a rhapsodist recite well the Iliad and Odyssey, or one of the Hesiodic poems, and would award an overwhelming victory to him. But, who would really be the victor?—that is the question.

CLEINIAS. Yes.

AN ATHENIAN STRANGER. Clearly you and I will have to declare that those whom we old men adjudge victors ought to win; for our ways are far and away better than any which at present exist anywhere in the world.

CLEINIAS. Certainly.

AN ATHENIAN STRANGER. Thus far I too should agree with the many, that the excellence of music is to be measured by pleasure. But the pleasure must not be that of chance persons; the fairest music is that which delights the best and best educated, and especially that which delights the one man who is preeminent in virtue and education. And therefore the judges must be men of character, for they will require wisdom and have still greater need of courage; the true judge must not draw his inspiration from the theatre, nor ought he to be unnerved by the clamor of the many and his own incapacity; nor again, knowing the truth, ought he through cowardice and unmanliness carelessly to deliver a lying judgment, with the very same lips which have just appealed to the gods before he judged. He is sitting not as the disciple of the theatre, but, in his proper place, as their instructor, and he ought to be the enemy of all pandering to the pleasure of the spectators. The ancient and common custom of Hellas was the reverse of that which now prevails in Italy and Sicily, where the judgment is left to the body of spectators, who determine the victor by show of hands. But this custom has been the destruction of the poets themselves; for they are now in the habit of composing with a view to please the bad taste of their judges, and the result is that the spectators instruct themselves;—and also it has been the ruin of the theater; they ought to be receiving a higher pleasure, but now by their own act the opposite result follows.[11]

Plato continues his discussion of judges, emphasizing their necessary character and wisdom and the wide span of knowledge they must have. As for the latter he mentions a few of the kinds of errors in the performance of music that the adjudicator must understand and recognize. This includes considerations of choral performance as well.

> AN ATHENIAN STRANGER. Surely then he who would judge correctly must know what each composition is; for if he does not know what is the character and meaning of the piece, and what it actually represents, he will never discern whether the intention is correct or mistaken.
> CLEINIAS. Certainly not.
> AN ATHENIAN STRANGER. And will he who does not know what is true be able to distinguish what is good and bad? My statement is not very clear; but perhaps you will understand me better if I put the matter in another way.
> CLEINIAS. How?
> AN ATHENIAN STRANGER. There are ten thousand likenesses which we apprehend by sight?
> CLEINIAS. Yes.
> AN ATHENIAN STRANGER. Even in their case, can he who does not know what the exact object is which is imitated, ever know whether the resemblance is truthfully executed? I mean, for example, whether a statue has the proportions of a body, and the true situation of the parts; what those proportions are, and how the parts fit into one another in due order; also their colors and conformations, or whether this is all confused in the execution: do you think that anyone can know about this, who does not know what the animal is which has been imitated?
> CLEINIAS. Impossible.
> AN ATHENIAN STRANGER. But even if we know that the thing pictured or sculptured is a man, who has received at the hand of the artist all his proper parts and colors and shapes, shall we therefore know at once, and of necessity, whether the work is beautiful or in any respect deficient in beauty?
> CLEINIAS. If this were true, stranger, we should almost all of us be judges of beauty.
> AN ATHENIAN STRANGER. Very true; and may we not say that in everything imitated, whether in drawing, music, or any other art, he who is to be a competent judge must possess three things;—he must know, in the first place, of what the imitation is; secondly, he must know that it is true; and thirdly, that it has been well executed in words and melodies and rhythms?
> CLEINIAS. Certainly.
> AN ATHENIAN STRANGER. Then let us not faint in discussing the peculiar difficulty of music. Music is more celebrated than any other kind of imitation, and therefore requires the greatest care of them all. For if a man makes a mistake here, he may do himself the greatest injury by welcoming evil dispositions, and the mistake may be very difficult to discern, because the poets are artists very inferior in character to the Muses themselves, who would never fall into the monstrous error of assigning to the words of men the intonation and song of women; nor after combining the melodies with the gestures of freemen would they add on the rhythms of slaves and men of the baser sort; nor, beginning with the rhythms and gestures of freemen, would they assign to them a melody or words which are of an opposite character; nor would they mix up the voices and sounds of animals and of men and instruments, and every other sort of noise, as if they were all one. But human poets are fond of introducing this sort of inconsistent mixture, and so make themselves ridiculous in the eyes of those

---

[11] *Laws*, 657d.

who, as Orpheus says, 'are ripe for true pleasure.' The experienced see all this confusion, and yet the poets go on and make still further havoc by separating the rhythm and the figure of the dance from the melody, setting bare words to meter, and also separating the melody and the rhythm from the words, using the lyre or the aulos alone. For when there are no words, it is very difficult to recognize the meaning of the harmony and rhythm, or to see that any worthy object is imitated by them. And we must acknowledge that all this sort of thing, which aims at only swiftness and smoothness and a brutish noise, and uses the aulos and the lyre not as the mere accompaniments of the dance and song, is exceedingly coarse and tasteless. The use of either instrument, when unaccompanied, leads to every sort of irregularity and trickery. This is all rational enough. But we are considering now how our choristers, who are from thirty to fifty years of age, and may be over fifty, are not to use the Muses, but how they are to use them. And the considerations which we have urged seem to show that these fifty-years-old choristers who are to sing, will require something better than a mere choral training. For they need have a quick perception and knowledge of harmonies and rhythms; otherwise, how can they ever know whether a melody would be rightly sung to the Dorian mode, or the rhythm which the poet has assigned to it?

CLEINIAS. Clearly they cannot.

AN ATHENIAN STRANGER. The many are ridiculous in imagining that they know what is proper harmony and rhythm, and what is not, when they can only be made by force to sing to the aulos and step in rhythm; it never occurs to them that they are ignorant of what they are doing. Now every melody is right when it has suitable harmony and rhythm, and wrong when unsuitable.

CLEINIAS. That is most certain.

AN ATHENIAN STRANGER. But can a man who does not know a thing, as we were saying, know that the thing is right?

CLEINIAS. Impossible.

AN ATHENIAN STRANGER. Then as now, as would appear, we are making the discovery that our newly appointed choristers, whom we hereby invite and, although they are their own masters, compel to sing, must be educated to such an extent as to be able to follow the steps of the rhythm and the notes of the song, that they may review the harmonies and rhythms, and be able to select what are suitable for men of their age and character to sing; and may sing them, and have innocent pleasure from their own performance, and also lead younger men to receive the virtues of character with the welcome which they deserve. Having such training, they will attain a more accurate knowledge than falls to the lot of the common people, or even of the poets themselves. For the poet need not know the third point, viz. whether the imitation is good or not, though he can hardly help knowing the laws of melody and rhythm. But our critics must know all the three, that they may choose the best, and that which is nearest to the best; for otherwise they will never be able to charm the souls of young men in the way of virtue.[12]

Now Socrates turns to presenting his ideas on how an ideal festival might be organized. He is nevertheless pragmatic, discussing such things as the inclusion of variety to keep the spectators interested and the employment of wine to break down the hesitation of the old men so they too will participate.

---

[12] Ibid., 668c.

AN ATHENIAN STRANGER. Our choruses shall sing to the young and tender souls of children, reciting in their strains all the noble thoughts of which we have already spoken ... the sum of them shall be, that the life which is by the Gods deemed to be the happiest is also the best;—thus we shall both affirm what is most certainly true, and the mind of our young disciples will be more likely to receive these words of ours than any others which we might address to them.

CLEINIAS. I assent to what you say.

AN ATHENIAN STRANGER. First will enter in their natural order the choir of the Muses, composed of children, which is to sing lustily the heaven-taught lay to the whole city. Next will follow the choir of young men under the age of thirty, who will call upon the God Paean to testify to the truth of their words, and will pray him to be gracious to the youth and to turn their hearts. Thirdly, the choir of elder men, who are from thirty to sixty years of age, will also sing. There remain those who are too old to sing and they will tell stories, illustrating the same virtues, as with the voice of an oracle.

CLEINIAS. Who are those who compose the third choir, stranger? I do not clearly understand what you mean to say about them.

AN ATHENIAN STRANGER. And yet almost all that I have been saying has been said with a view to them.

CLEINIAS. Will you try to be a little plainer?

AN ATHENIAN STRANGER. I was speaking at the commencement of our discourse, as you will remember, of the fiery nature of young creatures: I said that they were unable to keep quiet either in limb or voice, and they they called out and jumped about in a disorderly manner; and that no other animal attained to any perception of order in these two things, but man only. Now the order of motion is called rhythm, and the order of voice, in which high and low are duly mingled, is called harmony; and both together are termed choric song. And I said that the Gods had pity on us, and gave us Apollo and the Muses to be our playfellows and leaders in the dance; and Dionysus, as I dare say that you will remember, was the third.

CLEINIAS. I quite remember.

AN ATHENIAN STRANGER. Thus far have I spoken of the chorus of Apollo and the Muses; the third and remaining chorus must be called that of Dionysus.

CLEINIAS. How is that? There is something strange, at any rate on first hearing, in a Dionysiac chorus of old men, if you really mean that those who are above thirty, and may be fifty, or from fifty to sixty years of age, are to dance in his honor.

AN ATHENIAN STRANGER. Very true; and therefore it must be shown that there is good reason for the proposal.

CLEINIAS. Certainly.

AN ATHENIAN STRANGER. Are we agreed thus far?

CLEINIAS. About what?

AN ATHENIAN STRANGER. That every man and boy, slave and free, both sexes, and the whole city, should never cease charming themselves with the strains of which we have spoken; and that there should be every sort of change and variation of them in order to take away the effect of sameness, so that the singers may always receive pleasure from their hymns, and may never weary of them?

CLEINIAS. Everyone will agree.

AN ATHENIAN STRANGER. Where, then, will that best part of our city which, by reason of age and intelligence, has the greatest influence, sing these fairest of strains in such a way as to do most good. Shall we be so foolish as to neglect this regulation, which may have a decisive effect in making the songs most beautiful and useful?

CLEINIAS. But, says the argument, we cannot neglect it.

AN ATHENIAN STRANGER. Then how can we carry out our purpose with decorum? Will this be the way?

CLEINIAS. What?

An Athenian Stranger. When a man is advancing in years, he is afraid and reluctant to sing;—he has no pleasure in his own performances; and if compulsion is used, he will be more and more ashamed, the older and more discreet he grows;—is not this true?

Cleinias. Certainly.

An Athenian Stranger. Well, and will he not be yet more ashamed if he has to stand up and sing in the theater to a mixed audience?—and if moreover when he is required to do so, like the other choirs who contend for prizes, and have been trained under a singing master, he is pinched and hungry, he will certainly have a feeling of shame and discomfort which will make him very unwilling to perform.

Cleinias. No doubt.

An Athenian Stranger. How, then, shall we reassure him, and get him to sing? Shall we begin by enacting that boys shall not taste wine at all until they are eighteen years of age; we will tell them that fire must not be poured upon fire, whether in the body or in the soul, until they begin to go to work—this is a precaution which has to be taken against the excitableness of youth;—afterwards they may taste wine in moderation up to the age of thirty, but while a man is young he should abstain altogether from intoxication and from excess of wine; when, at length, he has reached forty years, after dinner at a public mess, he may invite not only the other gods, but Dionysus above all, to the mystery and festivity of the elder men, making use of the wine which he has given men to lighten the sourness of old age; that in age we may renew our youth, and forget our sorrows; and also in order that the nature of the soul, like iron melted in the fire, may become softer and so more impressible. In the first place, will not anyone who is thus mellowed be more ready and less ashamed to sing,—I do not say before a large audience, but before a moderate company; nor yet among strangers, but among his familiars, and, as we have often said, to chant, and to enchant?

Cleinias. He will be far more ready.

An Athenian Stranger. There will be no impropriety in our using such a method of persuading them to join with us in song.

Cleinias. None at all.

An Athenian Stranger. And what strain will they sing, and what muse will they hymn? The music should clearly be of some kind suitable to them.

Cleinias. Certainly.

An Athenian Stranger. And what strain is suitable for heroes? Shall they sing a choric strain?

Cleinias. Truly, stranger, we of Crete and Lacedaemon know no strain other than that which we have learnt and been accustomed to sing in our chorus.

An Athenian Stranger. I dare say; for you have never acquired the knowledge of the most beautiful kind of song, in your military way of life, which is modeled after the camp, and is not like that of dwellers in cities; and you have your young men herding and feeding together like young colts. No one takes his own individual colt and drags him away from his fellows against his will, raging and foaming, and gives him a groom to attend to him alone, and soothes and rubs him down, and sees that nothing is missing in his education which will make him not only a good soldier, but also a governor of a state and of cities. Such a one, as we said at first, would be a greater warrior than he of whom Tyrtaeus sings; and he would honor courage everywhere, but always as the fourth, and not the first part of virtue, either in individuals or states.

The poets of ancient Rome have left us a very broad view of their secular festivals and the music one might have heard in them. Many of these poems recall ancient rituals based on the cycles of agriculture, consisting of prayers to the gods for planting and harvesting. In Virgil's (70–19 BC) *Georgics*, a celebration of country life, we find the suggestion that these rural celebrations still continued among the peasants. He praises the land, olives, berries, and of course grapes.

> All hail, Saturnian Land, our honored Mother!
> For thee I broach these themes of ancient art
> And dare disclose the sacred springs of verse,
> Singing Hesiod's song through Roman towns …
> This soil is good for grapes, and for the juice
> We offer to the gods in cups of gold,
> As the sleek Etruscan plays his ivory pipe
> Beside the alters where we sacrifice
> With steaming entrails loaded high on plates.[13]

This rather rare mention of an 'ivory pipe' is, we judge, a reference to the aulos, which underwent numerous changes in ancient Rome. This instrument is mentioned again in a poem by Propertius (50–16 BC), a contemporary of Virgil. Here we have a festival dedicated to Apollo and it has the earmarks of a cult-religious celebration.

> Let there be silence, that the sacrifice fall well;
> the heifer is struck down now
> before the fire of my alter,
> with properly inspired consecration.
> Let the Roman wreath contend with the ivy berries of Philetas,
> let the jar splash me with Cyrenian water, give me
> mild myrrh & alluring olibanum,
> & wind the wool disk 3 times round the fire;
> pour the ablution down,
> let the ivory flute ring a tuneful song here by the new alter;
> Deception, depart; let evil float in another air.
> Smooth the singer's new path with laurel.
> Muse, we will bring anew
> the story of Palatine Apollo's shrine; Calliope,
> the work deserves your favor.
> I sing these songs in Caesar's name,
> & while Caesar is sung, I pray even Zeus be silent.[14]

Seneca (4 BC–65 AD) makes reference to more 'sophisticated' festivals, and does not look with favor on those which call for animal sacrifices.

> At the altars you'll make no fast and nimble
> Step, as the curved horn booms in stirring rhythms,
> Honoring barbaric temples with ancient dance.
> O form of death more grim than death itself.

---

[13] Virgil, *Georgics*, II, 174ff.

[14] Propertius, *Poems*, IV, 6.

Our walls will see a sight more piteous
Than great Hector's murder.[15]

Another festival associated with agricultural life was the festival in honor of Ceres, the goddess of agriculture. Again, we especially find the genuine rural picture of this celebration in Virgil's *Georgics*.

> See that your country folk adore the goddess:
> For her let milk and honey flow, and wine,
> And lead the sacrificial victims round the crops
> Three times, to bring good fortune, let a chorus
> Follow the procession, singing hymns
> To Ceres, ask her blessing on their homes;
> Let no one lay his sickle to the grain
> Until, with festive oak wreath on his brow,
> He honors Ceres' name in dance and song.[16]

Ovid (43 BC–17 AD) in a poem celebrating the festival of Ceres mentions a great variety of wildlife and crops. We quote the beginning and ending of this poem.

> Now comes the yearly festival of Ceres,
> And my love lies alone in bed at night.
> O golden goddess, garlanded with wheatears,
> Why must your feast inhibit our delight? …
>
> A feast day calls for song and wine and women;
> Those are the gifts the lordly gods should gain.[17]

Ovid provides more musical information relative to the festival of Juno, who was the mythical daughter to Saturn and wife to Jupiter. The poem is also interesting for the details of the procession and the references to its Greek origin.

> The orchard town Camillus took, Falerii,
> Was my wife's birthplace; we came there one day.
> Juno's chaste feast was being celebrated,
> With games and sacrifice the place was gay;
> A feast well worth the visit, though the journey
> Is difficult, a steep and toilsome way.
>
> A grove stands there, ancient and dense and gloomy;
> The place must be a god's, one can be sure.
> The faithful offer incense at an alter,
> An artless alter reared in days of yore.

---

[15] Seneca, *Trojan Women*, III, 780.

[16] Virgil, *Georgics*, I, 344ff.

[17] Ovid, *Amores*, III, 10.

Here, to the sound of auloi and solemn chanting,
The long procession passes every year
Through streets bedecked, with white Falerian heifers
From their own fields, while all the people cheer ...

Young men and shy girls go before the goddess,
Their trailing vestments sweeping the wide street.
The girls' hair is adorned with gold and jewels,
And stately gowns half-hide their gilded feet.

High on their heads they bear the holy vessels,
White-robed according to the old Greek rites.
The crowd is hushed as June in her golden
Procession comes behind her acolytes.

The form of the procession comes from Argos.
On Agamemnon's death Halaesus fled
The murder and his father's wealth and wandered
Long over land and sea as exile led ...[18]

Calpurnius Siculus (third century AD) has also left a poem referring to the rural celebration of Faunus, god of field, flock and tillage, which includes the following lines.

Corydon
Wherever you call I follow, Ornytus; for my
Leuce by saying No to embraces and night's joys
Allows me access to horned Faunus' holy place.
Out with your reeds then and the songs you've stored away.
My panpipe will not fail you, which resourceful Ladon
Lately put together for me of seasoned reed.[19]

Tibullus has also composed a hymn to these ancient country celebrations which would develop in time into the more familiar festival of Bacchus. The reference to the curved pipes means the panpipe, the larger versions of which were made to curve around the player in order to speed up the process of finding the individual tube to blow.

This is a hymn for them alone, the country gods ...
The sweaty farmer, tired of plowing in hot noon sun,
 would rest in the shade and make words that fitted a tune,
 or, his belly full, would finger the stop on an oaten pipe
 to win the ear of a god whose image he tried to shape.
It was such a man, great Bacchus, his face vermilion-dyed,
 who beat a rustic measure for rustic feet to tread ...
Come, bless our country feast, most holy—but leave behind
 your arrows; as for your torch, do not let it fire this land!
Hark when we sing you songs to pray for our flocks' increase

---

[18] Ibid., III, 13.

[19] *Eclogue I*, 13.

> and beg you blessings, aloud, for them; in a whisper, for us—
> or aloud for ourselves as well; no man will be able to hear
> in that noisy crowd where the curved pipes play a Phrygian air.[20]

Tibullus, in another poem, suggests that the origin of festivals centering on the celebration of grapes and wine was not in Greece but in Egypt with the worship of Osiris.

> The river-god and Osiris—theirs is a double altar
> where hymns to the ox make a wild barbaric strain.
> It was Osiris in truth who was the plow's inventor,
> turning the virgin earth with an iron share;
> he was the first to drop seed in the furrow, and gather
> from nameless trees the fruit they began to bear.
> He learned, and taught to men, how the vine is tied to the pole,
> and how the hook must lop the leaves from the vine.
> Out of the grape clusters that heavy feet had trampled,
> none before him had ever brought forth wine—
> and men, having drunk it, were moved to what would someday be singing,
> once they had smoothed it out, and to rustic dance ...
> Osiris, yours was never a province of misfortune;
> in your land love and mirth and song are law.[21]

The festival of Bacchus is the one which these Roman lyric poets focused on most frequently in their poetry, no doubt due to the romantic associations of love and wine. Virgil's his references to Bacchus are still framed in the older rural setting.

> Now, Bacchus, I shall sing
> Of you and of the woodlands, of the shrubs,
> Of the slowly growing olive's progeny.
> Approach, Lenaean Father: here all things
> Are brimming with your gifts, for you the farmlands
> Flourish, large with Autumn's trailing vine,
> The vintage foams in swelling vats.
>
>   ......
>
> To Bacchus at each shrine, and tragedies
> Of old came on the stage, and Theseus' sons
> Gave prizes out for local wit in towns
> And crossroads, and they danced in mellow fields
> On well-oiled goatskins, tipsy; and Ausonians,
> A people sent from Troy to settle here,
> Sport their disheveled verses, crude guffaws,
> And don their grisly masks of hollow cork
> And sing to you, O Bacchus, happy songs,
> And hang your swaying mask on lofty pines,

---

[20] Tibullus, *Poems*, II, i.

[21] Ibid., I, vii.

> That as the god inclines his noble head
> In each direction, ripening vineyards grow,
> Hollow vales and deepened glades fill out.
> We shall, then, sing, in native songs, our debut
> Of praise to Bacchus, bring on cakes and plates
> And lead in by the horns a sacred goat
> To stand beside the altar, and proceed
> To roast his fertile flesh on hazel spits.[22]

Some of these poetic descriptions emphasize the mythical aspect of Bacchus as in this example by Horace (65–8 BC).

> I did see Bacchus, high in a mountain glen—
> Believe me, future hearers!—instructing nymphs
> In dithyrambs of his, and goat-foot
> Satyrs all cocking their ears to learn them.
>
> Evoe! My mind still reels from that recent dread
> And in my heart, by Bacchus possessed, I fell
> Wild joy. Evoe. But spare me, Liber,
> Spare me the goad of your painful thyrsus!
>
> I feel a strong compulsion to sing in praise
> Of dancers dancing tirelessly, fountain jets
> Of wine and milk, abounding brooks, and
> Honey that drips from the hollow reed-wands;
>
> I feel compelled to sing of the blessed spouse
> Immortalized in stars,[23] and the palace hall
> Of Pentheus toppled to a ruin,
> And of the Thracian Lycurgus's downfall.[24]

In the only other description of the Bacchus celebration by Horace there is the suggestion that wine lifts the quality of his work to new heights of creativity.

> Whither, Bacchus, am I swept on,
> Thus possessed by your wine? What are the groves and caves
> This new self of mine must behold?
> By what grottoes shall I, singing, be heard to tell
> Caesar's eminent glory set
> High in Jupiter's hall up with eternal stars?
> Fame conferring, unheard of song,
> New and strange, shall be mine ...
> Nothing common shall I compose,

---

[22] Virgil, *Georgics*, 1ff and 380ff.

[23] Bacchus/Dionysus found Ariadne on the island of Naxos and upon marrying her turned her bridal crown into a constellation [see also the finale of *Ariadne auf Naxos* by Strauss].

[24] Horace, *Odes*, II, 19.

Nothing destined to die. Sweet is the peril braved,
Wine-press god, in your footsteps' wake,
While with tendrils of green grapevine my brows are crowned.

A poem by Propertius (50–2 BC) also touches on the changes in man (and women) caused by wine.

Wine imperils glamour & gets the better of manhood,
 & a woman in the heat of wine may forget her proper lover.
But ... I speak too harshly, I don't mean it.
Bacchus cannot change you, so imbibe and look lovely;
 the fruit of the vine becomes you.
Your trailing laurel hangs over the cup
 & my music lifts your soft voice.[25]

In the following generations references to the festival of Bacchus by Ovid (43 BC–17 AD) maintain the rural character but now seem to take on a more sinister character centering on the secret rites of women. Ovid gives us a vivid picture of the ritual dress of the women in this episode when Procne invades this female ceremony looking for her sister.

It was the time when all the Thracian mothers
Held festival for Bacchus, and the night
Shared in their secrets; Rhodope by night
Resounded as the brazen cymbals clashed,
And so by night the queen went from her palace,
Armed for the rites of Bacchus, in all the dress
Of frenzy, trailing vines for head-dress, deer-skin
Down the left side, and a spear over the shoulder.
So, swiftly through the forest with attendants,
Comrades and worshipers in throngs, and driven
By madness, terrible in rage and anger,
Went Procne, went the Bacchanal, and came
At last to the hidden cottage, came there shrieking,
'Hail, Bacchus!' broke the doors in, found her sister,
Dressed her like all the others, hid her face
With ivy-leaves, and dragged her out, and brought her
Home to the palace.[26]

In another references to this festival, Ovid speaks of this hidden ritual continuing for ten days[27] and with a larger participation of musical instruments.

When suddenly timbrels sounded, unseen timbrels
Harsh in their ears, flutes piped, and horns resounded

---

[25] Propertius, *Poems*, II, 33.

[26] Ovid, *Metamorphoses*, VI, 585ff.

[27] Ibid., XI, 96.

> And cymbals clashed, and all the air was full
> Of the smell of myrrh and saffron, and their weaving
> Turned green, and the hanging cloth resembled ivy
> Or grape-vines, and the threads were tendrils clinging.[28]

Virgil's references to the Bacchus festival in his epic poem, *The Aeneid*, no longer describes of a simple rural celebration, but now something wild and out of control.

> When she saw Latinus was stubborn, and deep in her heart
> The maddening serpent's venom had sunk and spread over
> Her entire body, then truly the unhappy woman,
> Disturbed by gigantic horrors, ran out of control
> And raged through the wide-sprawling city …
> Even into the forests she ran, pretending the power
> Of Bacchus controlled her, to commit a greater sin
> Against heaven, a greater madness. She hid her daughter
> In leafy mountains, to snatch her from Trojan marriage
> And delay its torches. 'Euhoe, Bacchus,' she shouted,
> Calling you worthy alone of the girl; for you
> She was seizing the pliant thyrsus, for you she was dancing
> In chorus, growing a sacred hair-lock for you.
> The news of Amata flew far. Each mother was fired
> With madness to seek in like fashion new homes. They deserted
> Their old ones and, baring their necks and hair to the winds,
> The filled the air with a tremulous howling. Their dresses
> Were animal-skins, they carried vine-stalks as spears.
> In their midst Amata brandished a flaming pine-torch
> And chanted a wedding-song for her daughter.
> ……
>
> But you are not sluggish
> For love and its nightly combat nor when the curved flute
> Announces the Bacchic dance. Be eager for feasts
> And wine on a groaning board—this is love, this you long for.[29]

It is in the satirical poetry of Juvenal (late first–early second century) that we find some hint of the extent of the decay of these festivals. First, in what seems to be a reference to the Bacchus festival, he writes,

> Of the Good Goddess, when aulos -music stirs the loins,
> And frenzied women, devotees of Priapus,
> Sweep along in procession, howling, tossing their hair,
> Wine-flown, horn-crazy, burning with the desire
> To get themselves laid.[30]

---

[28] Ibid., IV, 391ff.

[29] Virgil, *The Aeneid*, VII, 375ff and XI, 736ff.

[30] *Satire VI*, 313.

And in the same poem, a reference to another important festival, that of Cybele.

> And now in comes a procession,
> Devotees of the frenzied Bellona, and Cybele, Mother of Gods,
> Led by a giant eunuch, the idol of his lesser
> Companions in obscenity. Long ago, with a shard,
> He sliced off his genitals: now neither the howling rabble
> Nor the kettledrums can outshriek him.[31]

We are inclined to believe there is some long lost link between the reference above 'He sliced off his genitals' and a practice among some priests which is mentioned in a curious poem of the second century. Here there is mentioned the *thalame,* which were receptacles in which the organs of castrated priests were deposited.

Otherwise, this poem describes the celebration of Cybele, with the sound of a drum which we may presume was used in these ceremonies. It must have been some drum for it frightened away a lion (in Italy!)

> Chaste Atys, the gelded servant of Cybele, in frenzy giving his wild hair to the wind, wished to reach Sardis from Phrygian Pessinus; but when the dark of evening fell upon him in his course, the fierce fervor of his bitter ecstasy was cooled and he took shelter in a descending cavern, turning aside a little from the road. But a lion came swiftly on his track, a terror to brave men and to him an inexpressible woe. He stood speechless from fear and by some divine inspiration put his hand to his sounding tambor. At its deep roar the most courageous of beasts ran off quicker than a deer, unable to bear the deep note in its ears, and he cried out, 'Great Mother, by the banks of the Sangarias I dedicate to thee, in thanks for my life, my holy *thalame* and this noisy instrument that caused the lion to flee.'[32]

These large festivals became a particular target of the Church, for by the second century AD, these festivals were still popular. Aside from the behavior described above, they were a rival of the Church in the competition for the attention of the public. Justin Martyr (100–165 AD) admonished the faithful Greeks of this time as follows:

> I have come to detest even your public festivals. There you indulge in immoderate banquets, listen to finely polished aulos which incite you to lustful actions, and you needlessly submit to elaborate anointing with perfume, while your heads are crowned with flowers. With such an accumulation of evil practices you determine your reverence. With such practices are your minds filled, while your intemperance excites you to Bacchic frenzy, whence you indulge in your customary unholy and mad intercourse. I would like to make another observation. Why do you, who are Greeks, become angered when your son, in imitation of Jupiter, turns against you and robs you of your own wife? … Why do you complain of your wife's infidelity, yet honor Venus with temples? If these events had been narrated by others, they could be presumed to have been false and slanderous accusations, but even now your own poets extol them in song, and your histories blatantly describe them.[33]

---

[31] Ibid., 512.

[32] Dioscorides, in *The Greek Anthology*, VI, 220.

[33] 'Discourse to the Greeks,' trans. in *Saint Justin Martyr* (New York: Christian Heritage), IV.

Not withstanding the Church's condemnation, by the fourth century these festivals were still popular and so it is no surprise to find the Church attacking in even stronger language. St. John Chrysostom (347–407 AD) finds a passage in the Old Testament where, he warns us, God did not like festivals of any kind—not to mention instrumental music!

> But do their festivals have something solemn and great about them? They have shown that these, too, are impure. Listen to the prophets; rather, listen to God, and with how strong a statement he turns his back on them. 'I have found your festivals hateful, I have thrust them away from myself.'[34]
>
> Does God hate their festivals and do you share in them? He did not say this or that festival, but all of them together. Do you wish to see that God hates the worship paid with percussion, lyres, harps and other instruments? God said: 'Take away from me the sound of your songs and I will not hear the canticle of your harps.'[35] If God said: 'Take them away from me,' do you run to listen to their trumpets?[36]

---

[34] Amos 5:21. The *Revised Standard Version* reads, 'I hate, I despise your feasts, and I take no delight in your solemn assemblies.'

[35] Amos 5:23. The *Revised Standard Version* reads, 'Take away from me the noise of your songs; to the melody of your harps I will not listen.'

[36] St. John Chrysostom, 'Discourses Against Judaizing Christians,' trans. Paul W. Harkins (Washington, D.C.: The Catholic University of American Press), 26.

On Ancient Concert Halls

IN THIS BOOK WHEN WE SPEAK OF PERFORMANCE or concerts we speak only of art music, not popular music. Our knowledge of art music in the ancient world, as with other subjects is limited to a relatively small amount of surviving literature. The Christian Church not only destroyed a great deal of the ancient literature, but during the one thousand years or so which we generally call the 'dark ages,' they controlled the production of books. As a result, their hostile stand against theaters of all kinds prevented the writing of books which might have given us irreplaceable information about musical production in large halls. In addition, the Church discouraged the early Christians from being fond of art of all kinds, with the argument that God gets the credit, not the artist.

The above explains, in part, why the reader has probably not heard about concert halls in the ancient world, an important topic for the inference of lost information about concerts which must have taken place in them. Nevertheless, there are a few references to concert halls in the ancient world and, in view of the above, they serve to make one regret even more the lost accounts of early concerts.

In ancient Greece, in addition to great public festivals, there were apparently more intimate performance sites called *symposia*, where, much like concerts today, the works of the older lyric poets were sung as 'classics.'[1] Indeed, we find evidence of this tradition for the performance of such older repertoire in *The Clouds* by Aristophanes, produced in 423 BC.

> *Strepsiades.*
> … I bade him
> Take up his lyre and give me the good song
> Of old Simonides, 'The ram was shorn.'[2]

These symposia offered the opportunity as well for both solo and choral performance by non-professionals.[3] The interior civic space where these choruses performed was called the *Khoros* and the conductor was called, *khoregos*.[4] We have invaluable documentation for one of these ancient Greek concert halls in the study of Pericles by Plutarch (46–119 AD). He reports the Athenian statesman, Pericles (495–429 BC) was responsible for constructing as a special hall for the performance of music.

---

[1] Geoffrey S. Conway, *The Odes of Pindar* (London: Dent, 1972), 113.
[2] *Clouds*, 1355–1358.
[3] Gregory Nagy, *Pindar's Homer* (Baltimore: Johns Hopkins University Press, 1982), 342.
[4] Ibid., 399, 345.

> The Odeum, or concert hall, which in its interior was full of seats and ranges of pillars, and outside had its roof made to slope and descend from one single point at the top, was constructed, we are told, in imitation of the king of Persia's Pavilion.[5]

There are several other early references to this very concert hall. First, it is probably the concert hall in Athens which is mentioned by Aristotle.[6] Second, we are told that the Stoic philosopher, Chrysippus (282–206 BC) died just after taking his students to a performance at the Odeum. Finally, this concert hall is mentioned in a fragment of dialogue of a lost play by Sotion. Athenaeus preserves the following dialog from the play, *The Teacher of Profligacy*, which reflects a general decay in the quality of art music during the ancient Greek period and in which a character says,

> What's this nonsense you are talking, forever babbling, this way and that, of the Lyceum, the Academy, and the Odeum gates—mere sophists' rubbish? There's no good in them. Let's drink, and drink our fill, Let's have a good time while we may still keep the life in our bodies. Whoop it up, Men! There's nothing nicer than the belly.[7]

While some writers assign to the Romans a 'rather uncouth and vulgar' taste in music,[8] the distinguished Roman specialist, Alfred Sendrey, writes of a vigorous musical practice throughout all levels of Roman society. The reader will notice he mentions concert halls.

> In general, contemporary records indicate that the tendency to practice music prevailed, at least in public life, in gigantic proportions. Music teachers and music schools furnished dilettantes *en masse*; it belonged to the *bon ton* of every bourgeois family to give their daughters instruction in lyre playing. Rich people employed multitudes of slaves, who made music day and night, to the despair of their neighbors. At banquets there was no longer any conversation, since music drowned out every attempt at it. A veritable invasion of virtuosi of all kinds flooded the theaters and concert halls, bringing with them all their idiosyncrasies, vanities, and intrigues.[9]

Moreover, we have some specific extant information on early Roman concert halls, specifically the ones built by various emperors. Domitian (81–96 AD) installed the Capitolinian Plays in 86 AD, which included musical contests, including 'those of the lyre players, between choruses

---

5   *Lives*, 'Pericles.'

6   *Metaphysica*, 1010b.12.

7   Athenaeus, *Deipnosophistae*, VIII, 336. In Book VIII, 339, Athenaeus also mentions a profligate harp player.

8   Paul Henry Lang, *Music in Western Civilization* (New York, 1941), 31.

9   Alfred Sendrey, *Music in the Social and Religious Life of Antiquity* (Rutherford: Fairleigh Dickinson University Press, 1974), 379.

of such players and in the lyre alone, without singing.'¹⁰ For these he built a large concert hall on the Campus Martius. Trajan (52–117 AD) also constructed a music hall on the Forum and Maximian (286–305 AD) also built a concert hall.¹¹

The poet Juvenal (55–127 AD) mentions concert halls in passing in a discussion of the deaf.

> How can the deaf appreciate music? The standard
> Of the performance eludes them: a top-line soloist,
> Massed choirs in their golden robes, all mean less than nothing.
> What does it matter to them where they sit in the concert hall
> When a wind band blowing its guts out is barely audible?¹²

Sendrey summarizes the wide spectrum of Art Music during the Empire Period of Rome.

> In the pantomimes, *symphoniae* were inserted, which meant that a choir sang and danced to the accompaniment of a group of instrumentalists. Sometimes an actor sang a solo aria; in other instances a professional singer sang the lyrics, while a mime interpreted the words with gestures and appropriate dances. The pantomimes were frequently presented in gigantic proportions; sometimes 3000 singers and 3000 dancers participated in them.
>
> There were numerous instrumental virtuosi, and the number of good average artists was legion. From all parts of the empire musicians converged on Rome, attracted by the gold of the capital of the world. The huge number of musically educated slaves made it possible for their masters to maintain large choirs and orchestras with almost no expense ...¹³
>
> Many wealthy persons had their own permanent music groups. Some had their especially gifted musicians sent to famous teachers for further education.
>
> Professional virtuosi were in great demand and undertook extended concert tours in all parts of the empire. They were highly paid and often became the idols of the audiences. For several of them monuments or statues were erected ... Women of high society adored them and paid large sums for their love; other female admirers fought for the possession of a plectrum the admired artist had used in the concerts; others offered sacrifices to the gods to insure victory for their favorites in the festival contests ... The victors in poetical and musical contests received the coveted oak wreath from the hands of the emperor ...
>
> The honoraria of some of the traveling virtuosi bordered on the fantastic ...
>
> In a fresco of Herculaneum (now in the Naples Museum) a concert is depicted in the home of a wealthy man. It shows a female aulos player ... and accompanied by a kithara player. That it is a real house concert and not merely a private musical entertainment is evident from the large audience depicted in this fresco.¹⁴

---

10 Ibid., VIII, iv.

11 The poet, Calpurnius Siculus, in *Eclogue VII*, 23ff., gives an interesting first-hand description of one of the outdoor theaters.

12 Juvenal, *Satire X*, 211.

13 Painting, however, was reserved for those of noble birth. Pliny the Elder says slaves were forbidden to be instructed in it and he observes that in both painting and sculpture there were no famous works executed by a slave.

14 Sendrey, *Music in the Social and Religious Life of Antiquity*, 387ff.

The mention, above, of three thousand singers, while extraordinary, only reflects the great number of practicing musicians in Rome. Such numbers seem confirmed in 284 AD in the works of Carinus, who presented a series of plays in which he used, among other things, one hundred trumpeters and one hundred horn players.[15] And Seneca (4 BC–65 AD), referring to a large indoor 'auditorium,' mentioned that sometimes it seemed that there were more people on the stage than there used to be in the audience.[16]

> Do you not see how many voices there are in a chorus? Yet out of the many only one voice results. In that chorus one voice takes the tenor, another the bass, another the baritone. There are women, too, as well as men, and the aulos is mingled with them. In that chorus the voices of the individual singers are hidden; what we hear is the voices of all together. To be sure, I am referring to the chorus which the old-time philosophers knew; in our present day exhibitions we have a larger number of singers than there used to be spectators in the theaters of old. All the aisles are filled with rows of singers; brass instruments surround the auditorium; the stage resounds with auloi and instruments of every description; and yet from the discordant sounds a harmony is produced.

As mentioned above, because of the Church's control over the production and survival of written materials during the Medieval Period there is a general lack of knowledge of all performing arts during that time. But we can, in some cases, imagine that performances continued nevertheless. We have no accounts of drama during the dark ages, but as there was a robust tradition before, and a 'reappearance' which can be documented in the late Middle Ages. It seems impossible that some form of drama accompanying civic festivals did not occur throughout the interval of years in between. The same can be said for the highly organized and elaborate horse shows before audiences, which are documented before and after the dark ages. All this is to say that perhaps concerts and concert halls existed throughout the Medieval Period and were simply not accounted for in extant records. Otherwise, how can one explain the existence of such intriguing accounts as the one by Cavalieri during the early seventeenth century in Italy. With respect to hearing the singer, Cavalieri recommends performance in a hall seating no more than one thousand! Otherwise,

> If it is presented in very large halls it is not possible to hear all the words; and the singer would have to force his voice, which lessens the emotional effect; also, so much music with the words not being audible becomes tiresome.[17]

As we live in a time when the construction of concert halls is tending toward downsizing, it may be difficult for the reader to imagine early concert halls so vast that Cavalieri would recommend circumstances which would require a hall seating *only* one thousand. But such a vast hall seems to have existed as we see by another reference from the seventeenth century which

---

[15] Ibid., 412.

[16] *Epistolae*, 84.10.

[17] Emilio de' Cavalieri, *Rappresentazione di Anima, et di Corpo*, Preface, quoted in Carol MacClintock, *Readings in the History of Music in Performance* (Bloomington: Indiana University Press, 1979), 184.

refers to a theater holding ten thousand persons! Monteverdi wrote the music for an allegorical tournament celebrating the marriage of Duke Odoardo Farnese of Parma and Margherita de' Medici of Florence in 1628. An eyewitness to the occasion reports,

> As soon as Signora Settimia, representing Aurora, began to sing, all conversation among the spectators ceased ... All ears were so consoled by the sweetness of the voice and the divine quality of the song, that among the 10,000 people seated in the theater, there was no one...who did not grow tender at the trills, sigh at the sighs, become ecstatic at the ornaments, and who was not stupefied and transfixed by the miraculous beauty and song of an heavenly siren.[18]

If that is not surprising, then consider a letter by Franz Liszt, written in 1872, when he refers to a hall to be built in Boston.

> An American came to invite me, at all costs, to the Boston Festival, to take place in June, and for which a colossal hall is being built with a capacity of nearly 100,000 people.[19]

---

[18] Quoted in Tim Carter, 'The North Italian Courts,' in *The Early Baroque Era* (Englewood Cliffs: Prentice Hall, 1994), 39.

[19] Letter to Olga von Meyendorff, Oct. 10, 1872.

Memories of Ancient Concerts

THE PRESENT ESSAY will present some first-hand observations on ancient concerts as well as giving the reader a general view of the venues in which such concerts took place. One of the earliest venues for serious art music was the banquet, the banquet itself being a basic aristocratic activity in a world which still had a relatively limited choice in entertainment. At a banquet for a guest noble, let us imagine, there would be a great variety of functional music, including music to announce that the meal is ready, even music to wash hands, music to accompany dishes from the kitchen and of course dinner music. But a very frequently described moment came at the end of the eating and drinking, always designated in the literature by a phrase, 'when the tables were cleared.' It was this window, after the meal when the guests *listened* to a performance of music. Judging by the many accounts, it may have been brief, but it was a real concert in the modern sense of the word (minus tuxes, programs and turning off the lights). There are accounts which tell of fine musicians refusing to play if there were continued eating or drinking. We can gain a glimpse of how seriously the musicians took this performance by a passage in *The Clouds*, a play by the great playwright of ancient Greece, Aristophanes (448–385 BC) Here we have the host of the banquet, Strepsiades, and the musician, Phidippides. The musician has refused to play because some were still drinking and his refusal led to a fight with the host. The Leader of the Chorus asks, 'But how did the fight begin?

Strepsiades
I will tell you what was the start of the quarrel. At the end of the meal, as you know, I bade him take his lyre and sing me the song of Simonides, which tells of the fleece of the ram. He replied bluntly, that it was stupid, while drinking, to play the lyre and sing, like a woman when she is grinding barley.

Phidippides
Why, by rights I ought to have beaten and kicked you the very moment you told me to sing![1]

From this same period of ancient Greece there is a wonderful passage in *Ion*, the book by Plato (427–347 BC) which relates a conversation between Socrates and Ion, a rhapsodist. The ancient rhapsodist was a performing artist who in a kind of sung-speech presented memorized epic poetry before an audience. It was these people who preserved Homer until such time that the invention of the written form of the Greek language permitted it to be written down. In this passage, Socrates gives a brilliant analogy to explain how in music there is a direct communication from composer through the performer to the listener.

---

[1] *The Clouds*, 1352ff.

SOCRATES. The gift which you possess of [singing] excellently about Homer is not an art, but, an inspiration; there is a divinity moving you, like that contained in the stone which Euripides calls a magnet, but which is commonly known as the stone of Heraclea. This stone not only attracts iron rings, but also imparts to them a similar power of attracting other rings; and sometimes you may see a number of pieces of iron and rings suspended from one another so as to form quite a long chain: and all of them derive their power of suspension from the original stone. In like manner the Muse first of all inspires men herself; and from these inspired persons a chain of other persons is suspended, who take the inspiration.

......

Do you know that the spectator is the last of the rings which, as I am saying, receive the power of the original magnet from one another? Yourself, and the actor, are intermediate links, and the poet himself is the first of them.[2]

There must have been specialists who sang solo art songs in very ancient times. By the ancient Roman period there are accounts, such as the following by the poet, Juvenal (55–127 AD), which suggest that these performers were nothing less than virtuosi in the modern sense. Here Juvenal wonders why the gods have nothing better to do than to listen to prayers for such singers by aristocratic women.

> If your wife has musical tastes, she'll make the professional
> Singers come when she wants. She's forever handling
> Their instruments, her bejeweled fingers sparkle
> Over the lute, she practices scales with a vibrant
> Quill once employed by some famous virtuoso—
> It's her mascot, her solace, she lavishes kisses on it,
> The darling object.
> A certain patrician lady,
> Whose lutanist protege was due to compete in
> The Capitoline Festival, made inquiry of Janus
> And Vesta, offering wine and cakes, to find out
> If her Pollio could aspire to the oakwreath prize
> For the best performance. What more could she have done
> If her husband was sick, or the doctors shaking their heads
> Over her little son? She stood there at the altar,
> Thinking it no disgrace to veil her face on behalf of
> This cheapjack twangler. She made the proper responses
> In traditional form, and blanched as the lamb was opened.
> Tell me now, I beg you, most ancient of deities,
> Old Father Janus, do such requests get answered? There must
> Be time to spare in heaven. From what I can see
> You Gods have nothing on hand to keep you occupied.[3]

---

[2] *Ion*, 533d, 535e.

[3] Juvenal, *Satire VI*, 379ff.

In another place, Juvenal mentions the singer who performs recitals describing and praising the exploits of former leaders and generals. Much of this was in the form of sung poetry. Juvenal starts to tell the story of one of the earlier Greek battles, and then says, 'O well, the rest,'

> You can hear when some tame poet, sweating under the armpits,
> Gives his wine-flown recital.[4]

With the arrival of the Renaissance in Italy we find the old functional civic musicians now beginning to perform art music. The impetus for this change was a growing sense of civic pride, not unrelated to Humanism, which led to the construction in many towns of the city hall, the *Palazzo Comunale*, beginning in the late thirteenth century. The *palazzo* stood in competition with the cathedral, in pride if not in scope, representing the affairs of the present life rather than those of the next life. It was this civic pride which was the object of such compositions in praise of cities such as Johannes Ciconia's (1335–1411) 'O Padua' and 'Venetia mundi splendor.'

It is also in the fourteenth century, following the same sense of civic identity, that many Italian towns began to expand their corps of civic musicians to now include more specialized ensembles. By the end of this century Florence maintained not only the usual ceremonial trumpet players, but now a shawm ensemble [*pifferi*] and an ensemble called *trombadori*. Several towns already had uniforms for their civic bands by the fourteenth century and the musicians of Pisa were subject to a fine if they forgot to wear their official red gowns.

In addition to appearances of the usual functional nature (the Bologna *pifferi* had to perform each day at three o'clock in the morning!) there are hints which suggest concerts, meaning music to be listened to. A fourteenth-century contract for the Perugia civic band, for example, after listing various functional duties, says that they must also play in the civic square 'for the joy of the public.' A similar document of Florence dated July 1333 mentions,

> Since in almost every noble city, whether in Lombardy or Tuscany, fine singers are retained for the delight and joy of the citizens.[5]

And even in the relatively small town of Treviso, we read in a document of 1395 that money will be given to Pietro di Bartolomeo Boldrani to buy a trumpet, 'for the presence of artists increases the honor of the whole community.'[6]

---

4   *Satire X*, 178.

5   Quoted in John Larner, *Culture and Society in Italy, 1290–1420* (New York: Scribner's, 1971), 171.

6   Quoted in Don L. Smithers, *The Music and History of the Baroque Trumpet* (London: Dent), 75ff.

Another form of art music which flourished during the Renaissance, yet scarcely is mentioned in general music history texts, was the solo art song. It seems to be little understood that most poetry was still sung, not read. Hence today one finds a great artist like Petrarch not in the Music Building but exiled to the Romance Languages Building. In fact, a fifteenth-century authority credits Petrarch himself for reviving the art song of ancient Greece.

> Those forms of poetry usually are numbered which consist of eight lines [strambotti] or three lines [elegies], which type Francesco Petrarch is said to have first established among us as he *sang* his exalted poems with a lute.[7]

Additional evidence that the poetry of Petrarch was sung and not read is found in a note in his own hand in the margin of his copy of his *Canzoniere*, which reads,

> I must make these two verses over again, singing them and I must transpose them: 3 o'clock in the morning, October the nineteenth.[8]

The ability of young aristocrats to sing poetry is documented in the *The Decameron*. Larner believes that the majority of middle-class men and women also sang and performed on instruments.[9] We especially like one of the tales of the anonymous 'Il Novellino,' which speaks of an unhappy knight whose lady had rejected him.

> Then he composed a very beautiful song; and in the morning early went up into the pulpit and began to sing his song as best he knew, and well he knew how to sing it.

The members of the church, upon hearing this song, 'cried out mercy, and the lady pardoned him.'[10]

Among the working class, the songs of Sacchetti enjoyed great popularity. He himself was a good musician and set many of his poems to music himself. Symonds suggests that these pastoral part-songs were a harbinger of the madrigal as we know it in the sixteenth century.[11]

In fourteenth-century England one finds the record of a large number of solo art singers in the works of Chaucer. There is the singer of the epic song, in which the singer sings of the deeds of heroes of the past, as in the tale of 'Sir Thopas,' where a minstrel is called for to sing

---

7   Cortesi, 'De Cardinalatu,' quoted in John D'Amico, *Renaissance Humanism in Papal Rome* (Baltimore: Johns Hopkins University Press, 1983), 106.
8   Quoted in John Larner, *Culture and Society in Italy*, 163.
9   Quoted in Ibid., 172.
10 'Il Novellino,' trans. Edward Storer (London: Routledge), LXIV.
11 John Addington Symonds, *Renaissance in Italy* (New York: Capricorn Books, 1964), I, 135.

tales of royalty, popes and cardinals.[12] In this same tradition are nineteen ladies who sing and dance a ballade, in 'carol style,'[13] the lyrics of which include reference to the Old Testament, Greece and Rome and Cleopatra.

A description of the solo song which we do not find in the thirteenth century is 'loud' singing, which we take to mean enthusiasm. In the 'Canterbury Tales,' the carpenter's wife sang 'loud and lively'[14] and we are told that even a trumpet was not half so loud as the two-part songs sung by the Pardoner and the Sumner.[15] The parish clerk, Absalom, sometimes sang in a 'loud treble,'[16] but when he was thinking of love he sang in a small and gentle voice with good harmony from his gittern.

> He syngeth in his voys gentil and smal,
> 'Now, deere laady, if thy wille be,
> I praye yow that ye wole rewe on me,'
> Ful wel acordaunt to his gyternynge.[17]

A singer we find especially attractive is Nicholas, the 'poor scholar' of Oxford. He sang only at night, in his room, for himself, sweetly singing to the accompaniment of his psaltery. But he sang a varied repertoire, some sacred songs and some secular ones, such as 'The King's Note.'

> And al above ther lay a gay sautrie,
> On which he made a-nyghtes melodie
> So swetely that all the cyhambre rong;
> And *Angelus ad virginem* he song;
> And after that he song the kynges noote.[18]

There are also a few references to art music by ensembles in Chaucer. In one place we have a little concert by a wind ensemble and we are told 'it was like heaven to listen to them.'

> Toforn hym gooth the loude mynstralcye,
> Til he cam to his chambre of parementz,
> Ther as they sownen diverse instrumentz,
> That it is lyk an heavene for to heere.[19]

---

[12] 'Sir Thopas,' 845ff.
[13] 'The Legend of Good Women,' 200ff.
[14] 'The Miller's Tale,' 3257.
[15] 'Prologue, The Canterbury Tales,' 669.
[16] 'The Miller's Tale,' 3332.
[17] Ibid., 3360. This musical parish clerk, could also serve as a barber, surgeon, lawyer and dance twenty different ways in the 'Oxford manner.'
[18] 'The Miller's Tale,' 3213.
[19] 'The Squire's Tale,' 268ff. In early English 'loud minstrels' meant wind instruments.

And as mentioned above there was traditionally time for a brief concert at the end of banquets. We find such a description in 'The Squire's Tale,' where after the third course, the king sat listening to his minstrels play their things deliciously before him at the table.

> Whil that this kyng sit thus in his nobleye,
> Herknynge his mynstralles hir thynges pleye
> Biforn hym at the bord deliciously.[20]

By the fifteenth century there are more records of civic ensembles playing concerts for the public. An extant document of Florence required the civic band to play every Sunday at the city hall.[21] Similarly, the civic players of Perugia at this time were also required by contract to play 'for the enjoyment of the public.'[22] An eyewitness from Turin describes such a concert, an hour long concert from an arcade of the town hall.

> Ma che alegrezza se alde tutto il zorno de quel pifari de la signoria che sona in cima a un pergolo del palazzo un'ora de longo.[23]

It is the fifteenth century when one sees the patronage of music shift from the towns to the newly powerful aristocrats—beginning with the pope, who now had his own wind band, known under the name 'i Musici Capitolini e i tamburini del Popolo Romano.'

In Ferrara we gain a glimpse of the importance of the court wind ensemble in a letter of Borso d'Este's wife, written in response to a request by Bianca Maria Sforza to borrow the ensemble to help celebrate her daughter's wedding.

> Because the wedding will occur in April, which coincides with our own festival in honor of San Zorzo, the piffari are needed, indeed most needed to help honor our Saint. If the illustrious Bianca Maria Sforza would therefore accept our excuse we would be most content and if there are any other possibilities of repaying the declined favor we would be most happy.[24]

The two amazing sisters, Beatrice d'Este (1475–1497) and Isabella d'Este (1474–1539) were both musicians, singers and harpsichordists, and were responsible for courts filled with art music. Lorenzo the Magnificent in Florence had the composer Heinrich Isaac in residence, who composed the beautiful 'Quis dabit' for Lorenzo's funeral.

Art song was maturing and one account of a recital at the end of the fifteenth century in Italy certainly documents the contemplative listener.

---

[20] Ibid., 78.

[21] L. Cellesi, 'Documenti per la storia musicale di Firenze,' in *Rivista Musicale Italiana* (1927), 285.

[22] Alessandro Vessella, *La Banda* (Milan, 1935), 44.

[23] Andrea Calmo, *Lettere*, ed. V. Rosso (Turin, 1888), 331.

[24] Quoted in E. Motta, *Musici alla Corte degli Sforza: ricerche e documenti milanesi* (Milano, 1887), 22ff.

> No sooner were we seated at the table than Fabio was ordered to sing ... and immediately he filled our ears, or rather our hearts, with a voice so sweet that ... I was almost transported out of my senses, and was touched beyond doubt by the unspoken feeling of an altogether divine pleasure.[25]

An account of a similar artistic recital in fifteenth-century France also mentions the contemplative listeners.

> The ladies were seated throughout the chambers in great comfort and delight, for a master of the viol, who knew how to perform very well indeed, sang them a courtly lay in a voice of very good tone that was in such harmony with the viol that it was truly a song to be listened to and enjoyed.[26]

Even the Church dramas now contain ensemble pieces of art music. In Arnoul Greban's *Mystere des Actes des apostres* we read,

> Bringing Dame Poetry to bear
> On sounds harmonious and sweet;
> Motets and chansons sing to us,
> Full of the sweetest melody;
> And let forthwith each render lays
> As sumptuous as may be found,
> And in your voices' harmony ...[27]

The *Mystere de Saint Louis*, by the Count of Provence, mentions a wind band performing 'a beautiful motet.'

Due to the strong interest and support of music by Philip the Good, it is especially in the Low Countries where one finds numerous accounts of art music. The annual Ommegang in Termonde in 1405 enjoyed seventeen visiting ensembles who performed not only in the civic procession but in concerts before the city hall.[28]

When important nobles visited they were often the guests of honor for a town banquet. A typical example was the performance by the Brussels civic band in 1495 after a banquet honoring Philip, son to Maximilian I, in a concert reported the repertoire to have consisted of various 'chansons de musique.'[29]

Some town bands were giving regular public concerts by the fourteenth century, such as those in Bruges by 1350 in the town plaza. A contract for this same town band of the fifteenth century gives interesting details of these concerts.

---

[25] Quoted in Nino Pirrotta and Elena Povoledo, *Music and Theatre from Poliziano to Monteverdi* (Cambridge: Cambridge University Press, 1982), 36.

[26] Thomas E. Vesce, trans., *The Knight of the Parrot* (New York: Garland, 1986), 84.

[27] Translated in Gustave Reese, *Music in the Renaissance* (New York: Norton, 1959), 151.

[28] Wytsman, *Anciens airs et chansons populaires de Termonde*, quoted in Edmond Vander Straeten, *La Musique aux Pays Bas avant le XIXe Sicle* (New York, 1959), IV, 198.

[29] *Archives generales du royaume*, quoted in Ibid., IV, 159ff.

> Each [of the civic musicians] is obligated to play at the front of the old hall at the customary place on all Sundays and Holy Days at 11:00 before noon and at 6:00 in the evening from Easter to *Baefmesse* [Feast of St. Bava], and from *Baefmesse* to Easter at 3:00 in the afternoon; they are to play two chansons [*liedekens*] or motets [*moteten*] at each performance; each performer is to appear in uniform and sign the work book.[30]

When a group of musicians from Brabant were hired as the town band in Utrecht in 1489, their contract stipulated that they were to perform motets from the church tower on all Holy Days and to play in the Church for the Marian services.[31] In Bruges, the master of the children at St. Donaes, Casin de Brauwer, was commissioned by the city in 1484 to prepare a collection of motets for use by the city band in the Marian services.[32]

One can see how important these concerts had become to the city fathers in an interesting document regarding a performance at the Bruges market-fair of 1500 involving the famous Obrecht, who, as chapel master at St. Donaes, was in charge. This document by the town fathers complains about the performance, mentioning 'great confusion ... lack of communication ... absence of singers ... and the embarrassment to the city,' and demanding correction.[33]

With the sixteenth century one finds numerous records of concerts of art music. The famous Italian, Benvenuto Cellini, in his autobiography, describes a typical post-dinner concert.

> The supper was followed by a short concert of delightful music, voices joining in harmony with instruments; and forasmuch as they were singing and playing from the book ...[34]

Two listeners in particular, Cellini, reports 'dropped their earlier tone of banter, exchanging it for well-weighed terms of sober heartfelt admiration.'

Pietro Aretino also left us an interesting description of an art singer who accompanied herself on the lute:

> There is no doubt ... that our pleasures are the panders of our senses, and that being the case, the things which Franceschina sang yesterday to the tune of her lute, penetrated my heart with so sweet a sort of musical persuasion, that I must needs come to the point of amorous conjunction.

In another book, this author describes a chamber ensemble in a private home.

> While I was being so greatly complimented, the great virtue of music arrived, music which went to the core of my soul. There were four singers, who were looking in a book, and another fellow with a silver lute, which was tuned to their voices. They sang: 'Divine eyes, so calm, so pure.'[35]

---

30 Louis Gilliodts-Van Severen, 'Les menestrels de Bruges,' in *Essais d'Arceologie Brugeoise* (Bruges, 1912), II, III.

31 Keith Polk, 'Ensemble Instrumental Music in Flanders—1450–1550' [Unpublished], 22.

32 Ibid., 23.

33 Ibid., 22.

34 John Addington Symonds, trans., *The Life of Benvenuto Cellini* (New York: Scribner's, 1914), I, xxx.

35 Pietro Aretino, *Dialogues*, trans. Raymond Rosenthal (New York: Marsilio, 1971), 54ff.

In terms of larger scale vocal music, we must not forget that the famous Camerata, which we associate with the birth of opera, had its beginnings in the sixteenth century. It seems clear that an important focus of the Camerata's discussions on music, aside from their dreams of a Classical revival, was relative to the communication of feelings. Some of the music of the earliest prototype operas is lost, making it difficult to appreciate the immediate application of this idea. However, Peri said of Cavalieri's work that its purpose was to use the stage to underline action and emotion and an account of Cavalieri's lost *La Disperazione di Fileno* mentions that the singing of Archilei 'moved the audience to tears.'[36]

This movement can be seen even earlier than the meetings of the Camerata. An anonymous chronicler of a performance of the tragedy *Alidoro,* given in Reggio in 1568 includes the following description:

> An infinite number of singers and instrumentalists started performing together in a truly divine manner; you could hear at once from the gravity of the sound, which was by turns terrible and sad, that the play that was being performed could not be other than tragic ... Not only the music of the opening but all the music heard later [was made] to reflect the terrible and sad qualities of the tragedy and to point to every change of mood.[37]

By the sixteenth century virtually all the more prosperous towns in the Low Countries had regularly employed wind bands of at least six members. The Antwerp civic wind band enjoyed a large collection of city owned instruments and received uniforms. One of the members of this band was the famous Hans Nagel. Soon after Susato joined this wind band he himself transcribed thirty-three volumes of six-part music, running to about four hundred folio pages![38] His famous instrumental dances, published in four part-books in 1551 are almost certainly taken from the repertoire of this band.

Another town which had a fine wind band was Mechelen, which profited from the presence of the court of Margaret of Austria. An extant contract for these players, from 1505, says they were to play on cornetts and other instruments during solemn masses; they were to perform concerts at the town hall late mornings, every Saturday, Sunday, holiday and on days preceding public festivities and they were to play for civic banquets and could not refuse to participate in any service required by the town. In order to maintain a desirable standard of performance, they were ordered to rehearse together at least twice weekly and to obey a leader.[39] A later contract for Mechelen, in 1568, calls for concerts on Sundays, Holy Days, and feast days.[40]

---

[36] Nino Pirrotta, in *Music and Culture in Italy from the Middle Ages to the Baroque* (Cambridge: Harvard University Press, 1984), 225.

[37] Ibid., 230ff.

[38] John Murray, *Antwerp in the Age of Platin and Brueghel* (Norman: University of Oklahoma Press, 1970), 147.

[39] Robert Wangermee, *Flemish Music and Society in the Fifteenth and Sixteenth Centuries* (New York, 1968), 180.

[40] Raymond Van Aerde, *Menestrels Communaux ... a Malines, de 1312 a 1790* (Mechelen, 1911), 39ff.

A contract of the Mons civic band, of 1532, demands the performance of concerts for the citizens twice a day, at eleven o'clock in the morning and at six o'clock in the evening.[41] By 1588, in Mons, new members were now expected to play string instruments, in addition to shawm, cornett and recorder, in the performance of 'such songs as the masters see fit to choose.'[42] A similar contract for the Bruges civic wind band requires concerts each Sunday at eleven o'clock in the square in front of the city hall and in the St. Donaes Church after the evening prayer.[43] The repertoire for these concerts was specified as sacred and devotional.

In Italy Giambattista Marino's (1569–1625) *Adonis* had a 'play within a play,' which represents the post banquet concert, but here with an ensemble providing the music.

> Lo, now a concert of musicians next
> begins in low, in high, in blended strains,
> and concords sound from various instruments,
> some played by hand and others played by mouth;
> in tempi bright and quick, then grave and slow,
> the verses swell for those blest banqueters;
> from choruses of nymphs responsive sound
> the echoes of a symphony of Love.[44]

With the arrival of the Baroque Period in Germany the citizens were hearing music that we still perform frequently today. A comment which Johann Heinichen (1683–1729) wrote in 1711 is not only the harbinger of the modern music era but should be engraved in stone above the stage door of every theater today:

> Whoever plays in a concert must play for the honor and perfection of the performance and not for his own particular honor. It is no longer a concert when each plays only for himself.[45]

There was in Germany a growing middle-class which was beginning to be consumers of art music. It is of them that Georg Muffat was thinking of in the Foreword of his *Auserlesene Instrumental-Music* (1701) when he writes,

> These concerti, suited neither to the church ... nor for dancing [but] are composed only for the express refreshment of the ear, may be performed most appropriately in ... assemblies of musical amateurs and virtuosi.[46]

---

[41] Leopold Devillers, *Essai sur l'historie de la musique a Mons* (Mons, 1868), 16.

[42] Wangermee, *Flemish Music and Society in the Fifteenth and Sixteenth Centuries*, 182.

[43] Louis Gilliodts-Van Severen, 'Les menestrels de Bruges,' in *Essais d'Archeologie Brugeoise* (Bruges, 1912), II, 134.

[44] Giambattista Marino, *L'Adone* [1623], trans. Harold Priest (Ithaca: Cornell University Press, 1967), V, 146.

[45] Johann David Heinichen, *General-Bass Treatise* [1711], quoted in George Buelow, *Thorough-Bass Accompaniment according to Johann David Heinichen* (Ann Arbor: UMI Research Press, 1986), 215.

[46] Quoted in Oliver Strunk, *Source Readings in Music History* (New York: Norton, 1950), 449.

And it was for this new public as well that we find similar references on the title pages of Bach's *Clavier Ubung,* Part III, and the 'Goldberg Variations,' where he gives the purpose to 'refresh the spirits.'

After the general interruption of the Thirty Years War at the beginning of the seventeenth century, the resumption of performances of art music was at first led by the aristocrats themselves. Both emperors, Ferdinand III and Leopold I, were active composers and in the court at Munich, Carl Albrecht (1726–1745) was a fan of Italian opera produced at court and sometimes conducted the rehearsals himself.

The courts were busy with music, as they would remain so throughout the Classical Period. One court musician who served in Weissenfels, Johann Beer (1655–1700), who dreamed of an easier life as a civic musician, gives us a player's view of this activity.

> With the court you've got to be in one place today, tomorrow in another. Day and night, unfortunately, makes no difference. Tempest, rain, sunshine—it's all the same. Today you've got to go into church, tomorrow to the dining hall, the day after tomorrow to the theater. Compared to all this disturbance, life is somewhat more peaceful in the towns …
>
> Many princely musicians long for the city, because the service in the court is so insecure and he must be ready to move if the support for music by the noble fails or if he decides to cut back. What good are riches without stability? I say continued poverty could be called better luck than irregular riches, where one may go from a horse to an ass and from the ass even to sit in the dust …
>
> In the city one can hope for quicker advancement … this has the civic musician, but at court even if he had a doctorate in all three faculties he waits without hope. The more excellent he is, the more he will remain in his station which he once accepted, to remain used, all feathers plucked from his wings so he can not hope to soar higher.[47]

But, as they say, 'the grass is always greener on the other side of the fence.' Bach, in 1730, submitted a memorandum to the Leipzig Councilmen complaining about the difficulties of life as a German civic musician. Quite the reverse of Beer, Bach contemplates how nice it would be to be a court musician, as for example in Dresden.

> It is somewhat strange that German musicians are expected to be capable of performing at once and *ex tempore* all kinds of music, whether it comes from Italy or France, England or Poland, just as may be done, say, by those virtuosos for whom the music is written and who have studied it long beforehand, indeed, know it almost by heart, and who, *quod notandum,* receive good salaries besides, so that their work and industry thus is richly rewarded; while, on the other hand, this is not taken into consideration, but the German musicians are left to look out for their own wants, so that many a one, for worry about his bread, cannot think of improving—let alone distinguishing—himself. To illustrate this statement with an example one need only go to Dresden and see how the musicians there are paid

---

47 Johann Beer, *Musicalische Diskurse* (Nürnberg, 1710), 18ff. Beer, in fact, was accidentally shot and killed while playing for a hunt in 1700. Metastasio, in a letter of 1732, relates some details of a similar accident in which the emperor of Austria accidentally shot and killed Prince Schwaisemberg during a hunt. [See Charles Burney, *Memoirs of the Life and Writings of the Abate Metastasio* (New York: Da Capo Press, 1971), I, 87.]

> by His Royal Majesty; it cannot fail, since the musicians are relieved of all concern for their living, free from *chagrin*, and obliged each to master but a single instrument: it must be something choice and excellent to hear.[48]

The traditional civic wind band reaches a high artistic peak during the seventeenth century in Germany, but this is the story for another book. A new and very important form of civic music begins in the Baroque in Germany and in some ways it is one of the forerunners of public concerts as we know them. The civic *collegium musica* were meetings of students and local musicians who met, sometimes in coffee houses, for the performance and enjoyment of music. The Leipzig *collegium musicum* under Telemann began to meet on a regular weekly basis and gave concerts for the citizens. In a letter to a friend, Telemann is enthusiastic to find strong support for concerts among the leaders of the city.

> A great advantage is added to this by the fact that, besides the presence of many persons of rank here, also the most prominent men of the city—including the entire city council—do not absent themselves from public concerts. Likewise the reasoned judgment of so many connoisseurs and intelligent people give opportunity for concerts.[49]

Bach began to become involved with the Leipzig *collegium musicum* after 1729, when he seems to have become more interested in secular music in general and a number of his secular cantatas and instrumental works appear to have been composed for these performances. There is extant an announcement for his public concerts in 1736 which includes several interesting details.

> Both the public musical Concerts or Assemblies that are held here weekly are still flourishing steadily. The one is conduced by Mr. Johann Sebastian Bach, Kapellmeister to the Court of Weissenfels and Music Director at the Thomas-Kirche and Nicolai-Kirche in this city, and is held, except during the Fair, once a week in Zimmerman's coffeehouse in the Cather-strasse, on Friday evenings from 8 to 10 o'clock …
>
> The participants in these musical concerts are chiefly students here, and there are always good musicians among them, so that sometimes they become, as is known, famous virtuosos. Any musician is permitted to make himself publicly heard at these musical concerts, and most often, too, there are such listeners as know how to judge the qualities of an able musician.[50]

During the late years of the seventeenth century another town famous for its public concerts was Lübeck. Its *Abendmusiken*, given in the Marienkirche, were even advertised by the city fathers for the purpose of attracting visitors. In Leipzig soon after the beginning of the eighteenth century local publishers began to print music expressly intended for amateur performance by the middle class.

---

[48] Quoted in Hans T. David and Arthur Mendel, *The Bach Reader* (New York: Norton, 1966), 123.

[49] H. Grosse and H. R. Jung, ed., *Georg Philipp Telemann Briefwechsel* (Leipzig, 1972), 213.

[50] Quoted in David and Mendel, *The Bach Reader*, 149.

By the end of the Baroque there must have been much musical activity among the upper middle-class merchants in Germany, although this topic, with the exception of the Fugger family of Munich, has received little attention to date. The reader will recall that the great Gabrieli of Venice had dedicated his *Concerti* of 1587 to Jakob Fugger.

Before leaving Germany, we should also mention that the extraordinary achievements of the civic wind band in Germany during the seventeenth century declined severely in the early years of the eighteenth century. And it was of the decline of these ancient guilds that Johann Scheibe wrote the following in 1739:

> You absurd guild which loves only laziness,
> Which denominates as masters those who are yet unskilled,
> Which in fact wants much written; yet never thinks,
> Which dispatches musical foolishness into the world day and night,
> Which so frightfully tortures and torments the sensitive ear,
> Which almost rejects music's cause out of tastelessness,
> Must throw down pen and paper, reflect,
> and examine yourself.[51]

In the court at Paris most of the musical activity was intended only for entertainment. However, on occasion, it would appear that these 'divertissements' may have included a performance which was more in the character of art music. An example is an account of a performance conducted by Lully in 1668.

> If one takes the Music, there is nothing which does not perfectly express all the passions, delighting the spirit of the Hearers. But what was never before seen is that pleasing harmony of voices, that symphony of instruments, that delightful union of different choruses, those sweet songs, those tender and amorous dialogues, those echoes, in short, that admirable conduct in every part, in which it might always be seen from the first words that the Music was increasing, and having begun with a single voice, it concluded with a concert of over one hundred persons, seen all at once upon the same Stage, uniting their instruments, their voices and their steps in a harmony and cadence that brings the Play to an end, leaving everyone in a state of admiration that cannot be adequately expressed.[52]

From Baroque England we have a distinguished critic and amateur musician, Roger North (1653–1734), who left us an important contemporary chronicle of the first public concerts in London. In these early public concerts, North was first bothered by what he perceived to be a lack of aesthetic order. Whether it be a fireworks display, or comedy or tragedy, he attributed the success with the audience with a plan in which the event began slowly and gradually increased in intensity. But in concerts he found only disorganized variety.

---

[51] Poem in honor of the publication of Johann Mattheson, *Der vollkommene Capellmeister* [1739], trans. Ernest Harriss (Ann Arbor: UMI Research Press, 1981), 73.

[52] Marcelle Benoit, in 'Paris, 1661–87: the Age of Lully,' in *The Early Baroque Era* (Englewood Cliffs: Prentice Hall, 1994), 243.

> A song, fugue, a solo or any single piece may be very good in their several kinds, but for want of a due coherence of the whole, the company will not be pleased. And thus it is with the music exhibited in London publicly for a half crown. A combination of masters agree to make a consort as they call it, but do not submit to the government of any one, as should be done, to accomplish their design. And in the performance, each takes his parts according as his opinion is of his own excellence. The master violin must have its solo, then joined with a lute, then a fugue, or sonata, then a song, then the trumpet and oboe, and so other variety, as it happens ... And the company know not whether all is ended, or anything is more to come, and what.[53]

An even worse idea for programming, in the view of North, was competition. While he admits the importance of aristocratic money in supporting music, he was much opposed to a current trend in London whereby nobles contributed money to a 'pot' to be given to the performer who pleases them best in a concert. Competition in music, he says, has largely negative results.

> Instead of encouraging the endeavors of all, the happy victor only was pleased, and all the rest were discontented and some who thought they deserved better, were almost ready to [give up music] ... So much a mistake it is to force artists upon a competition, for all but one are sure to be malcontents.[54]

After concluding, from his own experience, that no concert should last more than one hour,[55] North writes of some of his additional objections to the new emphasis on professional concerts. First, he observes that since performance is itself a pleasurable activity, the players enjoy a pleasure 'which the audience cannot pretend to.' Second, because the performers play so well, the members of the audience who may be amateur performers become discouraged, wishing to achieve such a level of performance themselves but knowing they cannot.

Another source of puzzlement for the aristocratic audience may have been related to their deportment. In what must be regarded as a hallmark of a new era, North points to an Italian violinist, Nicolai Matteis, whose popularity in London was hampered by his artistic demands when he played at court, for he,

> behaved himself *fastously*; no person must whisper while he played, which sort of attention had not been the fashion at Court.[56]

And he was quite correct about the past tradition. One can see many court paintings of a large palace room in which musicians, dressed in elegant clothes, are playing. Generally a few people are standing near listening, but most of the people in the room are sitting at tables playing

---

53 John Wilson, *Roger North on Music* (London: Novello, 1959), 13ff.
54 Roger North, *Memoirs of Music*, ed. Edward Rimbault (London: Bell, 1846), 118ff.
55 In a letter by Franz Liszt to Marie zu Sayn-Wittgenstein, July 15, 1854, Liszt mentions,
   This evening after the end of the third and last Concert—which parenthetically, will last from 4 to 5 hours ...
56 North, *Memoirs of Music*, 123.

cards or conversing. We once stayed in an old hotel in Italy that had a public room with an ancient sign reading, 'Sala per musiche e conversatione.' It was not quite time for a room to be designated just 'Room for Music.'

This social environment got better, but did not disappear during the Classical Period. One of the deep dark secrets of music history is that a great deal of the chamber music we call 'classical music' was first heard as background music.

But musicians, like the above Nicolai Matteis, were making an important point: music was now worth listening to. The next generation confirmed this. Mozart knew *his* music was worth listening to and so it is no surprise to find he demanded the same audience decorum as did Maestro Matteis. After Mozart's death, one of his friends, the English tenor, Michael Kelly, recalled,

> He was kind-hearted, and always ready to oblige; but so very particular, when he played, that if the slightest noise were made, he instantly [stopped playing].[57]

And so it was great music which changed concerts from entertainment events to something more important. By about the time of World War II the formality of classical concerts began to ease. We once heard two elder gentlemen talking during the intermission of a Philadelphia Orchestra concert in the Academy of Music, Philadelphia. One gentleman said to the other, 'Oh! It is a pity that people no longer dress for concerts!' He meant that he regretted that the public no longer came in white tie and tails like the orchestra.

So, one might say the pendulum has begun to swing back. Indeed, recently as we sat in the audience of a university concert in Los Angeles we noticed that two young people sitting in front of us were playing cards during the concert much as one might have found during the Baroque.

---

[57] Michael Kelly, *Reminiscences* (London, 1826).

On the Ancient Greek Chorus

And the sound of the voice which reaches and educates the soul,
we have ventured to term music.[1]

THERE ARE ACCOUNTS OF PERFORMANCES by choral ensembles from very remote times and they are nearly always associated with religion. This reflects not only the long association of music with religion, based in part on the mystery conveyed by the fact that music is the only art you cannot see, but the fact that early historical records were often written by church clerics. Usually, as in the case of information engraved on a stone slab of Assur, dating ca. 800 BC, they were described as being accompanied by instruments.

> The precentors a chant to the drum shall sing.
> To the sacred *lilis* shall sing.
> To the aulos and tambourine shall sing.[2]

There are also accounts of surprisingly large choral ensembles from Sumeria (ca. 3,000 BC), as for example a list of the names of 164 liturgical singers for a single year and another document which lists sixty-four female temple slaves for the temple at Lagash.[3] The titles of some of these musicians indicate one was in charge of supervising the choir and another responsible for the rehearsal of the choir. Farmer mentions a similar document from Akkad (also up to 3,000 BC) in which some temple musicians are described as those who 'know the melodies' and are 'masters of the musical movements.'[4] This last reference reminds us that ancient choirs often are associated with movement of some kind. Some early philosophers considered dance as the 'sixth part' of music, meaning it was the part of music that you could see.

An account from Babylonia (2,000–562 BC) speaks of lamentations sung with 'flutes of crystal' and harps during the Festival of Tammuz.[5] This festival also included some 'epic' productions which told of the marriage, death and resurrection of the god Tammuz, sung antiphonally by choirs.[6]

---

1   Plato, *Laws*, 672e.

2   Henry G. Farmer, 'The Music of Ancient Mesopotamia,' in *The New Oxford History of Music* (London: Oxford University Press, 1966), 234. Farmer gives 'timpani' for lilis.

3   Alfred Sendrey, in *Music in the Social and Religious Life of Antiquity* (Rutherford: Fairleigh Dickinson University Press, 1974), 32.

4   Farmer, 'The Music of Ancient Mesopotamia,' 235.

5   Sendrey, *Music in the Social and Religious Life of Antiquity*, 55.

6   Ibid., 58.

Beginning with the Old Kingdom (2,686–2,181 BC) of Egypt we can see a testimonial to the importance of individual musicians in the hieroglyphic texts which accompany the tomb paintings. Some of these descriptions seem likely to be associated with choral music in the temples, as for example 'leader of ritual music' and 'inspector of vocal music.' In rare cases we even know their names, including Nikaure, 'instructor of the singers of the pyramid of King Userkaf,' and Rewer, 'teacher of the royal singers,' who lived during the Fifth Dynasty (2,563–2,423 BC). During the Sixth Dynasty we find several musicians named Snefrunufer, one of whom had a tomb at Giza which identifies him as 'instructor of singers in The Great House.'

A remarkable painting from the Middle Kingdom tomb of an 'instructor of singers' and 'overseer of prophets' named Khesuwer, located at Kom el-Hisn in the Delta, pictures the instructor actually teaching. We see him teaching ten ladies in sistrum-playing and in another scene teaching ten ladies in hand-clapping.

When female musicians appear in the New Kingdom (1,567–1,085 BC), some of them also have apparent positions in the temple, with titles such as 'Chief of the Singers.' The tomb painting tells us of music in the temple by both solo and choral singers, dances accompanied by instruments, and processions around the altar.

Athenaeus,[7] speaking of the period of Ptolemy (285–246 BC), quotes a reference to a 'choral band of 600 men,' with three hundred harp players participating in the music for a festival.

The Old Testament also includes references to large numbers of singers among the Hebrews, as for example.

> God had given Heman fourteen sons and three daughters. They were all under the direction of their father in the music in the house of the Lord with cymbals, harps, and lyres ... The number of them who were trained in singing to the Lord, all who were skillful, was two hundred and eighty-eight.[8]

The apocryphal book of Ecclesiasticus gives credit to David for the formal establishment of the tradition of using vocal music in the service.

> In all his works he praised the Holy One most high with words of glory;
> with his whole heart he sang songs, and loved him that made him.
> He set singers also before the altar, that by their voices they might make
> sweet melody, and daily sing praises in their songs.[9]

Regarding the actual organization of the music of the Temple, the Old Testament several times mentions surprisingly large numbers of musicians performing together,[10] as for example in an extraordinary description of praise associated with thanksgiving:

---

7 Athenaeus, in *Deipnosophistae*, V, 201.

8 1 Chronicles 25:5ff.

9 Ecclesiasticus 47:8ff.

10 1 Chronicles 15:16ff; 25:5ff; Ezra 1:40, 65; and Nehemiah 7:43. 1 Esdras 7:22 says the Temple musicians paid no taxes!

> ... and all the Levitical singers, Asaph, Heman, and Jeduthun, their sons and kinsmen, arrayed in fine linen, with cymbals, harps, and lyres ... with a hundred and twenty priests who were trumpeters; and it was the duty of the trumpeters and singers to make themselves heard in unison in praise and thanksgiving ... and when the song was raised, with trumpets and cymbals and other musical instruments, in praise to the Lord.[11]

By 'unison' here we believe is meant rather 'together,' for it is unlikely the great numbers of singers and instruments were always heard in unison. This supposition seems confirmed by the reference to a 'great variety *of sounds*' in the following description of the Temple music:

> The singers also sang praises with their voices, with great variety of sounds was there made sweet melody.[12]

Another passage[13] speaks of cymbals, harps, lyres, trumpets, and singing altogether in the service. Psalm 68 even gives us the order of a procession: singers in front, then 'maidens playing timbrels,' and finally the instrumentalists.

Because we have far more surviving literature from ancient Greece than from any of the other areas, it is here that we find the most information on ancient choral performance. Extant information appears to date the solo lyric song with lyre or aulos from the seventh century, with the choral ensembles joining the lyric singers, and singing independently, from the sixth century BC. In the following century we can identify actual choral schools of Melanippides (ca. 450–413 BC), Philoxenus (435–380 BC) and Timotheus (end of the fifth and beginning of the fourth centuries).

This body of literature [lyric poets] was performed in public by the solo singer with lyre (*kitharoidos*), the solo singer with aulos[14] (*auloidos*) and by both professional and non-professional choirs (*khoros*). Athenaeus says *khoregus* originally was used to mean the conductor of the chorus, not, as later, the administrator, or 'provider.'[15] These choruses should be thought of as representatives of their cities. Indeed, the Spartans actually called the interior civic space the *Khoros*. Nagy explains this civic association.

> As a representative of the polis, the chorus is concerned partly with local interests, and it can therefore serve as a formal vehicle of ritual ... which constitute part of the ritual chain of athletics. The range, however, of choral self-expression in matters of ritual is certainly not limited to the Games. Besides epinician odes, a given chorus in a given polis may perform a wide variety of other kinds of compositions related to various local or civic rituals.

......

---

[11] 2 Chronicles 5:12ff. Other references to songs of thanksgiving are found in 1 Chronicles 16:7, Nehemiah 12:27ff ('with singing, with cymbals, harps and lyres'), Psalm 26:7, Psalm 95, Psalm 107, Isaiah 51:3ff, which gives the complete text of a thanksgiving song, 1 Maccabees 13:51 and 1 Esdras 5:59ff.

[12] Ecclesiasticus 50:18.

[13] 2 Chronicles 29:25ff.

[14] The aulos was the double-pipe familiar in Greek vases.

[15] *Deipnosophistae*, XIV, 633,

> As a microcosm of society, it is equally important to note the khoros is also a microcosm of social hierarchy. Within the hierarchy that is the chorus ... a majority of younger members act out a patter of subordination to a minority of older leaders; this acting out conforms to the role of the chorus as an educational collectivization of experience ... the concept of older leaders, within the hierarchy of the chorus, is in most instances embodied in the central persona of the *khoregos* 'chorus leader.'[16]

We have a little information on the organization of an ancient choir, a boy's choir, in a speech, known as 'On the Chorus Boy,' which Antiphon (480–411 BC) wrote for an unknown defendant who was in charge of the chorus at Thargelia in 412 BC. This speech provides valuable details regarding the establishment and provisions of a boy's chorus.

> When I was appointed in charge of the chorus [*choregus*] at Thargelia ..., I performed the office as well and conscientiously as I could. In the first place, I provided a room for training in the most convenient part of my house, where I used to train when I was *choregus* at the Dionysia. Secondly, I enrolled a chorus in the best way I could, not penalizing anyone nor forcibly exacting security nor making an enemy of anyone; but, as was most agreeable and convenient to both parties, I made my requests and demands, while the parents sent their sons with good grace and willingly ...
>
> I appointed Phanostratus to look after the chorus in case they needed anything. Phanostratus is a fellow demesman of the prosecutors and a kinsman of mine, in fact, my son-in-law, and I expected him to look after them well. A appointed two other men too, Ameinias of the tribe Erechtheis, whom the tribesmen themselves regularly elected to enroll and look after the tribe, a man with a good reputation; and the second man from the Cecropid tribe, who regularly convened that tribe. Then I appointed a fourth, Philippus, who was commissioned to buy and spend any money necessary on the authority of the poet or of an other of the officials, so that the boys should enjoy the best possible *choregia* and should go in want of nothing because of my inability to give them my attention.

Plato, in a charming description of the philosopher Hippias (fl. ca. 450 BC),[17] tells us that he was also a composer and that he gave an elegy on the loss of a Messenian boys' chorus who died crossing a river, but this is not extant. Herodotus, the great fifth century BC historian, tells of a similar tragedy:

> The Chians had sent a choir of a hundred young men from Delphi; ninety-eight of them caught the plague and died and only two returned.[18]

The beginning of the period of the great Greek stage tragedies overlaps the period of the last of the lyric poets. When Aeschylus died, in 456 BC, Pindar had at least ten years of activity left and Bacchylides was still in middle life. To some degree it was the narrative dithyramb[19] of the lyric poets which expanded and became fifth-century tragedy. Due to references as late

---

[16] Gregory Nagy, *Pindar's Homer* (Baltimore: The Johns Hopkins University Press, 1982), 399, 345.

[17] Plato, *Hippias Minor*, 368b.

[18] Herodotus, *The Histories*, VI, 29.

[19] Nagy, *Pindar's Homer*, 105, fn. 118, notes, 'By the time that Aristotle was composing his *Poetics*, about 330 BC, the dithyramb seems to have been the only kind of choral lyric that was still alive enough to deserve his notice in that work.'

as Aristophanes (448–385 BC) of actual lyric poets, we have every reason to suppose that older choral repertoire works were still known and performed during the fifth century BC. A line in Euripides (480–406 BC) confirms that this was the case.

> For I sing this day to Dionysus
> The song that is appointed from of old.

The choral odes of the older poets, those works sung in public festivals and choral competitions, become the 'choruses' of the fifth-century dramatists and their stage directions indicate, contrary to productions today, that they were still *sung* choruses. An example of one of these choruses which seems to us to be very much in the style of the old choral odes is one found in *Alcestis* by Euripides.

> *Chorus (singing)*
> O house of a bountiful lord,
> Even open to many guests,
> The God of Pytho,
> Apollo of the beautiful lyre,
> Designed to dwell in you
> And to live a shepherd in your lands!
> On the slope of the hillsides
> He played melodies of mating
> On the Pipes of Pan to his herds.
>
> And the dappled lynxes fed with them
> In joy at your singing;
> From the wooded vale of Orthrys
> Came a yellow troop of lions;
> To the sound of your lyre, O Phoebus,
> Danced the dappled fawn
> Moving on light feet
> Beyond the high-crested pines,
> Charmed by your sweet singing.[20]

Moreover, the choruses in these plays may have continued to dance, as well as sing, again in the tradition of the older choral odes. Athenaeus quotes Chamaeleon as saying,

> Aeschylus was the first to give poses to his choruses, employing no dancing masters, but devising for himself the figures of the dance, and in general taking upon himself the entire management of the piece.[21]

---

[20] *Alcestis*, 568. Unless otherwise indicated, all translations for these four dramatists are quoted from Whitney J. Oates, ed., *The Complete Greek Drama* (New York: Random House, 1938).

[21] Athenaeus, *Deipnosophistae*, I, 22.

Nothing is of more interest to modern musicians than the nature of these movements which are so often mentioned as part of ancient Greek choral performances. Some descriptions suggest that these movements were not just mere decorations, as one sees on 'show choirs' of our time, but were used somehow to amplify the emotions or meaning of the text. Athenaeus, for example, lists Thespis, Pratinas, Cratinus, and Phrynichus among older playwrights who 'relied upon the dancing of the chorus for the interpretation of their plays.'[22]

References to the earliest period, 700 BC, when the chorus was singing the odes with the lyric poets, the movement references often mention dancing by the chorus. Athenaeus, for instance, states that these singers traditionally had few facial expressions, but were more active with the feet, 'both in marching and in dance steps.'[23]

This was clearly dancing to the music, and not music for dancing, as is clarified in Pindar's *Ode for Hieron of Aetna*, Winner of the Chariot Race.

> O glorious lyre, joint treasure of Apollo
> And of the Muses violet-tressed,
> Your notes the dancers' step obeys ...[24]

In addition sometimes the solo performer danced together with the chorus. In one of the poems of Alkman, for example, the singer complains that he is too old and weak to dance with the chorus.[25]

Herodotus, the great fifth century BC historian, writes that it was the choral conductors who trained the dancers for the religious ceremonies.[26] Beyond the appearances performing with lyric poets and in the theater in plays, the Greek choirs also performed in concerts. There are a few contemporary references to such concerts and the pure musical activity of the choirs. The more intimate performance occasions were called *symposia*, where, much like concerts today, the works of the older lyric poets were performed as 'Classics.' These symposia offered the opportunity as well for both solo and choral performance by non-professionals.[27]

Plutarch provides us with a nice story about Damonidas, a member of one of these choruses, which reflects on the serious attitude of one singer. When the chorus master placed him in the lowest place for the choral dance, Damonidas is said to have responded, 'Well, sir, you have found a way to make this place, which was infamous before, noble and honorable!'[28]

---

22 Ibid.
23 Ibid..
24 Geoffrey S. Conway, *The Odes of Pindar* (London: Dent, 1972), 81.
25 Nr. 42, in Guy Davenport, *Archilochos, Sappho, Alkman* (Berkeley: University of California Press, 1980).
26 Herodotus, *The Histories*, V, 82.
27 Gregory Nagy, *Pindar's Homer*, 342.
28 Quoted in Plutarch, 'Laconic Apophthegms.'

On the Ancient Greek Chorus 61

In several places in this book the reader will find contemporary references to the decay in culture in Greece perceived by the ancient philosophers. Perhaps this decline was in part responsible for a complaint by the famous orator of this period, Demosthenes (385–322 BC). First he refers to a common complaint by some early philosophers that music only lasts a brief period (during performance) and then disappears! We find this in one of his speeches where he comments that he too was not hearing choral performances of lasting impression. He regrets the large amount of money spent on choral performances 'which affords those of us who are in the theater gratification for a fraction of a day.'[29] On the other hand, in another place he indicates that the annual Spring Festivals were still being given on a lavish scale.

> Larger sums are lavished upon them than upon any one of your [military] expeditions [and] they are celebrated with bigger crowds and greater splendor than anything else of the kind in the world.[30]

Festivals were no doubt a common place for the ancient Greek choirs to perform. Although we do not know very much about them from a musical standpoint, one stage direction in the play, *The Bacchae*, by Euripides reflects an ancient Egyptian origin.

> There comes stealing in from the left a band of fifteen Eastern Women, the light of the sunrise streaming upon their long white robes and ivy-bound hair. They wear fawn-skins over the robes, and carry some of them timbrels, some pipes and other instruments. Many bear the thyrsus, or sacred Wand, made of reed ringed with ivy.

Plutarch also has given us an illustration of choral repertoire sung at a festival which reflects an importance placed on the participation of persons of all ages.

> At all their public festivals these songs were a great part of their entertainment, where there were three companies of singers, representing the three several ages of nature. The old men made up the first chorus, whose business was to present what they had been after this manner:
>
>> *That active courage youthful blood contains*
>> *Did once with equal vigor warm our veins.*

To which the chorus, consisting of young men only, thus answers:

> *Valiant and bold we are, let who will try:*
> *Who dare accept our challenge soon shall die.*

The third, which were of young children, replied to them in this manner:

> *Those seeds which Nature in our breast did sow*
> *Shall soon to generous fruits of virtue grow;*
> *Then all those valiant deeds which you relate*
> *We will excel, and scorn to imitate.*[31]

---

[29] 'Against Leptines,' trans. J. H. Vince (Cambridge: Harvard University Press, 1954), 509.
[30] 'The First Philippic,' Ibid, 89.
[31] 'Customs of the Lacedaemonians.'

This illustration also reflects an earlier discussion by Plato on the organization of music at festivals. He writes in great detail of the requirements of the singers, the educational purpose, the values to society and even such practical issues as how to get older persons to overcome their reluctance to sing.

> AN ATHENIAN STRANGER. Then let us not faint in discussing the peculiar difficulty of music. Music is more celebrated than any other kind of imitation, and therefore requires the greatest care of them all. For if a man makes a mistake here, he may do himself the greatest injury by welcoming evil dispositions, and the mistake may be very difficult to discern, because the poets are artists very inferior in character to the Muses themselves, who would never fall into the monstrous error of assigning to the words of men the intonation and song of women; nor after combining the melodies with the gestures of freemen would they add on the rhythms of slaves and men of the baser sort; nor, beginning with the rhythms and gestures of freemen, would they assign to them a melody or words which are of an opposite character; nor would they mix up the voices and sounds of animals and of men and instruments, and every other sort of noise, as if they were all one. But human poets are fond of introducing this sort of inconsistent mixture, and so make themselves ridiculous in the eyes of those who, as Orpheus says, 'are ripe for true pleasure.' The experienced see all this confusion, and yet the poets go on and make still further havoc by separating the rhythm and the figure of the dance from the melody, setting bare words to meter, and also separating the melody and the rhythm from the words, using the lyre or the flute alone. For when there are no words, it is very difficult to recognize the meaning of the harmony and rhythm, or to see that any worthy object is imitated by them. And we must acknowledge that all this sort of thing, which aims at only swiftness and smoothness and a brutish noise, and uses the flute and the lyre not as the mere accompaniments of the dance and song, is exceedingly coarse and tasteless. The use of either instrument, when unaccompanied, leads to every sort of irregularity and trickery. This is all rational enough. But we are considering now how our choristers, who are from thirty to fifty years of age, and may be over fifty, are not to use the Muses, but how they are to use them. And the considerations which we have urged seem to show that these fifty-years-old choristers who are to sing, will require something better than a mere choral training. For they need have a quick perception and knowledge of harmonies and rhythms; otherwise, how can they ever know whether a melody would be rightly sung to the Dorian mode, or to the rhythm which the poet has assigned to it?
>
> CLEINIAS. Clearly they cannot.
>
> AN ATHENIAN STRANGER. The many are ridiculous in imagining that they know what is proper harmony and rhythm, and what is not, when they can only be made by force to sing to the flute and step in rhythm; it never occurs to them that they are ignorant of what they are doing. Now every melody is right when it has suitable harmony and rhythm, and wrong when unsuitable.
>
> CLEINIAS. That is most certain.
>
> AN ATHENIAN STRANGER. But can a man who does not know a thing, as we were saying, know that the thing is right?
>
> *Cleinias*. Impossible.
>
> AN ATHENIAN STRANGER. Then as now, as would appear, we are making the discovery that our newly appointed choristers, whom we hereby invite and, although they are their own masters, compel to sing, must be educated to such an extent as to be able to follow the steps of the rhythm and the notes of the song, that they may review the harmonies and rhythms, and be able to select what are suitable for men of their age and character to sing; and may sing them, and have innocent pleasure from their own performance, and also lead younger men to receive the virtues of character with the welcome which they deserve. Having such training, they will attain a more accurate knowledge than falls to

the lot of the common people, or even of the poets themselves. For the poet need not know the third point, viz. whether the imitation is good or not, though he can hardly help knowing the laws of melody and rhythm. But our critics must know all the three, that they may choose the best, and that which is nearest to the best; for otherwise they will never be able to charm the souls of young men in the way of virtue.

......

AN ATHENIAN STRANGER. Our choruses shall sing to the young and tender souls of children, reciting in their strains all the noble thoughts of which we have already spoken...the sum of them shall be, that the life which is by the Gods deemed to be the happiest is also the best;—thus we shall both affirm what is most certainly true, and the mind of our young disciples will be more likely to receive these words of ours than any others which we might address to them.

CLEINIAS. I assent to what you say.

AN ATHENIAN STRANGER. First will enter in their natural order the choir of the Muses, composed of children, which is to sing lustily the heaven-taught lay to the whole city. Next will follow the choir of young men under the age of thirty, who will call upon the God Paean to testify to the truth of their words, and will pray him to be gracious to the youth and to turn their hearts. Thirdly, the choir of elder men, who are from thirty to sixty years of age, will also sing. There remain those who are too old to sing and they will tell stories, illustrating the same virtues, as with the voice of an oracle.

CLEINIAS. Who are those who compose the third choir, stranger? I do not clearly understand what you mean to say about them.

AN ATHENIAN STRANGER. And yet almost all that I have been saying has been said with a view to them.

CLEINIAS. Will you try to be a little plainer?

AN ATHENIAN STRANGER. I was speaking at the commencement of our discourse, as you will remember, of the fiery nature of young creatures: I said that they were unable to keep quiet either in limb or voice, and they they called out and jumped about in a disorderly manner; and that no other animal attained to any perception of order in these two things, but man only. Now the order of motion is called rhythm, and the order of voice, in which high and low are duly mingled, is called harmony; and both together are termed choric song. And I said that the Gods had pity on us, and gave us Apollo and the Muses to be our playfellows and leaders in the dance; and Dionysus, as I dare say that you will remember, was the third.

CLEINIAS. I quite remember.

AN ATHENIAN STRANGER. Thus far have I spoken of the chorus of Apollo and the Muses; the third and remaining chorus must be called that of Dionysus.

CLEINIAS. How is that? There is something strange, at any rate on first hearing, in a Dionysiac chorus of old men, if you really mean that those who are above thirty, and may be fifty, or from fifty to sixty years of age, are to dance in his honor.

AN ATHENIAN STRANGER. Very true; and therefore it must be shown that there is good reason for the proposal.

CLEINIAS. Certainly.

AN ATHENIAN STRANGER. Are we agreed thus far?

CLEINIAS. About what?

AN ATHENIAN STRANGER. That every man and boy, slave and free, both sexes, and the whole city, should never cease charming themselves with the strains of which we have spoken; and that there should be every sort of change and variation of them in order to take away the effect of sameness, so that the singers may always receive pleasure from their hymns, and may never weary of them?

CLEINIAS. Everyone will agree.

AN ATHENIAN STRANGER. Where, then, will that best part of our city which, by reason of age and intelligence, has the greatest influence, sing these fairest of strains in such a way as to do most good. Shall we be so foolish as to neglect this regulation, which may have a decisive effect in making the songs most beautiful and useful?

CLEINIAS. But, says the argument, we cannot neglect it.

AN ATHENIAN STRANGER. Then how can we carry out our purpose with decorum? Will this be the way?

CLEINIAS. What?

AN ATHENIAN STRANGER. When a man is advancing in years, he is afraid and reluctant to sing;—he has no pleasure in his own performances; and if compulsion is used, he will be more and more ashamed, the older and more discreet he grows;—is not this true?

CLEINIAS. Certainly.

AN ATHENIAN STRANGER. Well, and will he not be yet more ashamed if he has to stand up and sing in the theater to a mixed audience?—and if moreover when he is required to do so, like the other choirs who contend for prizes, and have been trained under a singing master, he is pinched and hungry, he will certainly have a feeling of shame and discomfort which will make him very unwilling to perform.

CLEINIAS. No doubt.

AN ATHENIAN STRANGER. How, then, shall we reassure him, and get him to sing? Shall we begin by enacting that boys shall not taste wine at all until they are eighteen years of age; we will tell them that fire must not be poured upon fire, whether in the body or in the soul, until they begin to go to work—this is a precaution which has to be taken against the excitableness of youth;—afterwards they may taste wine in moderation up to the age of thirty, but while a man is young he should abstain altogether from intoxication and from excess of wine; when, at length, he has reached forty years, after dinner at a public mess, he may invite not only the other gods, but Dionysus above all, to the mystery and festivity of the elder men, making use of the wine which he has given men to lighten the sourness of old age; that in age we may renew our youth, and forget our sorrows; and also in order that the nature of the soul, like iron melted in the fire, may become softer and so more impressible. In the first place, will not anyone who is thus mellowed be more ready and less ashamed to sing,—I do not say before a large audience, but before a moderate company; nor yet among strangers, but among his familiars, and, as we have often said, to chant, and to enchant?

CLEINIAS. He will be far more ready.[32]

The Greek choirs were also active in participation at contests, in part, no doubt, for the reason given by Antiphon, a famous fifth century BC orator, in a fragment of a speech,

> For honors, prizes, the baits which God has given to mankind, bring them to the necessity of great toil and sweat.[33]

We read of these contests as early as Aristophanes,

> To thee, oh Phoebus, I dedicate my most beauteous songs; to thee,
> the sacred victor in the poetical contests.[34]

---

[32] *Laws*, 668c.

[33] Quoted in Rosamond Kent Sprague, *The Older Sophists* (Columbia: University of South Carolina Press, 1972), 228.

[34] *The Themophoriazusae*, 108.

There was also an important role played by choral music in education and this has also been addressed by Plato.

> AN ATHENIAN STRANGER. The whole choral art is also in our view the whole of education; and of this art, rhythms and harmonies form the part which has to do with the voice.
> CLEINIAS. Yes.
> AN ATHENIAN STRANGER. The movement of the body has rhythm in common with the movement of the voice, but gesture is peculiar to it, whereas song is simply the movement of the voice.
> CLEINIAS. Most true.
> AN ATHENIAN STRANGER. And the sound of the voice which reaches and educates the soul, we have ventured to term music.[35]

In another reference to this relationship, Plato also explains how accountability may be measured.

> AN ATHENIAN STRANGER. And the uneducated is he who has not been trained in the chorus, and the educated is he who has been well trained?
> CLEINIAS. Certainly.
> AN ATHENIAN STRANGER. And the chorus is made up of two parts, dance and song?
> CLEINIAS. True.
> AN ATHENIAN STRANGER. Then he who is well educated will be able to sing and dance well?
> CLEINIAS. I suppose that he will.
> AN ATHENIAN STRANGER. Let us see; what are we saying?
> CLEINIAS. What?
> AN ATHENIAN STRANGER. He sings well and dances well; now must we add that he sings what is good and dances what is good?
> CLEINIAS. Let us make that addition.
> AN ATHENIAN STRANGER. We will suppose that he knows the good to be good, and the bad to be bad, and makes use of them accordingly: which now is the better trained in dancing and music—he who is able to move his body and use his voice in what he understands to be the right manner, but has no delight in good or hatred of evil; or he who is scarcely correct in gesture and voice and in understanding, but is right in his sense of pleasure and pain, and welcomes what is good, and is offended at what is evil?
> CLEINIAS. There is a great difference, stranger, in the two kinds of education.
> AN ATHENIAN STRANGER. If we know what is good in song and dance, then we truly know also who is educated and who is uneducated; but if not, then we certainly shall not know wherein lies the safeguard of education, and whether there is any or not.[36]

The dance, which was apparently accompanied by the aulos, was in Plato's view especially valuable in the relief of certain powerful emotions.

> The affection both of the Bacchantes and of the children is an emotion of fear, which springs out of an evil habit of the soul. And when someone applies external agitation to affections of this sort, the motion coming from without gets the better of the terrible and violent internal one, and produces a

---

35 *Laws*, 672e.

36 Ibid., 654b.

> peace and calm in the soul, and quiets the restless palpitation of the heart, which is a thing much to be desired, sending the children to sleep, and making the Bacchantes, although they remain awake, to dance to the pipe with the help of those gods to whom they offer acceptable sacrifices, and producing in them a sound mind, which takes the place of their frenzy.[37]

The historian Polybius recalled this educational purpose when he departed from his description of the internal wars of the period 220–216 BC to give a fervent testimonial to the role music plays in shaping the character of entire peoples and a plea that the Cynaetheans return to this use of music to save themselves. In the course of his argument he mentions the role of contests in ancient Greece.

> For it is a well-known fact, familiar to all, that it is hardly known except in Arcadia, that in the first place the boys from their earliest childhood are trained to sing in measure the hymns and paeans in which by traditional usage they celebrate the heroes and gods of each particular place; later they learn the measures of Philoxenus and Timotheus, and every year in the theater they compete keenly in choral singing to the accompaniment of professional aulos players, the boys in the contest proper to them and the young men in what is called the men's contest.[38]

Finally, we must mention that nearly all the ancient philosophers make a point to mention the decline in art music in ancient Greece and which was much in evidence during the final, Alexandrian Period. Athenaeus, for one, summarizes the current state of this decline.

> It happened that in ancient times the Greeks were music lovers; but later, with the breakdown of order when practically all the ancient customs fell into decay, this devotion to principle ceased, and debased fashions in music came to light, wherein every one who practiced them substituted effeminacy for gentleness, and license and looseness for moderation. What is more, this fashion will doubtless be carried further if some one does not bring the music of our forebears once more to open practice.[39]

Athenaeus finds only the Spartans have preserved the old values.

> Of all the Greeks the Spartans have most faithfully preserved the art of music, employing it most extensively, and many composers of lyrics have arisen among them. Even to this day they carefully retain the ancient songs, and are very well taught in them and strict in holding to them ... For people [are] glad to turn from the soberness and austerity of life to the solace of music, because the art has the power to charm.[40]

Among the most noble of the old traditions were the choral odes of the sixth century BC. Now we also see a rather dismal stage of their evolution.

---

[37] Ibid., 791.

[38] Polybius, *The Histories*, IV.20.5ff, trans. W. R. Paton (Cambridge: Harvard University Press, 1954).

[39] Athenaeus, *Deipnosophistae*, XIV, 633.

[40] Ibid., XIV, 632.

Pratinas of Phlius, when hired aulos players and dancers usurped the dancing places, became indignant at the way in which the aulos players failed to accompany the choruses in the traditional fashion, and choruses now sang a mere accompaniment to the aulos players; ... 'What uproar is this? What dances are these? What outrage hath assailed the alter of Dionysus with its loud clatter? ... 'Tis the song that is queen, established by the Pierian Muse; but the aulos must be second in the dance, for he is even a servant; let him be content to be leader in the revel only, in the fist-fights of tipsy youngsters raging at the front door. Beat back him who has the breath of a mottled toad, burn up in flames that spit-wasting, babbling raucous reed, spoiling melody and rhythm in its march, that hireling whose body is fashioned by an auger!'[41]

---

[41] Ibid., XIV, 617.

On the Ancient Roman Chorus

IN TERMS OF ART MUSIC, as well as a great deal of the culture itself, musical traditions traveled generally from Greece to Rome. In particular many slave musicians were Greeks who fled to Rome after the conquest of Macedonia in 167 BC and the destruction of Corinth in 144 BC. It was for this reason that the historian Nepos (100–22 BC) wrote that the practice of music and singing was not appropriate to a man of distinction.[1] In any case, this vast number of slaves made possible some very large performing forces. A procession in the time of Ptolemaeus Philadelphus (283–246 BC), for example, included no fewer than six hundred singers and three hundred kithara players.[2]

It seems likely that early Roman choral music used for religious-cult ceremonies was much influenced by similar practice in earlier Greece. Livy, for example, describes a very early (eighth century BC) religious procession by women which seems very Greek in character. This instance is of particular interest for as they are moving down the street they are doing a dance in a triple meter.

> … in the service of Mars Gradivus … they were given the uniform of an embroidered tunic and bronze breastplate, and their special duty was to carry the *ancilia*, or sacred shields, one of which was fabled to have fallen from heaven, as they moved through the city chanting their hymns to the triple beat of their ritual dance.[3]

One of the later first century AD emperors re-established festivals which included choral competition. Domitian created a five-year festival which included sports, choral performances, solo performance on various instruments and in singing and public speaking.[4]

During the Empire Period (14–476 AD) the upper class began to become interested in performing music. According to Sendrey, by,

> around 50 AD music in Rome was recognized as an art form valued for itself. From then on, it became an essential element in the education of every distinguished Roman, male or female; women especially passed entire days practicing music, singing, and even composing new songs. Even the emperors were affected by the music mania …
>
> Lyric poems had to be performed with musical accompaniment—art music was composed mainly for this purpose.

---

[1] Alfred Sendrey, *Music in the Social and Religious Life of Antiquity* (Rutherford: Fairleigh Dickinson University Press, 1974), 407.

[2] Ibid., 411.

[3] Livy, *The Early History of Rome*, I. 20.

[4] Suetonius, *The Twelve Caesars* (New York: Penguin, 1989), 302.

> In the pantomimes, *symphoniae* were inserted, which meant that a choir sang and danced to the accompaniment of a group of instrumentalists. Sometimes an actor sang a solo aria; in other instances a professional singer sang the lyrics, while a mime interpreted the words with gestures and appropriate dances. The pantomimes were frequently presented in gigantic proportions; sometimes 3000 singers and 3000 dancers participated in them.
>
> There were numerous instrumental virtuosi, and the number of good average artists was legion. From all parts of the empire musicians converged on Rome, attracted by the gold of the capital of the world. The huge number of musically educated slaves made it possible for their masters to maintain large choirs and orchestras with almost no expense …
>
> Many wealthy persons had their own permanent music groups. Some had their especially gifted musicians sent to famous teachers for further education.
>
> Professional virtuosi were in great demand and undertook extended concert tours in all parts of the empire. They were highly paid and often became the idols of the audiences. For several of them monuments or statues were erected … Women of high society adored them and paid large sums for their love; other female admirers fought for the possession of a plectrum the admired artist had used in the concerts; others offered sacrifices to the gods to insure victory for their favorites in the festival contests … The victors in poetical and musical contests received the coveted oak wreath from the hands of the emperor … The honoraria of some of the traveling virtuosi bordered on the fantastic …
>
> In a fresco of Herculaneum (now in the Naples Museum) a concert is depicted in the home of a wealthy man. It shows a female aulos player … and accompanied by a kithara player. That it is a real house concert and not merely a private musical entertainment is evident from the large audience depicted in this fresco.[5]

The mention, above, of three thousand singers, while extraordinary, only reflects the great number of practicing musicians in Rome. In 284 AD, Carinus presented a series of plays in which he used, among other things, one hundred trumpeters and one hundred horn players.[6] Seneca mentioned that sometimes it seemed that there were more people on the stage than there used to be in the audience.

> Do you not see how many voices there are in a chorus? Yet out of the many only one voice results. In that chorus one voice takes the tenor, another the bass, another the baritone. There are women, too, as well as men, and the aulos is mingled with them. In that chorus the voices of the individual singers are hidden; what we hear is the voices of all together. To be sure, I am referring to the chorus which the old-time philosophers knew; in our present day exhibitions we have a larger number of singers than there used to be spectators in the theaters of old. All the aisles are filled with rows of singers; brass instruments surround the auditorium; the stage resounds with auloi and instruments of every description; and yet from the discordant sounds a harmony is produced.[7]

---

5   Ibid., 387ff.

6   Ibid., 412.

7   *Epistolae*, 84.10.

Choral performance became more popular during this period and in addition to performances for plays,⁸ weddings, religious celebrations, there were also public concerts of both choral and solo performances. Juvenal, in commenting on the fact that deaf people cannot appreciate music, mentions that the choirs were already wearing robes, as well as references to concert halls and famous soloists.

> How can the deaf appreciate music? The standard
> Of the performance eludes them: a top-line soloist,
> Massed choirs in their golden robes, all mean less than nothing.
> What does it matter to them where they sit in the concert hall
> When a wind band blowing its guts out is barely audible?⁹

The Greek tradition of singing art music at banquets, after the tables were cleared, seems to have been practiced in Rome as well. There is an account of Aulus Gellius (ca. 117–ca. 180 AD) in which he describes such a concert consisting of choral groups singing poems of Anacreon and Sappo, as well as contemporary love-elegies.¹⁰

We should also mention here a curious reference by Pliny the Elder, while discussing geography, of a curious promontory in Illyria.

> There are also small islands at Nymphaeum called the Dancing Islands, because they move to the foot-beats of persons keeping time with the chanting of a choral song.¹¹

The most dramatic transformation by the Romans was in the nature of the quasi-religious celebrations. While Horace reports numerous aulos and lyres accompanying songs in the temple of Venus, much in the style of the Greek tradition, most Roman religious cult celebrations were violent and dangerous. There are a number of extant descriptions of these cult ceremonies,¹² but we shall allow one described by Livy, which documents the presence of a Roman chorus, to represent them all.

> It was common knowledge that for the past two years no one had been initiated who was over the age of twenty. As each one was introduced, he became a kind of sacrificial victim for the priests. They led the initiate to a place which resounded with shrieks, with the chanting of a choir, the clashing of cymbals and the beating of drums, so that the victim's cries for help, when violence was offered to his chastity, might not be heard.

---

8   *The Trojan Women* by Seneca includes a chorus in the Greek tradition, which mentions both lamentations (I, 77) and a wedding hymn (II, 202).

9   Juvenal, *Satire X*, 211.

10 Sendrey, *Music in the Social and Religious Life of Antiquity*, 408.

11 Pliny the Elder, *Natural History*, II, xcvi, 209. In VIII, lxx, 185, he mentions a festival in Egypt which includes a chorus of boys singing praises of the Ox.

12 Most frequently described are the Roman Bacchanalia, for the Roman god, Bacchus, which had its origins in the Greek Dionysus celebrations.

In 186 BC the testimony of a woman came to the attention of one of the consuls and led to an investigation of this cult. Her understanding was that until recent years it has been a three-day festival for women only, with matrons chosen in rotation as priestesses. She identified the priestess, Paculla Annia, as the one who altered this tradition, ostensibly on the advice of the gods. She changed from three days per year to five days per month held at night.

> From this time when the rites were held promiscuously, with men and women mixed together, and when the license offered by darkness had been added, no sort of crime, no kind of immorality, was left unattempted. There were more obscenities practiced between men than between men and women. Anyone refusing to submit to outrage or reluctant to commit crimes was slaughtered as a sacrificial victim ... Men, apparently out of their wits, would utter prophecies with frenzied bodily convulsions; matrons, attired as Bacchantes, with their hair disheveled and carrying blazing torches, would run down to the Tiber, plunge their torches into the water and bring them out still alight—because they contained a mixture of live sulfur and calcium. Men were said to have been carried off by the gods—because they had been attached to a machine and whisked away out of sight to hidden caves.

She indicated that many people were involved in these rites, including members of the aristocracy. Indeed, when the larger government investigation began there was such a flight of people from Rome that legal proceedings became temporarily impossible.

The government, naturally, feared that any covert society of this size might have the potential to become a political threat to the state itself. In time the Senate arranged for one of its members to speak to the public to help mitigate the general sense of fear and panic caused by the wide-ranging investigations. He placed the blame on the women.

> The Bacchic rites have for a long time been performed all over Italy, and recently they have been celebrated even in many places in Rome itself; I am quite sure that you have been made aware of this not only by rumors but also by the bangings and howlings heard in the night, which echo throughout the city ...
>
> As for their number, if I tell you that there are many thousands of them, you are bound to be scared out of your wits, unless I go on to describe who they are and what kind of people they are. In the first place, then, a great part of them are women, and they are the source of this evil thing; next, there are males, scarcely distinguishable from females.

The government eventually determined that more than seven thousand persons were involved in these rites, and Livy tells us that many committed suicide and that the number condemned to death and executed outnumbered those who were thrown into prison.

In addition to these kinds of cult celebrations, there were special rites held for a wide variety of special occasions. For example, Livy, mentions a special nine-day rite to bless troops preparing to leave Rome, ca. 210–207 BC. On this occasion twenty-seven virgins marched through the city singing a hymn composed for the occasion by Livius.

In the forum the procession stopped, and the virgins, linked together by a cord passed through their hands, moved on, beating time with their feet to the music of their voice. They then proceeded ... to the Temple of Juno Regina; where two victims were immolated.[13]

From the pen of Horace (65–8 BC) we have a love song addressed not to his lover but to the mistress of Caesar. This poem is one of several which contain hints that the movements of the Greek choral tradition were also continued by the Romans.

> My sweet Muse bids me sing lady Licymnia's
> Praise, describing the fair light of her lustrous eyes
> And the mutual trust holding her heart and yours
> In the bonds of devoted love.
>
> Stiff constraint does not keep her from the choral dance,
> Nor from the light repartee, nor from entwining arms
> With the maidens attired grandly before the throngs
> On Diana's most holy day.[14]

A similar hint that the choral dance tradition was still known in the first century AD is found in a reference by Lucilius to a banquet and a slave choir.

> You know the rule of my little banquets. Today, Aulus, I invite you under new convivial laws. No lyric poet shall sit there and recite, and you yourself shall neither trouble us nor be troubled with literary discussions.
>
> ......
>
> I never knew, Epicrates, that you were a tragedian or a choral aulos player or any other sort of person whose business it is to have a chorus with them. But I invited you alone; you, however, came bringing with you from home a chorus of dancing slaves, to whom you hand all the dishes over your shoulder as a gift. If this is to be so, make the slaves sit down at the table and we will come and stand at their feet to serve.[15]

Perhaps some choral performances were less disciplined than others. Lucian (second century AD), in one of his satires, describes what the earth might look like from heaven above and compares it to the chaos of a poor choral performance. While this description is not intended to be of a real chorus, the fact that he employs this analogy suggests he must have seen such things.

> MENIPPUS. You must try to conceive what a queer jumble it all made. It was as if a man were to collect a number of choristers, or rather of choruses, and then tell each individual to disregard the others and start a melody of his own; if each did his best, went his own way, and tried to drown his neighbor, can you imagine what the musical effect would be?
> A FRIEND. A very ridiculous confusion.

---

[13] Livy, *History of Rome*, XXVII, 37.

[14] Horace, *Odes*, II, 12.

[15] *The Greek Anthology*, trans. W. R. Paton (Cambridge: Harvard University Press, 1939), IV, 10, 11.

> MENIPPUS. Well, friend, such are the earthly dancers; the life of man is just such a discordant performance; not only are the voices jangled, but the steps are not uniform, the motions not concerted, the objects not agreed upon—until the impresario dismisses them one by one from the stage, with a 'not wanted.' Then they are all alike, and quiet enough, confounding no longer their undisciplined rival melodies. But as long as the show lasts in its marvelous diversity, there is plenty of food for laughter in its vagaries.[16]

In another place, Lucian gives a similar description of an undisciplined chorus.

> For not only the sounds they make are out of tune, but also their attitudes are unlike, and their movements contradictory, and in their purposes they are utterly at variance, until the conductor of the chorus drives every one of them off the stage, declaring that he has no further use for them.[17]

Tacitus (55–117 AD), perhaps forecasting the decay of cultural traditions, mentions a 'lascivious chorus' in connection with a wine festival.[18]

A reference from the very end of the period of the Roman Empire still speaks of very large numbers of musicians in the theaters, including choruses. Ammianus Marcellinus, observes,

> The vast and magnificent theaters of Rome were filled by three thousand female dancers, and by three thousand singers, with the masters of the respective choruses. Such was the popular favor which they enjoyed, that, in a time of scarcity ... the merit of contributing to the public pleasures exempted them from a law, which was strictly executed against the professors of the liberal arts.[19]

A passing comment by St. Gregory of Nazianzus (330–390 AD) possibly gives us an important insight into the placement on stage of these large ancient choirs and their conductors.

> I thought, in my vain imaginings, that once I had control of this throne (outward show carries great weight) I could act like a chorus leader between two choruses. Putting the two groups chorus-fashion, one on this side of me, the other on that, I could blend them with myself and thus weld into a unity what had been so badly divided.[20]

Finally, one of the letters of Pliny the Younger discusses the paid claques who were hired to applaud orators and in passing mentions that these groups were conducted by a choral conductor—a fringe benefit![21]

---

[16] Lucian, *Icaromenippus*.

[17] Winthrop D. Sheldon in *A Second Century Satirist* (Philadelphia: Drexel Biddle, 1901), 361.

[18] Tacitus, *Annals*, XI, 31.

[19] Quoted in Edward Gibbon, *The History of the Decline and Fall of the Roman Empire* (Philadelphia: Coates), III, 32.

[20] Saint Gregory of Nazianzus, 'Concerning his own Life,' trans. Denis Meehan (Washington, D.C.: The Catholic University of America Press), 119.

[21] *The Letters of the Younger Pliny* (New York: Penguin, 1969), 73.

On Music of Ancient Courts

PERHAPS THE BEST KNOWN ACCOUNT of a musical ensemble in an ancient court is the Babylonian one of Nebuchadnezzar which is described in detail in the Old Testament Book of Daniel, 3:5 and 3:15. This account suffers from the problem one encounters in attempting to consider the older parts of the Old Testament as literal history. The Book of Daniel was written four hundred years after the events it describes and so it is prone to all the mistakes and exaggerations of oral tradition. Furthermore, the names of the actual instruments mentioned in Daniel, *karna, mashrokita, kathros, sambyke, pesanterin,* and *sumponyah,* are expressed in several languages, including Greek, and at least two of them have no agreed upon modern meaning.[1] In view of these difficulties, translators have tended to simply make up names of instruments which might be familiar to readers. Thus, the *King James Version* gives us a band, consisting of typical Renaissance instruments, including cornett, flute, harp, sackbut, psaltery, and dulcimer! The *Revised Standard Version* (1952) invents a nonsense ensemble that no one would ever want to listen to: a horn, pipe, lyre, trigon, harp, and bagpipe.

Our most descriptive accounts of the entertainments of the Persians (600–330 BC) are written by their rivals the Greeks and thus they emphasize the more extravagant aspects of court life. Athenaeus records two anecdotes relative to the dinner music of the court of Cyrus the Great (585–529 BC). First he quotes the *Persian History* by Heracleides of Cumae:

> In most cases the king breakfasts and dines alone, but sometimes his wife and some of his sons dine with him. And throughout the dinner his concubines sing and play the lyre; one of them is the soloist, the others sing in chorus.[2]

Athenaeus does not mention how many concubine musicians performed for these dinners here, but in another place he says '300 women watch over him.'[3] Annarus, the viceroy under Cyrus, wore women's clothes and ornaments, according to Athenaeus, and, although he himself was technically a slave of the king, his dinners were always accompanied by one hundred and fifty women, playing on harps and singing.[4]

Presumably this tradition continued for two centuries, for several accounts mention that when the Greeks finally brought an end to this empire by the defeat of Darius III in 330 BC, they carried away 329 concubine musicians from the court.[5]

---

[1] Curt Sachs, *The History of Musical Instruments* (New York, 1940), 83ff.

[2] Athenaeus, *Deipnosophistae*, IV, 145.

[3] Ibid., XII, 514.

[4] Ibid., XII, 530.

[5] Henry G. Farmer, 'The Music of Ancient Mesopotamia,' in *The New Oxford History of Music* (London: Oxford University Press, 1966), 239.

It is not clear if Plutarch's reference to these kings refers to these older ones or kings of his generation, but it sounds as if he is retelling a tale told many times and improved upon each time with the telling.

> The Persian kings, when they contain themselves within the limits of their usual banquets, suffer their married wives to sit down at their tables; but when they once design to indulge the provocations of amorous heats and wine, then they send away their wives, and call for their concubines, their gypsies, and their songstresses, with their lascivious tunes and wanton galliards. Wherein they do well, not thinking it proper to debauch their wives with the tipsy frolics and dissolute extravagances of their intemperance.[6]

Another interesting comment by Athenaeus, which may apply to these people, refers to the use of music for diplomacy!

> Many of the barbarians [those who do not speak Greek well] also conduct diplomatic negotiations to the accompaniment of aulos and harp to soften the hearts of their opponents.[7]

Herodotus, the great fifth century BC historian describes entertainment music of a rather high level among the ancient Greeks.

> When dinner was over, the suitors began to compete with each other in music and in talking in company ... Hippocleides ... asked the aulos player to play him a tune and began to dance to it.[8]

And, of course, we must assume that there was much music by the slaves and servants of the Greek nobles. Polybius tells a nice story about Cleomenes III, a King of Sparta in the third century BC. When one Nicagoras arrived at Alexandria by ship with a cargo of horses to sell, Cleomenes said to him,

> You would have done much better to bring a cargo of male prostitutes and girls to play the harp; that is the kind of cargo to please this King![9]

Arrian, in his history of Alexander the Great, writes that he had an extra-large chariot built so that in traveling he could recline on his couch with his intimate friends listening to the music of auloi.[10]

In Egypt one can still see in the paintings on the walls of the ancient tombs numerous small court ensembles. One king, Amenophis IV (also known as Ikhnaton) seems to have been an especially enthusiastic sponsor of music. One extraordinary tomb painting from ca. 1,570

---

[6] 'Conjugal Precepts.'

[7] Athenaeus, *Deipnosophistae*, XIV, 627. In XIV, 631, Athenaeus gives the form name of this kind of music as 'apostolic (also called parthenioi) ...'

[8] Herodotus, *The Histories*, VI, 128.

[9] Polybius (second century BC), *The Rise of the Roman Empire*, V, 37.

[10] Arrian, *The Campaigns of Alexander*, VI, 28. Alexander also had military trumpets playing as the fires consumed important leaders in their last rites. [Arrian, VII, 4]

BC shows a music school which he built in his capitol of Amarna. Here we see pictures of a collection of musical instruments spread over four rooms, in addition to scenes of instruction. Another painting from his court shows a concert by a double ensemble, which includes foreign guest artists, judging by their dress.

It is during the reign of this king, by the way, in which we see court scenes with apparently blind, or blindfolded, musicians. The significance of this is not known to modern scholars, some speculating that the blindfolds prevented slave musicians from seeing what was going on in the palace, others that the musician, being of a lower social order, was not permitted to look upon a god.

This is perhaps an appropriate place to mention that history has left us several accounts of additional wonderful blind musicians. One of these is documented in Homer's *The Odyssey*. The setting is a banquet, but, as this extraordinary passage makes clear, this is not the usual banquet music—this is music to be listened to. Indeed, we are told that only when everyone stopped eating and drinking did the singer begin to play and sing. In this case the singer was the blind Demodocus, 'to whom above all others has the god granted skill in song.' He is requested to 'give delight in whatever way his spirit prompts him to sing.'

> For him, the herald, set a silver-studded chair in the midst of the banqueters, leaning it against a tall pillar, and he hung the clear-toned lyre from a peg close above [the singer's] head, and showed him how to reach it with his hands. And beside him he placed a basket and a beautiful table [of food], and a cup of wine, to drink when his heart should bid him. So they put forth their hands to the good cheer lying ready before them. But when they had put from them the desire of food and drink, the Muse moved the minstrel to sing of the glorious deeds of warriors.[11]

As a testimonial to the contemplative listeners, Homer tells us that Odysseus [Ulysses] is moved to tears.

> This song the famous minstrel sang; but Odysseus grasped his great purple cloak with his stout hands, and drew it down over his head, and his comely face; for he had shame [that his guests, the Phaeacians, should see him] as he let fall tears from beneath his eyebrows. Yea, and as often as the divine minstrel ceased his singing, Odysseus would wipe away his tears and draw the cloak from off his head ... But as often as he began again, and the nobles of the Phaeacians bade him sing, because they took pleasure in his song, Odysseus would again cover his head and moan. Now from all the rest he concealed the tears that he shed.

Later, Demodocus is sent for again, for the purpose of having him play music for a dance. When the artist arrives, however, he 'struck the chords in prelude to his sweet lay and sang of the love of Ares and Aphrodite,' forcing the guests to listen rather than dance.[12]

---

[11] *The Odyssey*, trans. A. T. Murray (London: Heinemann, 1960), VIII, 60ff.

[12] Ibid, 250ff.

A third time[13] Demodocus is brought before the guests to perform and again Homer notes that the performance waited until the eating had stopped. Because of the impact Odysseus experienced from the first performance, he now begs the singer to 'change thy theme' and sing no more of the fate of the Achaeans, but rather of the 'building of the horse of wood.' This request the singer complies with, but apparently in such a way that Odysseus was again moved to tears.

> This song the famous minstrel sang. But the heart of Odysseus was melted and tears wet his cheeks beneath his eyelids. And as a woman wails and flings herself about her dear husband, who has fallen in front of his city and his people, seeking to ward off from his city and his children the pitiless day; and as she beholds him dying and gasping for breath, she clings to him and shrieks aloud, while the foe behind her smite her back and shoulders with their spears, and lead her away to captivity to bear toil and woe, while with most pitiful grief her cheeks are wasted: even so did Odysseus let fall pitiful tears from beneath his brows. Now from all the rest he concealed the tears that he shed, but Alcinous alone marked him and took heed, for he sat by him and heard him groaning heavily.

Finally this Alcinous says, 'Let the minstrel cease, that we may all make merry.' Before leaving these performances by this blind poet, we must also point out that some scholars believe Homer himself was blind.

Athenaeus provides a brief description of dancing presented as entertainment during a banquet. The music is provided the dancers by the same blind poet mentioned in *The Odyssey*.

> For Demodocus sang while 'boys in their first bloom' danced, and in the Forging of the Arms a boy played the lyre while others opposite him 'frisked about to the music and the dance.'[14]

Another blind poet-singer is found in an anonymous poem, ca. 800 BC, called, 'To Apollo.' In this poem the poet first gives us an interesting description of the talents of these poets, as well as a brief autobiographical note.

> After they first praise Apollo with a hymn
> > and now again Leto and arrow-pouring Artemis,
> > they tell of men and women who lived long ago
> > and sing a hymn, charming the races of men.
> The tongues of all men and their noisy chatter
> > they know how to mimic; such is their skill in composing the song
> > that each man might think he himself were speaking.
> But now may Apollo and Artemis be propitious;
> > and all you maidens farewell. I ask you to call me to mind
> > in time to come whenever some man on this earth,
> > a stranger whose suffering never ends, comes here and asks:
> > 'Maidens, which of the singers, a man wont to come here,
> > is to you the sweetest, and in whom do you most delight?'
> Do tell him in unison that I am he,

---

[13] Ibid., 470ff.

[14] Athenaeus, *Deipnosophistae*, I, 15.

a blind man, dwelling on the rocky island of Chios,
whose songs shall all be the best in time to come.[15]

Without any question, the most distinguished blind musician of music history was Francesco Landini (1335–1397), who became blind due to having smallpox in his youth. He was a well-rounded man, honored by King Peter I of Cyprus as a musician and poet. He was an exceptional composer, skilled in performance on many instruments, including the organ, and invented a number of instruments, including a sort of 'one-man band' called the 'Siren of Sirens.' Though employed in an ecclesiastical position, most of his *ballate* are concerned with love. He was remembered by Domenico da Prato, in his 'Paradiso degli Alberti,' as a leading humanist and as a performer on the *organetto* 'whose playing could attract the nightingale.'[16] Indeed there is a fine description of such a moment when birds stop their singing to listen to Landini.

> Now the sun rose higher and the heat of the day increased and the whole company remained in the pleasant shade; and as a thousand birds were singing among the verdant branches, someone asked Francesco to play the organ a little, to see whether the sound would make the birds increase or diminish their song. He did so at once, and a great wonder followed: for when the sound began many of the birds were seen to fall silent, and gather around as if in amazement, listening for a long time.[17]

To return to the Middle East, we can assume that much of the ancient musical traditions of the Hebrews came from the older civilization of Egypt, as was also the experience of ancient Greece. While the years the Hebrews spent in Egypt form a critical role in the drama of the Old Testament story, few actual details of this 430 year period are supplied. It is clear that most of this time the Hebrews lived freely in Egypt and were 'captives' in only the final eighty years of this period. During the first 350 years they were apparently free enough to conduct their own border wars,[18] independent of the Egyptians, enjoyed the economic freedom to maintain their own large herds of cattle[19] and enjoyed sufficient cultural respect that one of them actually married the daughter of a Pharaoh.[20] We can assume therefore that during this long period they were free to absorb much from the older Egyptian culture, including musical practices. In the case of Moses, we are told he 'was instructed in all the wisdom of the Egyptians.'[21]

---

15 'To Apollon,' 158–173, *The Homeric Hymns*, trans. Apostolos N. Athanassakis (Baltimore: Johns Hopkins University Press, 1976).

16 Quoted in Ibid., 170.

17 Giovanni da Prato, *Paradiso degli Alberti* [1389].

18 1 Chronicles 7:21.

19 Exodus 9:6, 7; 10:9.

20 1 Chronicles 4:18.

21 Acts 7:22.

The Old Testament also fails to give us much information about the period of captivity in Babylonia, after the destruction of Solomon's Temple in 537 BC. But again, it appears they were not 'captives' in the modern sense of the word, for when the 42,000 of them were allowed to return they brought back with them 7,337 slaves of their own, in addition to 245 male and female [slave] singers![22] One of the apocryphal books also mentions that they returned with all their musical instruments.[23] It is evident, in any case, that the Hebrews preserved their musical heritage during this period, as we can read in some of the most beautiful lines of the Old Testament.

> By the waters of Babylon,
>   there we sat down and wept,
>   when we remembered Zion.
> On the willows there
>   we hung up our lyres.
> For there our captors
>   required of us songs.[24]

As one would expect, there is little attention given in the Old Testament to the banquets accompanied by the music of the prostitute girls, who are so widely discussed in other ancient literature. But here and there are hints that the Hebrew aristocracy may have enjoyed the same kinds of entertainments found in neighboring countries. In one of those passages which are never read in church, even the wise King Solomon admits,

> I also gathered for myself silver and gold and the treasure of kings and provinces; I got singers, both men and women, and many concubines, man's delight.[25]

It is this type of female singer that is meant when we read,

> Use not much the company of a woman that is a singer, lest thou be taken with her attempts.[26]

Of course, we have a famous example of a royal person who was a practicing musician in the person of King David. In 1 Samuel 18:10 we are told David practiced everyday on his lyre and in Amos 6:5 we are told he also invented musical instruments.

One of the most extensive accounts of music in the Old Testament deals with the use of trumpet signals by the high priest to control the movements of great numbers of persons. This passage from the Book of Numbers is the most extensive discussion of its kind in ancient literature.

---

[22] Nehemiah 7:67 and 1 Esdras 5:42. Ezra 2:65 gives 200 singers.

[23] 1 Esdras 5:2. The apocryphal books appear in the early Septuagint and Vulgate versions of the Old Testament, but are not used by the modern Jewish and Protestant faiths.

[24] Psalm 137.

[25] Ecclesiastes 2:8.

[26] Ecclesiasticus 9:4.

> The Lord said to Moses, 'Make two silver trumpets; of hammered work you shall make them; and you shall use them for summoning the congregation, and for breaking camp. And when both are blown, all the congregation shall gather themselves to you at the entrance of the tent of meeting. But if they blow only one, then the leaders, the heads of the tribes of Israel, shall gather themselves to you. When you blow an alarm, the camps that are on the east side shall set out. And when you blow an alarm the second time, the camps that are on the south side shall set out. An alarm is to be blown whenever they are to set out. But when the assembly is to be gathered together, you shall blow, but you shall not sound an alarm. And the sons of Aaron, the priests, shall blow the trumpets. The trumpets shall be to you for a perpetual statute throughout your generations. And when you go to war in your land against the adversary who oppresses you, then you shall sound an alarm with the trumpets, that you may be remembered before the Lord your God, and you shall be saved from your enemies.
>
> On the day of your gladness also, and at your appointed feasts,[27] and at the beginnings of your months, you shall blow the trumpets over your burnt offerings and over the sacrifices of your peace offerings.[28]

First of all, we see here the silver trumpet, not the ram's horn instrument. Although the dating of all the material in the Old Testament is problematic, one can generally assume that the silver trumpets were carried away from Egypt, for these would be impossible to make in the desert. Over time, of course, these instruments would become worn out and the ram's horn became their surrogate.

With the signals being so influential as to cause great masses of people to move, it is easy to understand why we are told here that only the high priests can play them.[29] And what a variety of signals we have here, with even the implication of two-part signals, for two trumpets playing in unison would be indistinguishable from one trumpet heard from a distance.

These instruments must have produced enough sound to be heard for a considerable distance. In one place we read of a very impressive progression of trumpet volume, 'a long blast,' followed by 'a very loud blast,' and then 'the sound of the trumpet grew louder and louder.'[30] Perhaps an additional clue to the potential volume of sound capable of being produced by these early trumpets can be found in several symbolic references to the instrument. When, for example, all the scattered people will be called back from the various nations, 'In that

---

[27] Examples of this use of the trumpet can be found in Numbers 29:1, 2 Chronicles 29:25 and Leviticus 23:24 and 25:9.

[28] Numbers 10:1ff.

[29] A rare exception is found in 2 Samuel 20:1, where we read, 'Now there happened to be there a worthless fellow, whose name was Sheba, the son of Bichri, a Benjaminite; and he blew the trumpet.'

[30] Exodus 19:13ff.

day a great trumpet will be blown.'[31] Or again, 'Cry aloud, spare not, lift up your voice like a trumpet.'[32] Other kinds of trumpet signals mentioned are a welcome for King Solomon,[33] for the coronation of a king,[34] and for the taking of an oath.[35]

The musical history of ancient Greece was one which progressed from a time when music was practiced by members of the higher classes to a time when it became relegated to slaves. Once performance became the occupation of slaves, it then became something inappropriate for an aristocrat to be identified with. It is with this background that the reader can make sense of a story of Philip II, father to Alexander the Great. After hearing his son, a rare aristocratic musician, perform a composition in a charming and skillfully manner, he said to him, 'Are you not ashamed, son, to play so well?'[36]

An anonymous author from the early fourteenth century quotes a story about the music teacher of Alexander the Great.

> Antigonus, the teacher of Alexander [the Great], when one day the latter was having a cythera played for his delight, took hold of the instrument and cast it into the mud, saying 'at your age it behooves you to reign and not to play the cythera. For it may be said that luxury debases the body and the country, as the sound of the cythera enfeebles the soul. Let him then be ashamed who should reign in virtue, and instead delights in luxury.'
>
> King Porrus who fought with Alexander ordered during a banquet that the strings of a player's cythera should be cut, saying, 'it is better to cut than to play, for virtue departs with sweet sounds.'[37]

One of the few other Greek leaders who was a practicing musician, and of whom we have some extant background information, was one of the great political leaders of fifth century BC Athens, Pericles. According to Plutarch,

> The master that taught him music, most authors are agreed, was Damon. Although Aristotle tells us that he was thoroughly practiced in all accomplishments of this kind by Pythoclides.[38]

Plutarch also mentions his sponsorship of music competitions and his construction of a special concert hall for the performance of music.

---

[31] Isaiah 27:12.

[32] Isaiah 58. In Zechariah 9:14, we are told God was a trumpet player.

[33] 1 Kings 1:34ff.

[34] 2 Kings 9:13.

[35] 2 Chronicles 15:14.

[36] Plutarch, Lives, 'Pericles.'

[37] 'Il Novellino,' trans. Edward Storer (London: Routledge), XIII. Arrian, the second century AD historian in *The Campaigns of Alexander* (New York: Penguin Classics, 1978), 67, makes an extended comment on the fact that Alexander had no composer of choral odes or epic poems to sing his virtues, hence today we know relatively little about him.

[38] *Lives*, 'Pericles.'

The Odeum, or concert hall, which in its interior was full of seats and ranges of pillars, and outside had its roof made to slope and descend from one single point at the top, was constructed, we are told, in imitation of the king of Persia's Pavilion ...

Pericles, also, eager for distinction, then first obtained the decree for a contest in musical skill to be held yearly at the Panathanaea, and he himself, being chosen judge, arranged the order and method in which the competitors should sing and play on the aulos and harp. And both at that time, and at other times also, they sat in this music room to see and hear all such trials of skill.

The musical experience among the aristocrats of ancient Rome was the reverse of Greece. Here music began as the work of slaves but eventually became a practice of the upper class. For example, Sulla, though a harsh ruler, was a good singer. The consul Lucius Flaccus (fl. ca. 19 AD) was a diligent trumpet player, practicing daily it would appear.[39] And while we know nothing specific of Julius Caesar's interest in music, perhaps his sympathy for it is reflected in the fact that upon his death and ritual cremation, the musicians of Rome threw their professional clothes onto the fire as an expression of grief.[40]

Musical traditions in Rome owed a strong debt to the practice of music in ancient Greece. A poem by Ovid (43 BC–17 AD) describes a celebration of the festival of Juno, who was the mythical daughter to Saturn and wife to Jupiter. The poem is also interesting for the musical details of the procession and the references to its Greek origin.

> The orchard town Camillus took, Falerii,
> Was my wife's birthplace; we came there one day.
> Juno's chaste feast was being celebrated,
> With games and sacrifice the place was gay;
> A feast well worth the visit, though the journey
> Is difficult, a steep and toilsome way.
>
> A grove stands there, ancient and dense and gloomy;
> The place must be a god's, one can be sure.
> The faithful offer incense at an alter,
> An artless alter reared in days of yore.
>
> Here, to the sound of auloi and solemn chanting,
> The long procession passes every year
> Through streets bedecked, with white Falerian heifers
> From their own fields, while all the people cheer ...
> ......
>
> Young men and shy girls go before the goddess,
> Their trailing vestments sweeping the wide street.
> The girls' hair is adorned with gold and jewels,
> And stately gowns half-hide their gilded feet.
>
> High on their heads they bear the holy vessels,
> White-robed according to the old Greek rites.

---

39 Alfred Sendrey, *Music in the Social and Religious Life of Antiquity* (Rutherford: Fairleigh Dickinson University Press, 1974), 391.

40 Suetonius, *Lives of the Caesars*, Book I, lxxxiv.

> The crowd is hushed as June in her golden
> Procession comes behind her acolytes.
>
> The form of the procession comes from Argos.
> On Agamemnon's death Halaesus fled
> The murder and his father's wealth and wandered
> Long over land and sea as exile led.[41]

Ovid's poem, above, mentions 'young men and shy girls' participating in the rituals. This leads us to suppose that the children of the nobles of Rome had some music education. We note, for example, that one motion before the Senate relative to the funeral for Augustus was that, 'boys and girls of the nobility should sing his dirge.'[42] An indication of an even more challenging achievement is found in a procession in honor of Antiochus of Commagene organized by Caligula which called for 'children of noble birth chanting an anthem in praise of his virtues.'[43]

One has to be disappointed that the greatest Roman philosopher, Cicero (106–43 BC), wrote so little about music. When he did discuss music he usually assigns little worth to it and thinks of it merely something which might cause one to neglect the more important studies, like philosophy. For example, speaking of Epicurus, he contends,

> You are pleased to think him uneducated. The reason is that he refused to consider any education worth the name that did not help to school us in happiness. Was he to spend his time in perusing poets, who give us nothing solid and useful, but merely childish amusement? Was he to occupy himself like Plato with music and geometry, arithmetic and astronomy, which starting from false premises cannot be true, and which moreover if they were true would contribute nothing to make our lives pleasanter and therefore better? Was he to study arts like these, and neglect the master art, so difficult and correspondingly so fruitful, the art of living?[44]

Curiously, he nevertheless admits that Nature has left man unfinished[45] and that one should aspire to develop life to its full perfection.[46]

During the period of ancient Rome known as the 'Empire' (14–476 AD) we find a number of emperors who were also musicians. According to Suetonius, Titus (79–81 AD) was also educated in music and 'sang and played harp agreeably and skillfully.'[47] Elagabalus (205–222 AD) is recorded as having been a performer of the aulos and panpipes in religious-cult services honoring Baal and again during the ceremonies relative to his coronation. He also performed

---

[41] *Amores*, III, 13. Suetonius, *The Twelve Caesars* (New York: Penguin, 1989), 52, mentions that during the last rites for Julius Caesar the musicians were wearing robes of the emperor and removed them, throwing them into the fire. Herodotus, in his *Histories*, VI, 58, mentions a tradition whereupon on the death of a leader women make a procession beating cauldrons.

[42] Suetonius, Ibid., 110.

[43] Ibid., 161.

[44] Cicero, *De Finibus*, I, xxi, 72.

[45] Ibid., IV, xiii, 35.

[46] Ibid., V, ix, 27.

[47] Suetonius, *Lives of the Caesars*, VIII, iii.

on the trumpet, lute, water organ and sang. Severus Alexander (208–235 AD) sang, played the aulos, lyre, and organ, but performed only for the members of his family.[48] He also legalized the guild system, which included various musical guilds (*collegia*),[49] and allowed them to elect spokesmen. Maximian (286–305 AD) also built a concert hall. We also have a description of the private music of the emperor Valentinian (364–375 AD).

> He assumed the privilege, when he returned home after a dinner, of having a flute player play soft music before him.[50]

There were significant numbers of other members of the aristocracy who had a serious interest in music during the reign of the emperors. Among the members of the Senate, for example, we know of Caius Calpurnius Piso, one of the conspirators against Nero in 65 AD, who was an accomplished lyre player.[51]

But it is of the musical accomplishments of some of the emperors that we have the most extant information.[52] Caligula (12–41 AD) received an education which included both vocal and instrumental music and used to perform in private concerts before the aristocracy. Suetonius provides such an illustration:

> Once, at about midnight, he summoned three senators of consular rank to the Palace; arriving half-dead with fear, they were conducted to a stage upon which, amid a tremendous racket of flutes and clogs, Caligula suddenly burst, dressed in cloak and ankle-length tunic, performed a song and dance, and disappeared again.[53]

Caligula once asked a famous singer, Apelles, whether he considered him or Jupiter the greater. When the singer unfortunately hesitated in his answer, Caligula had him scourged, but complimented the musical quality of his voice during his cries of pain! We are also told that 'if anyone made even the slightest sound while his favorite was dancing, he had the person dragged from his seat and scourged him with his own hand.'[54] Caligula, when traveling at sea, had a large enough vessel that he could recline on his couch listening not only to songs but entire choruses.[55]

---

[48] *The Scriptores Historiae Augustae*, trans. David Magie (London: Heinemann, 1924), II, 231, 269. Regarding his interest in poetry, he once called Virgil, 'the Plato of poets,' and kept a portrait of him.

[49] Each instrument had its own guild. The aulos guild, *Collegium tibicinum,* enjoyed being fed at public expense in the temple of Jupiter. There was also a guild of concert artists, called *Synodus magna psaltum*. According to Plutarch these guilds began in the seventh century BC and the aulos guild was one of the oldest professional organizations in Rome [Grove, XVI, 147].

[50] Ammianus Marcellinus, *Constantius et Gallus*, trans. John C. Rolfe (London: Heinemann, 1935), II, 583.

[51] Sendrey, *Music in the Social and Religious Life of Antiquity*, 391.

[52] Ibid., 392ff.

[53] Suetonius, *The Twelve Caesars* (New York: Penguin, 1989), 180.

[54] Suetonius, *Lives of the Caesars*, Book IV, lv.

[55] *Twelve Caesars*, 172.

Nero (37–68 AD) was the most debauched and cruel of the emperors, having murdered his mother when age twenty-two! But, he also loved music, poetry and the theater. He studied the lyre with the foremost teacher of his time, Terpnos, as is described by Suetonius.

> Having gained some knowledge of music in addition to the rest of his early education, as soon as he became emperor he sent for Terpnos, the greatest master of the lyre in those days, and after listening to him sing after dinner for many successive days until late at night, he little by little began to practice himself, neglecting none of the exercises which artists of that kind are in the habit of following, to preserve or strengthen their voices. For he used to lie upon his back and hold a leaden plate on his chest,[56] purge himself by the syringe and by vomiting, and deny himself fruits and all foods injurious to the voice.[57]

Suetonius mentions an occasion, a banquet attended by a later emperor, Vitellius, when a popular flutist, as an encore, performed something from 'the Master's Book.' When the player finished, 'Vitellius jumped up delightedly and led the applause.'[58]

Finally, the Emperor Titus (first century AD) sang pleasantly and had mastered the harp.[59]

---

[56] This information comes from Pliny the Elder, *Natural History*, XXXIV, xliv, 167, who says,

> Nero, whom heaven was pleased to make emperor, used to have a plate of lead on his chest when singing songs *fortissimo*, thus showing a method for preserving the voice.

[57] Suetonius, *Lives of the Caesars*, Book VI, xxff.

[58] *Twelve Caesars*, 273.

[59] Ibid., 293. Polybius, *The Rise of the Roman Empire*, VIII, 4, points out that the harp was such a familiar and ancient musical instrument that even one of the military siege machinery works, the sambucae, was named for an early harp.

Theater Music in the Ancient World

*He who deceives is more honest than he who does not deceive
and he who is deceived is wiser than he who is not.*[1]

Gorgias (483–376 BC)

THE ABOVE IS ONE OF THE MOST FREQUENTLY QUOTED STATEMENTS of the fifth century BC. It refers to the theater and meant that one can be more honest with fiction, not running the personal risk involved in telling the truth in non-fiction. It is one of the strengths that theater shares with music, which deals *only* with Truth. The ancient painter or sculptor could not afford the risk of portraying his highness the way he really looked! It was a bad day for potentates when photography was invented.

It has often been observed that Shakespeare was careful to mirror real life in the sixteenth-century England. But this is also true of the first great school of drama, the ancient Greek tragedians, Aeschylus (525–456 BC), Sophocles (495–406 BC) and Euripides (480–408 BC), together with the first great master of comedy, Aristophanes (448–380 BC). The reflections of real life which we find in these plays include insights on musical practice, as for example *The Acharnians* of Aristophanes, which complains about,

> … this musician, who plagues us with his silly improvisations.[2]

The beginning of the period of the great Greek tragedies overlaps the period of the last of the lyric poets. When Aeschylus died, in 456 BC, Pindar had at least ten years of activity left and Bacchylides was still in middle life. It seems reasonable to believe that the choral odes of the older poets, those works sung in public festivals and choral competitions, became the models for the 'choruses' of the fifth-century dramatists and their stage directions indicate, contrary to productions today, that they were still *sung* choruses. An example of one of these choruses which seems to us to be very much in the style of the old choral odes is one found in *Alcestis* by Euripides.

> *Chorus (singing)*
> O house of a bountiful lord,
> Even open to many guests,
> The God of Pytho,
> Apollo of the beautiful lyre,
> Designed to dwell in you
> And to live a shepherd in your lands!

---

[1] Quoted in Giovanni Reale, *A History of Ancient Philosophy* (Albany: State University of New York Press, 1987), 171.

[2] 844.

> On the slope of the hillsides
> He played melodies of mating
> On the Pipes of Pan to his herds.
>
> And the dappled lynxes fed with them
> In joy at your singing;
> From the wooded vale of Orthrys
> Came a yellow troop of lions;
> To the sound of your lyre, O Phoebus,
> Danced the dappled fawn
> Moving on light feet
> Beyond the high-crested pines,
> Charmed by your sweet singing.[3]

That this older repertoire was used in the plays also seems evident in a line in Euripides:

> For I sing this day to Dionysus
> The song that is appointed from of old.[4]

The sung epic poetry that we read of in Homer, where the singer praised the heros of the past, must have still been known in the fifth century BC for this form is satirized by Aristophanes in a passage which begins,

> *Trygaeus*
> Hi! child! what do you reckon to sing? Stand there and give me the opening line.
>
> *Boy*
> 'Glory to the young warriors.'
>
> *Trygaeus*
> Oh! leave off about your young warriors, you little wretch; we are at peace and you are an idiot and a rascal.
>
> *Boy*
> 'The skirmish begins, the hollow bucklers clash against each other.'
>
> *Trygaeus*
> Bucklers! Leave me in peace with your bucklers.
>
> *Boy*
> 'And then there came groanings and shouts of victory.'
>
> *Trygaeus*
> Groanings! ah! by Bacchus! look out for yourself, you cursed squaller, if you start wearying us again with your groanings and hollow bucklers.[5]

---

3 *Alcestis*, 568. Unless otherwise indicated, all translations for these four dramatists are quoted from Whitney J. Oates, ed., *The Complete Greek Drama* (New York: Random House, 1938).

4 *The Bacchae*, 70. The stage note before this line gives us an interesting picture of the chorus.

> There comes stealing in from the left a band of 15 Eastern Women, the light of the sunrise streaming upon their long white robes and ivy-bound hair. They wear fawn-skins over the robes, and carry some of them timbrels, some pipes and other instruments. Many bear the thyrsus, or sacred Wand, made of reed ringed with ivy.

5 *Peace*, 1268ff.

There is another musical tradition which is reflected in the plays, the custom at the end of aristocratic banquets to pass an instrument around allowing each guest to perform and sing. This practice, of course, also reflects a time when the aristocrat was expected to have the training to be proficient in doing this. In a scene in Aristophanes' *The Wasps*, Bdelycleon is trying to teach Philocleon how to behave at a banquet. He must recline, 'in an elegant style,' then the meal, libations to the gods, and finally participate in the after dinner concert performed by the guests themselves. In this case, Philocleon is not cultured enough to do this.

> *Bdelycleon*
> The aulos player has finished the prelude. The guests are Theorus, Aeschines, Phanus, Cleon, Acestor; and beside this last, I don't know who else. You are with them. Shall you know exactly how to take up the songs that are started?
>
> *Philocleon*
> Quite well.
>
> *Bdelycleon*
> Really?
>
> *Philocleon*
> Better than any born mountaineer of Attica.
>
> *Bdelycleon*
> That we shall see. Suppose me to be Cleon. I am the first to begin the song of Harmodius, and you take it up: 'There never yet was seen in Athens …'
>
> *Philocleon*
> '… such a rogue or such a thief.'
>
> *Bdelycleon*
> Why, you wretched man, it will be the end of you if you sing that. He will vow your ruin, your destruction, to chase you out of the country.[6]

A more sophisticated aristocrat is mentioned in a lost play called *The Harper*, by Menander, when a character speaks of someone playing a musical instrument, 'He is very fond of music, and always practicing tunes in luxurious ease.'[7]

The plays of Aristophanes also offer valuable glimpses of the role of music in education. He mentions the 'teacher of choirs who forgets his position …'[8] and the student who refused to learn any but the Dorian style.

> You also know what a pig's education he has had; his school-fellows can recall that he only liked the Dorian style and would study no other; his music master in displeasure sent him away saying; 'This youth, in matters of harmony, will only learn the Dorian style because it is akin to bribery.'[9]

---

[6] 1218ff.

[7] Quoted in Athenaeus, *Deipnosophistae*, XII, 510.

[8] *The Frogs*, 360.

[9] *The Knights*, 990.

The reader will note the reference here to Dorian as a *style*, not a scale, reflecting as it did a people and not music theory. The reference to bribery, *dorodokos*, 'taker of bribes,' involved a play on words with the term *Doristi*, 'in the Dorian style.' A French translator captured it best in referring to it as the 'Louis d'or-ian mode.'

In *The Clouds*, Aristophanes, through the mouth of a character called Just Discourse, provides us with a stark vision of the nature of discipline in music education 'in the old days'— days when music education meant singing of the glories of one's elders and in music of the old style (none of this modern music!).

> Very well, I will tell you what was the old education, when I used to teach justice with so much success and when modesty was held in veneration. Firstly, it was required of a child, that it should not utter a word. In the street, when they went to the music school, all the youths of the same district marched lightly clad and ranged in good order, even when the snow was falling in great flakes. At the master's house they had to stand with their legs apart and they were taught to sing either, 'Pallas, the Terrible, who overturneth cities,' or 'A noise resounded from afar' in the solemn tones of the ancient harmony. If anyone indulged in buffoonery or lent his voice any of the soft inflections, like those which today the disciples of Phrynis take so much pains to form, he was treated as an enemy of the Muses and belabored with blows … At table, they would not have dared, before those older than themselves, to have taken a radish, an aniseed or a leaf of parsley, and much less eat fish or thrushes or cross their legs.

The product of this kind of education is praised by the Leader of the Chorus in *The Frogs*,

> So with men we know for upright, blameless lives and noble names,
> Trained in music and palaestra, freemen's choirs and freemen's games,[10]

and by a character in *The Thesmophoriazusae*, who tells us that one's choice of music reveals one's character.

> Answer me. But you keep silent. Oh! just as you choose; your songs display your character quite sufficiently.[11]

This is a reflection on the long held concept of the relationship between music and character, which is discussed at length by the ancient Greek philosophers. Euripides makes an interesting observation on composers which is related to this, here relative to the character of the composer and his art. He says, the composer who does not enjoy his own music cannot expect others to enjoy his music.

> He who maketh songs should take a pleasure in their making; for if it be not so with him, he will in no wise avail to gladden others, if himself have sorrow in his home; nay, 'tis not even right to expect it.[12]

---

[10] 728.

[11] 143.

[12] *The Suppliants*, 174.

In one of his comedies, Aristophanes also makes the point of poets, that their poetry reflects themselves.

> Besides, it is bad taste for a poet to be coarse and hairy. Look at the famous Ibycus, at Anacreon of Teos, and at Alcaeus, who handled music so well; they wore head-bands and found pleasure in the lascivious dances of Ionia. And have you not heard what a dandy Phrynichus was and how careful in his dress? For this reason his pieces were also beautiful, for the works of a poet are copied from himself.[13]

The ancient Greek plays also give us a few eye-witness reflections of the use of music in the various cult-religious celebrations. Euripides gives us two vivid descriptions of such celebrations, the first, from *Helen*, set in the time of the gods.

> Loudly rattled the Bacchic castanets in shrill accord, what time those maidens, swift as whirlwinds, sped forth with the goddess on her chariot yoked to wild creatures, in quest of her that was ravished from the circling choir of virgins …
>
> But when for gods and tribes of men alike she made an end to festal cheer, Zeus spoke out, seeking to soothe the mother's moody soul, 'Ye stately Graces, go banish from Demeter's angry heart the grief her wanderings bring upon her for her child, and go, ye Muses too, with tuneful choir.' Thereon did Cypris, fairest of the blessed gods, first catch up the crashing cymbals, native to that land, and the drum with tight-stretched skin, and then Demeter smiled, and in her hand did take the deep-toned aulos, well pleased with its loud note …
>
> Oh! mighty is the virtue in a dress of dappled fawn-skin, in ivy green that twineth round a sacred thyrsus, in whirling tambourines struck as they revolve in the air, in tresses wildly streaming for the revelry …[14]

And in *The Bacchae* we are given a similar description set in the present time.

> Uplift the dark divine wand,
> The oak-wand and the pine-wand,
> And don thy fawn-skin, fringed in purity
> With fleecy white, like ours …
>
> For thee of old some crested Corybant
> First woke in Cretan air
> The wild orb of our orgies,
> Our Timbrel; and thy gorges
> Rang with this strain; and blended Phrygian song
> And sweet keen pipes were there.
>
> But the Timbrel, the Timbrel was another's,
> And away to Mother Rhea it must wend;
> And to our holy singing from the Mother's
> The mad Satyrs carried it, to blend
> In the dancing and the cheer
> Of our third and perfect Year;
> And it serves Dionysus in the end! …

---

13 *The Thesmophoriazusae*, 161.

14 1302ff.

> Hither, O fragrant of Tmolus the Golden,
> Come with the voice of timbrel and drum;
> Let the cry of your joyance uplift and embolden
> The God of the joy-cry; O Bacchanals, come!
> With pealing of pipes and with Phrygian clamor,
> On where the vision of holiness thrills,
> And the music climbs and the maddening glamour ...[15]

The sense we have here of the power of wind instrument music is emphasized in a Chorus from *The Eumenides* by Aeschylus, where music is described as completely possessing the participant.

> But our sacrifice to bind,
> Lo, the music that we wind,
> How it dazeth and amazeth
> And the will it maketh blind,
> As it moves without a lyre
> To the throb of my desire;
> 'Tis a chain about the brain,
> 'Tis a wasting of mankind.[16]

One passage in Euripides mentions regular cult celebrations which were held at night.

> For thy worship is aye performed with many a sacrifice, and never art thou forgotten as each month draweth to its close, when young voices sing and dancers' music is heard abroad, while on our wind-swept hill goes up the cry of joy to the beat of the maidens' feet by night.[17]

The dancing was not always sedate, and hence a reflection of the character of the accompanying music, as we see in another comment by Euripides, 'lift high the nimble foot.'[18] In yet another place, Euripides also mentions that dancing was also done around the altar.[19]

We also have some reflection in these plays of the music used in battle, most often the noise and anxiety symbolized by the trumpet. An example from Aeschylus reads,

> Wild brazen bells make music of affright.[20]

In this same passage, by the way, we find a reference similar to those found in ancient Hebrew and Roman literature, of the change in the character of the horse when he hears the battle trumpet.

---

[15] 109ff.
[16] Lines 326.
[17] *The Heracleidae*, 777ff.
[18] *Electra*, 868.
[19] *Iphigenia in Aulis*, 675.
[20] *The Seven Against Thebes*, 386, trans. Murray.

> As some wild war-horse when the trumpets sound
> Stiffens and champs the curb and paws the ground.

Among these plays there are two references to a new kind of trumpet, which Euripides calls 'the Tuscan trumpet,'[21] and Sophocles the 'bronze-mouthed Tyrrhene trumpet.'[22] These are references to a new instrument developed by the Etruscans (Greek: *Tyrrhenians*) and which is known in Roman literature as the cornu, a great hoop-shaped instrument of bronze or iron, with transverse grip, looking somewhat like a capital letter 'G.'

The trumpet must have been common stage business. Indeed, Pliny the Younger, in the first century AD, mentions that most people had heard a trumpet *only* in the theater.[23]

We know also that the aulos was a basic instrument of the Greek army and there are two passages which document its presence in battle. In Aeschylus', *The Seven Against Thebes*,

> His fiery coursers eager to attack
> And die; but ever more he wheels them back,
> Their frontlets tossing, while the pipes beneath
> In barbarous music whistle to their breath.[24]

and in Euripides' *The Trojan Women*.

> And the noise of your music flew,
> Clarion and pipe did shriek.[25]

We also see in these plays references to occupational music. In Aristophanes' *The Acharnians*, for example, the character, Dicaeopolis, says,

> We hear nothing but the sound of whistles, of aulos and fifes to encourage the workers.[26]

In *The Frogs*, the same playwright speaks of music used to provide the beat for rowers.

> You'll row all right; as soon as you fall to,
> You'll hear a first-rate tune that *makes* you row.[27]

Finally, the occupation of the shepherd is mentioned twice and both times, of course, he appears with his traditional panpipe instrument. First, in Sophocles' *Philoctetes*,

---

[21] *The Phoenissae*, 1379.

[22] *Ajax*, 16.

[23] *The Letters of the Younger Pliny* (New York: Penguin, 1985), 64.

[24] Lines 460ff.

[25] 130.

[26] 555.

[27] 204.

> Like the shepherd with his rural pipe
> And cheerful song …[28]

and in Euripides' *Electra*,

> How on a day Pan, the steward of husbandry, came breathing dulcet music on his jointed pipe.[29]

There is some reference to entertainment music in these plays and one by Euripides is based on the following lines from Book X of *The Iliad*, by Homer.

> So often as [Agamemnon] gazed toward the Trojan plain, he marveled at the many fires that burned before the face of Ilios, and at the sound of aulos and pipes, and the din of men.

In his account of the same battle, Euripides includes the following description:

> A very weariness of joy
> Fell with the evening over Troy:
> And lutes of Afric mingled there
> With Phrygian songs: and many a maiden,
> With white feet glancing light as air,
> Made happy music through the gloom:
> And fires on many an inward room
> All night broad-flashing, flung their glare
> On laughing eyes and slumber-laden.[30]

Apart from all these reflections in the ancient Greek plays on the practice of music, it is some of the references to actual music that are most interesting. We wish we could actually hear what was meant by Aristophanes' expression, a 'soft Ionian Love song,'[31] not to mention Aeschylus',

> Through me too sorrow runs
> Like a strange Ionian Song.[32]

What could 'a *strange* Ionian Song' have meant? This adjective also occurs twice in Euripides,

> O Muse, be near me now, and make
> A strange song for Ilion's sake …[33]

......

---

[28] 239.
[29] 703.
[30] *The Trojan Women*, 543.
[31] *The Ecclesiazusae*, 881.
[32] *The Supplices*, 69.
[33] *The Trojan Women*, 510.

> A lad alone on Ida,
> Playing tunes on his pipe, strange melodies,
> Like the melodies Olympus sang.[34]

Neither can we know what is meant by 'songs of mystic melody,'[35] nor 'the harmony of aulos.'[36] And how we would love to hear once again that touching music which inspired Euripides, in *The Trojan Women*, to use three times the phrase 'a tune of tears.'

> My body rocketh, and would fain
> Move to the tune of tears that flow:
> For tears are music too, and keep
> A song unheard in hearts that weep.[37]

Aristotle, in his famous treatise on the writing of tragedy, *Poetics*, reminds us how important music was to the performance of ancient Greek plays. In his discussion of the elements of a good tragedy he writes,

> by 'language with pleasurable accessories' I mean that with rhythm and harmony or song superadded; and by 'the kinds separately' I mean that some portions are worked out with verse only, and others in turn with song.[38]

This passage tells us that music was very much part of the ancient Greek tragedies, but how little we know today. There may have been something equivalent to the aria, as Suetonius seems to infer when he tells us that Nero sang in tragedies.

> He did actually sing in tragedies, taking the parts of heroes and gods, sometimes even of heroines and goddesses, wearing masks wither modeled on his own face, or on the face of whatever woman he happened to be in love with at the time. Among his performances were *Canace in Childbirth*, *Orestes the Matricide*, *Oedipus Blinded* and *Distraught Hercules*.[39]

Tacitus, a contemporary of Nero, adds that, being jealous, he murdered Thrasea Paetus for having sung in a tragedy.[40]

---

34 *Iphigenia in Aulis*, 574.

35 Euripides, *The Bacchae*, 1056.

36 Aristophanes, *Peace*, 531.

37 118, 512, and 602:
> Even as the sound of a song
> Left by the way, but long
> Remembered, a tune of tears
> Falling where no man hears …

38 'Poetics,' 1449b.24.

39 Suetonius, *The Twelve Caesars* (New York: Penguin 1989), 225. Suetonius adds that the emperor Caligula also sang in the theater. [Ibid., 158]

40 Tacitus, *The Annals*, XVI, 21.

In any case, music is something entirely missing when we attend productions of these plays today. On the other hand, music was perhaps not so important as was thought by some during the Baroque Period who thought perhaps the entire plays were sung. They were probably wrong, but their error led to the invention of opera!

During the pre-Roman empire era, we read of Etruscan actors who performed with music as early as 389 BC.[41] From the earliest years of ancient Roman theater there is some evidence of the use of the aulos. There is a vase from this period (fourth century BC), now in the Hermitage, Moscow, which pictures an aulos player playing in the theater. An early actor and producer of theatrical works, Livius Andronicus (fl. ca. 240 BC), performed plays after the Greek models, including the use of the aulos as an accompanying instrument. On one occasion, when his voice failed, he had another singer perform with the aulos while he underscored the singing with mimical gestures—an event which is considered the beginning of pantomime.[42] A relief (Inv. Nr. 6687, Museo, Nazionale, Naples) from the second century BC also shows an aulos player in the theater.

In the plays of Terence (190–158 BC) there is extant information which actually gives us the name of the composer of the music for the play. In *The Girl from Andros*, for example, we read, 'Scored for equal auloi by Flaccus, freedman of Claudius.' This same composer composed the music for *The Brothers*, but here specified Etruscian ('Tyrian') auloi.

The music of the theater included an instrumental prelude, as well as music to underscore the drama and accompany the dancers. Often the production was preceded by a procession of cornu and lituus players. In the plays of Plautus (254–184 BC) there is an occasional song sung by an actor[43] and in one case even a chorus, in the Greek tradition, although here only three singers.[44]

Among the observers there seem to have been connoisseurs who, on hearing the first notes of a composition used in the theater, could identify the play—something which surprised Cicero (106–43 BC).[45] The style of music must have been changing, however, for Cicero complains of the loss of the 'austere sweetness' of music as it was heard in olden times on the stage. What he heard at present, he described as *delectatio puerilis* (childish amusement).[46] Cicero seemed to have a certain respect for actors, due in part to the very high standard that was expected by the public.

---

[41] Alfred Sendrey, in *Music in the Social and Religious Life of Antiquity* (Rutherford: Fairleigh Dickinson University Press, 1974), 424.

[42] Ibid., 424.

[43] For example, *The Twin Menaechmi*, Act V, Scene ii.

[44] *The Rope*, Act II, Scene i, where three fishermen 'chant their chorus in unison.'

[45] Cicero, *Academica*, II, vii, 20.

[46] Cicero, *De Finibus*, I, xxi, 72.

> If an actor makes a movement that is a little out of time with the music, or recites a verse that is one syllable too short or too long, he is hissed and hooted off the stage.[47]

Sometimes things did not go as planned in theatrical performances and the audiences were rather entertained than moved. An extraordinary case in point is related by the historian, Polybius (second century BC) who even provides the names of some of the famous aulos players of the theater. He tells of a special performance in the arena [Circus] organized by the Roman General, Lucius Anicius, to celebrate his defeat and capture of King Genthius of the Illyrians. It is clear here that General Lucius Anicius was not a connoisseur of music for he did not want a concert, but rather a musical representation of his battle.

> Having summoned the most distinguished artists of Greece and constructed a very large stage in the Circus, he first brought on the aulos players; there were Theodorus of Boeotia, Theopompus, Hermippus, Lysimachus, all of them the most distinguished. Posting them, then, at the front of the stage with the chorus, he directed them to play all together. As they started to perform their music to accompany the dance motions which corresponded to it, he sent word to them that they were not playing in the right way, and ordered them to whoop up the contest against one another. Since they were puzzled at this, one of the officials indicated that they should turn and advance upon one another and act as if they were fighting. Quickly the players caught the idea, and taking on motions in keeping with their own licentious characters they caused great confusion. For the aulos players by a concerted movement turned the middle choruses against those at the ends, while they blew on their auloi unintelligible notes, and all differing, and then they drew away in turn upon each other; and at the same time the members of the choruses clashed noisily against the players as they shook their gear at them and rushed upon their antagonists, to turn again and retreat. And so in one case a member of the chorus girded himself, and stepping out of the ranks he turned and raised his fists as if to box against the aulos player who plunged against him; and then, if not before, the applause and shouts that arose from the spectators knew no bounds. Furthermore, while these were contending in a pitched battle, two dancers entered with castanets, and four boxers mounted upon the stage accompanied by trumpeters and horn players. All these contests went on together, and the result was indescribable.[48]

The important Roman philosopher, Horace (65–8 BC), also provides some interesting comments regarding the role of music in the theater. First, with regard to subject and characterization, his concern seems to be that the music be genuine, suited to and contributing to the stage action.

> Let the Chorus sustain the part and strenuous duty of an actor, and sing nothing between acts which does not advance and fitly blend into the plot. It should side with the good and give friendly counsel; sway the angry and cherish the righteous. It should praise the fare of a modest board, praise wholesome justice, law and peace with her open gates; should keep secrets, and pray and beseech the gods that fortune may return to the unhappy, and depart from the proud.[49]

---

47 Cicero, *Paradoxa Stoicorum*, 26.

48 *Histories*, XXX.

49 Horace, *The Art of Poetry*, 467.

With regard to instrumental music in the theater, Horace reminds the reader of the history of this art. While it began with the role of amplifying the stage action, the popularity of the music itself soon led to its usurping the attention of the audience

> The aulos—not, as now, bound with brass and a rival of the trumpet, but slight and simple, with few stops—was once of use to lead and aid the chorus and to fill with its breath benches not yet too crowded, where, to be sure, folk gathered, easy to count, because few—sober folk, too, and chaste and modest. But when a conquering race began to widen its domain, and an ampler wall embraced its cities, and when, on festal days, appeasing the Genius by daylight drinking brought no penalty, then both time and tune won greater license. For what taste could you expect of an unlettered throng just freed from toil, rustic mixed up with city folk, vulgar with nobly born? So to the early art the aulos player added movement and display, and, strutting over the stage, trailed a robe in train. So, too, to the sober lyre new tones were given, and an impetuous style brought in an unwonted diction; and the thought, full of wise saws and prophetic of the future, was attuned to the oracles of Delphi.[50]

We must pause in our survey of music in the Roman theater to remind the reader that the early Church fathers of the first four centuries of the Christian Era were constantly attacking the theater and warning Christians not to attend. They were particularly concerned by the emphasis on emotions in the theater, warning that emotions were the first step toward sin!

The early Church father, Tertullian (155–230 AD), even attacked the traditional procession, in which the actors and their company would proceed through the town as a means of drawing spectators.

> A procession is held to the theater from the temples and alters, with that whole wretched business of incense and blood, to the tune of aulos and trumpets, under the direction of the two most polluted masters of ceremonies at funerals and sacrifices: the undertaker and soothsayer.[51]

In a passing reference to music in his attack on the theater, Tertullian makes a reference to music notation, which we presume to be the late Greek primitive notational system based on alphabet letters.

> Those features which are peculiar to, and characteristic of, the stage, that wantonness in gesture and posture, they dedicate to Venus and Liber, deities both dissolute: the former by sex perversion, the latter by effeminate dress.
> And all else that is performed with voice and melodies, instruments and musical notation, belongs to the Apollos and the Muses, the Minervas and Mercuries.[52]

---

[50] Ibid.

[51] Tertullian, 'Spectacles,' trans. Rudolph Arbesmann in *Disciplinary, Moral and Ascetical Works* (New York: Fathers of the Church, 1959), X, 2. In VII, 2, Tertullian describes more extensive processions to the circus, which included civic officials and various institutions of the city, again a familiar tradition throughout the Middle Ages. He also mentions that plays were already advertised through the use of posters.

[52] Ibid., X, 8. In Greek mythology Apollo was the god of music and patron of the voice; the Muses were in charge of music and dramatic performances; Minerva made the first flute and was the guardian of musical instruments; and Mercury, having invented letters, is cited here as the god of musical notation.

In a sarcastic vein, he wonders how any Christian who might be present can watch the action on the stage and keep his mind on appropriate thoughts.

> But, while the tragic actor is ranting, our good friend will probably recall the outcries of some prophet! Amid the strains of the effeminate flute-player, he will no doubt meditate on a psalm![53]

Merely by being present, Tertullian warns, the Christian is damned—for he cannot hide!

> What will you do when you are caught in that surging tide of wicked applause? Not that you are likely to suffer anything at the hands of men ... but consider how you would fare in heaven. Do you doubt that at the very moment when the Devil is raging in his assembly, all the angels look forth from heaven and note down every individual who has uttered blasphemy, who has listened to it, who has lent his tongue, who has lent his ears to the service of the Devil against God?[54]

During the third century, several Church fathers were very vocal in their attack on the theater. Commodianus attacks the theater and its music in a chapter entitled, 'Worldly Things to be Absolutely Avoided.'

> With an undisciplined mind you seek what you presume to be easily lawful, both your dear actors and their musical strains; nor do you care that the offspring of such an one should babble follies. While you think that you are enjoying life, you are improvidently erring.[55]

Novatian attacks the productions of the theater at length, especially for the treatment of women and the performances by the musicians. He reveals that plays were still widely attended at this time, but forbids Christians from going.

> Permit me now to pass on to the brazen witticisms of the stage. I am ashamed to tell you what is said there. I am embarrassed even to expose what things take place—the artificial turnings of the plots, the deceits of adulterers, the immoralities of women, the scurrilous jokes, the sordid parasites, even the toga-clad heads of households, at times simply silly, at other times morally disgusting—in all instances senseless, on certain counts shameless.
>
> No man—regardless of his background or profession—is spared by the despicable tongue of these rogues. Yet everyone still frequents the theater. Indecorum, commonly encountered, evidently delights to know and to learn of vice. There is a general rush to that despicable brothel of public shame, to the teaching of obscenity ...
>
> When one is accustomed to see such things, one also learns to act accordingly. As for those unfortunate women who have been debased in the service of public lewdness, they find concealment in their very location. In hiding they alleviate their shameful behavior. They who prostitute their virtue are ashamed to be seen doing so. But that public monstrosity takes place for all to see and surpasses the foulness of prostitutes. A method is sought whereby adultery may be committed with one's eyes!

---

[53] Ibid., XXV, 3.

[54] Ibid., XXVII, 2.

[55] Commodianus, quoted in *The Writings of Tertullianus* (Edinburgh: T. & T. Clark, 1895), III, 462.

> An evil quite worthy of it is added to this infamy: a completely broken down human being, a man soft beyond effeminacy, devoted to the art of expressing words with his hands. Because of one single I-don't-know-what, neither man nor woman, the entire city is excited so that the legendary orgies of bygone ages are carried out with frenzied dancing. So true is it that what is not permissible is eagerly sought after that what time itself has obscured is again remembered and brought to light.
>
> Since the evils of the present day do not suffice to glut the sensuality of our times, recourse has to be had in the theater where the aberrations of a past age are again presented. It is not permissible, I repeat, for faithful Christians to be present. It is absolutely unlawful even for these whom—to charm their ears—Greece sends everywhere to all who are instructed in her vain arts.
>
> One person tries to imitate the harsh war cry of the trumpet. A second person by blowing with his breath into pipes modulates their lugubrious sounds. A third, accompanied with dancing and a man's melodious voice, strains with his breath—laboriously drawn from the viscera to the upper parts of his body—to play upon the small openings of pipes. At times he releases and forces it into the air by means of fixed apertures. He even labors actually to speak with his fingers by breaking down the sound into definite rhythmic patterns. He is ungrateful to his Maker who gave him a tongue.
>
> Why should I even mention the wasted efforts of comedy and those senseless ravings of the tragic voice? Why mention the din made by the vibrating strings of instruments? Even if such things were not consecrated to idols, faithful Christians should not go there and look at them. Even if they were not sinful, their distinguishing characteristic is unspeakable vanity, unbefitting the faithful.[56]

The late third-century Church philosopher, Lactantius, mentions 'harmonious verses,' but his main concern is the lasting impact of the theater on the Christians who may be in attendance.

> What can young men or virgins do, when they see that these things are practiced without shame, and willingly beheld by all? They are plainly admonished of what they can do, and are inflamed with lust, which is especially excited by seeing; and every one according to his sex forms himself in these representations. And they approve of these things, while they laugh at them, and with vices clinging to them, they return more corrupted to their apartments; and not boys only, who ought not to be inured to vices prematurely, but also old men, whom it does not become at their age to sin.[57]

To return to the Roman stage itself, during the third century AD a report by the astronomer Firmicus Maternus mentions 'public musicians' who compose music for theatrical plays.[58] It is possible that some of these productions in the theater were of a very elevated artistic character, for Quintilian refers to the theater as 'a kind of temple for the solemnization of a sacred feast.'[59] Music contests were also introduced on the occasion of public theatrical plays.[60]

---

56 Novatian, 'The Spectacles,' trans. Russell J. DeSimone, in the *Fathers of the Church* (Washington, D.C.: The Catholic University of America Press), VI.

57 Lactantius, 'The Divine Institutes,' trans. William Fletcher in *The Works of Lactantius* (Edinburgh: T. & T. Clark, 1886), I, Book VI, xx.

58 Sendrey, *Music in the Social and Religious Life of Antiquity*, 391. The poet, Calpurnius Siculus, in *Eclogue VII*, 23ff., gives an interesting first-hand description of one of the outdoor theaters.

59 Quintilian, *The Education of an Orator*, III, viii, 30.

60 Sendrey, *Music in the Social and Religious Life of Antiquity*, 387.

According to a fourth-century Roman historian, Ammianus Marcellinus, the productions of the theater were extraordinary and employed enormous numbers of musicians.

> The vast and magnificent theaters of Rome were filled by three thousand female dancers, and by three thousand singers, with the masters of the respective choruses. Such was the popular favor which they enjoyed, that, in a time of scarcity … the merit of contributing to the public pleasures exempted them from a law, which was strictly executed against the professors of the liberal arts.[61]

We have some valuable insights regarding the use of music in the theater of the fourth century, found in the fragment of a treatise, 'On Comedy and Tragedy,' by Aelius Donatus. First, he says the music, 'arranged in measures,' was not composed by the author of the play, but by 'some one skilled in music of this sort.' We might judge that in some cases the composer was not only skilled, but famous, for Donatus mentions that the composer's name was placed above that of the author of the play and even the name of the play.

He indicates the music during the play was quite varied and that excerpts were performed before the play began, permitting many people, who recognized the music, to know what play was to be given even before it was announced.

Finally, there seems to have been subtleties associated with the instruments themselves which far surpass any such practice today.

> [Songs] were, moreover, played on 'equal' or 'unequal' aulos, and right- or left-handed. The right-handed, or Lydian, ones proclaimed the production of a comedy of serious and solemn character; the left-handed, or Serranian, ones announced humor in the comedy in the lightness of its catastrophe. In cases, though, where a 'right' and 'left' ceremony was required, it meant that the play combined seriousness and gaiety combined.[62]

Together with the general decline of the Roman Empire, the general impression one has is that the theaters remained popular, but that the quality of production had declined greatly. Gibbon remarks, 'the theaters might still excite, but they seldom gratified.'[63] The emperor Julian now saw them in the same category of low entertainment found in all kinds of public shows and states that he wished he could bring back the theater of old. These productions, as we have seen, were strongly criticized by the Church, but we gain the impression in a letter by Julian that individual priests were nevertheless joining the public in attending. Julian, taking the Church at its word, commands that no priest should go there!

> No priest must anywhere be present at the licentious theatrical shows of the present day, nor introduce one into his own house; for that is altogether unfitting. Indeed if it were possible to banish such shows absolutely from the theaters so as to restore Dionysus those theaters pure as of old, I should

---

[61] Quoted in Edward Gibbon, *The History of the Decline and Fall of the Roman Empire* (Philadelphia: Coates), III, 32.

[62] Aelius Donatus, 'On Comedy and Tragedy,' in Barrett H. Clark, *European Theories of the Drama* (New York: Crown, 1918), 45. Donatus defines Comedy as, 'a story treating of various habits and customs of public and private affairs, from which one may learn what is of use in life, and, on the other hand, what must be avoided.'

[63] Gibbon, *The History of the Decline and Fall of the Roman Empire*, III, 226.

certainly have endeavored with all my heart to bring this about; but as it is, since I thought that this is impossible, and that even if it should prove to be possible, it would not on other accounts be expedient, I forebore entirely from this ambition. But I do demand that priests should withdraw themselves from the licentiousness of the theaters and leave them to the crowd. Therefore let no priest enter a theater or have an actor or a chariot-driver for his friend; and let no dancer or mime even approach his door. And as for the sacred games, I permit anyone who will to attend those only in which women are forbidden not only to compete but even to be spectators. With regard to the hunting shows with dogs which are performed in the cities inside the theaters, need I say that not only priests but even the sons of priests keep away from them![64]

St. Augustine (354–430 AD) confirms the decline in the standards of the theater, but places the blame on the old pagan gods.

> The stage plays, those exhibitions of depravity and unbounded license, were not introduced in Rome by men's vices, but by the command of your gods ... If your mind retains enough sense to esteem the soul more than the body, then choose whom you should worship.[65]

With the 'victory' of the Christians over Rome, Western Europe entered the 'Dark Ages.' Rome, itself, was in total decay by 700, its great institutions forgotten (the Forum was used as a cow pasture already in the seventh century) and the great public buildings and temples were dismembered to provide building material for Christian churches and palaces. We have an eye-witness description of the city during the period of the first emperor of the sixth century, Justinian, who was certainly one of the strangest of all Roman emperors. He lived and dressed like a monk, fasting, praying, and discussing philosophy. As he wanted to become a musician and poet, we must assume his neglect of the educational institutions reported here was due more to his inclination to hoard money (he once increased his income by putting ashes in the peasant's bread). Procopius mentions the state of the theater under Justinian,

> Theaters, hippodromes, and circuses were almost all shut ... Both in private and in public there was grief and dejection, as if yet another visitation from heaven had struck them, and all laughter had gone out of life.[66]

There must have been some remaining theater in Rome for the Christian pope at the time, the famous Pope Gregory the Great (540–604 AD), makes an interesting argument against the Christian applauding in the theater, which can only be understood in the light of several centuries of earlier Church leaders forbidding attendance at all. In making a distinction between the 'kindly-disposed' person and one who is envious,[67] Gregory stipulates that the Christian

---

[64] Julian, 'Letter to a Priest,' in *The Works of the Emperor Julian*, trans. Wilmer Wright (London: Heinemann, 1913), II, 335.

[65] *The City of God*, trans. Gerald G. Walsh (New York: Fathers of the Church, 1954), I, xxxii.

[66] Procopius, *The Secret History* (Harmondsworth: Penguin Books, 1981), 169.

[67] Gregory the Great, 'Pastoral Care,' III, X, trans. Henry Davis (New York: Newman Press, 1978).

must applaud and imitate the good deeds they see in others. Indeed, to not do so, 'they stand to be smitten the more severely with punishment at the end of time.' On the other hand, one should not applaud the actor, whom one would not actually desire to imitate.

Cassiodorus (484–585 AD), one of our most important sources for information on music during the sixth century, provides a nostalgic history of the theater,

> When farmers, on the holidays, celebrated the rites of various deities in groves and villages, the Athenians were the first to raise this rustic beginning into an urban spectacle. To the place where they looked on, they gave the Greek name of theater, since the gathered throng, separated from the bystanders, could look on with no hindrance.
>
> But the back-drop of the theater was called the *scaena* from the deep shade of the grove where, at the start of spring, the shepherds sang various songs. Musical performances flourished there, and the precepts of a wise age. But it gradually came about that the respectable arts, shunning the company of depraved men, withdrew from that venue out of modesty.[68]

He then continues with some enlightening and rare comments on the use of music in Comedy and Pantomime.

> Comedy … is where the rustic actors made fun of human doings in merry songs. To these were added the speaking hands of dancers, their fingers that are tongues, their clamorous silence, their silent exposition. The Muse Polymnia is said to have discovered this, showing that humans could declare their meaning even without speech …
>
> Again, there is the pantomime actor, who derives his name from manifold imitations. When first he comes on stage, lured by applause, bands of musicians, skilled in various instruments, support him. Then the hand of meaning expounds the song to the eyes of melody, and, by a code of gestures, as if by letters, it instructs the spectator's sight; summaries are read in it, and, without writing, it performs what writing has set forth.

Another contemporary of the above was Isidore, Bishop of Seville (560–636 AD), the only writer known today representing Gothic Spain. His twenty-volume *Etymologiarum*, which is really the first encyclopedia, includes actors under 'vocal music,' which tells us that the ancient Greek tradition of using music in the theater must not have completely died.

> Harmonica is the modulation of the voice, it is the affair of comedians, tragedians, and choruses and all who sing. It produces motion of the mind and body, and from this motion sound. From this sound comes the music which in man is called voice.[69]

For the next several centuries of the 'dark ages' there is little extant literature to tell us of the fate of dramatic literature. General history texts sometimes declare it dead during these centuries, but we have always believed that some form of drama must have continued as part of civic celebrations. If the Church restrictions on literature have closed this chapter to us,

---

[68] Letter to the Patrician Symmachus, in *Variae*, trans. Thomas Hodgkin (London: Frowde, 1886), IV, li. In a document found in Ibid., VII, x.

[69] *Etymologiarum*, trans. W. M. Linsay, quoted in Oliver Strunk, *Source Readings in Music History* (New York: Norton, 1950), III, xx.

they compensated, to a degree, with some dramatic literature of their own. The ninth-century writer, Rabanus Maurus, for example, in his 'Life of Mary Magdalene,' assures us that Martha, after the death of Jesus, went to France and fought a dragon![70]

In view of the Church's condemnation of the theater during the first five centuries of the Christian Era, it is somewhat ironic that when drama 'returns' the first works known to us are Liturgical plays. Within this general body of dramatic literature there is one very interesting work which we must bring to the attention of the reader, the play, *Paphnutius*, by the tenth-century nun, Hrotswitha, which contains an extensive dialog on the subject of music.[71] The passage begins with a Disciple asking, 'What *is* music?' Paphnutius answers with a brief description of the place held by music among the liberal arts. The Disciples beg for more information and Paphnutius relents, 'since it is knowledge which monks don't have.'

Paphnutius, following the definition by Boethius, begins by telling the students that music is divided into three species: the celestial, the human, and that made with instruments.

> DISCIPLES. What does celestial music consist of?
> PAPHNUTIUS. Of the seven planets and the celestial sphere.
> DISCIPLES. How do you mean that?
> PAPHNUTIUS. Because, you see, they produce the same harmonious music as the strings of stringed instruments; For just as in the case of instruments, we find the same concordances and intervals of like number and length.
> DISCIPLES. And what are these 'intervals' you speak of?
> PAPHNUTIUS. They are the distances which exist between the planets, as between the notes of strings.

Upon further questions about the 'notes' just mentioned, Paphnutius begins to speak in the complex mathematical language of Boethius. The students object to this conceptual language and respond, 'What has this got to do with *music*?,' implying, we presume, that music has instead to do with feelings and emotions, not mathematics. The teacher's answer, like that of so many theory teachers today, is, 'But that is how you *talk* about music!' The reader will notice that he introduces here the word 'symphonia,' which the Greeks had used in place of our term 'harmony.'

> PAPHNUTIUS. A tone is formed of two sounds, of which the proportion is that of an *epothos* number, a sesquioctave: that is of nine to eight.
> DISCIPLES. (Discouraged.) The faster we try to keep up with you and follow the basic notions you give us, and technical terms of this discussion, the more you go on adding more difficult concepts for us to take in.
> PAPHNUTIUS. But that is how this kind of discussion is carried on.
> DISCIPLES. Well at least tell us something—but only the simplest account—about what they mean by concordances, just so we will know what the word means.
> PAPHNUTIUS. A concordance or 'symphonia' is a proper combination of sounds.

---

[70] *The Life of Saint Mary Magdalene and of her Sister Saint Martha*, trans. David Mycoff (Kalamazoo: Cistercian Publications, 1989), XL, 2365.

[71] *The Plays of Hrotswitha of Gandersheim*, trans. Larissa Bonfante (New York: New York University Press, 1979), 108ff.

The students now ask the difficult question, 'Why can't we hear the music of the spheres?' To this question, Paphnutius gives four possible explanations.

> DISCIPLES. Well, why can't we hear them, then?
> PAPHNUTIUS. Many different reasons are given to explain why we can't hear the music of the heavenly spheres. Some assert it can't be heard because the music never stops, and we become accustomed to its sound. Others say it is the density of the air, while there are some who claim that a sound of such grand volume cannot physically be taken in by the narrow passages of our human ears. And there are some who say that the spheres give forth a sound so sweet, of such great joy, that if men ever heard it, they would all join together, of one common accord, forget about themselves and any other interest, and be intent only on following this sound as it led them from the East to the Western regions.

Well, say the students, we have heard enough of the music of the spheres. Now tell us about 'human' music, and how it is produced.

> PAPHNUTIUS. Not only, as I said before, in the harmonious connection between body and soul, and in the deep bass or high pitched soprano voices, but even in the rhythmic throbbing of our veins, and in the measure and proportion of each of our limbs, as for example in the joints of our fingers, for which we find the same proportions when we measure off their sections. These are the same proportions, if you remember, which we talked of in our discussion of the meaning of 'symphonias,' because music is in fact an agreeable combination not only of voices, but of other unlike elements as well.
> DISCIPLES. (The have been looking at the joints of their fingers. They are quite frankly lost.) If we had only known before we asked, how knotty all these problems were for laymen like us, and how difficult to follow or resolve, we would have preferred never to have known about the 'lesser world' than try to learn such difficult lessons.
> PAPHNUTIUS. It did you no harm to try, for now you have learned things you did not know before.
> DISCIPLES. That's true. But we are exhausted from this philosophical lecture, since we are not able to understand the details of your explanation.

Perhaps because of the students' professed exhaustion, this discussion never continues on to the subject of instrumental music. The teacher brings the topic to a close by reminding the students of the true purpose of the acquisition of knowledge—to understand God.

> PAPHNUTIUS. For to whose praise does knowledge of all the arts redound more worthily and justly, if not to His, since He is the One who created all things knowable and gave us knowledge of them?

On Music Competition in the Ancient World

MAN CLEARLY HAS A RATIONAL SIDE OF HIS BEING, a collection of information he has absorbed from other sources and which for the most part are housed in the left hemisphere of the brain. It is equally clear that most of the knowledge housed there consists of agreed upon facts; there is only one way to spell 'cat' in English and everyone in the world learns that 2 + 2 = 4. Therefore, it follows that one can organize a competition in math or spelling and there will emerge an undisputed winner.

The other half of our person, and brain, is experiential knowledge, knowledge we have learned from our *own personal* experience. Hence while a concept like 'love' has a general agreed upon dictionary meaning, its *real* meaning for any person is a *personal* definition resulting from his own life experience with love. The experiential, emotional nature of music is analogous. Everything being based on personal experience, and not facts, one problem with the right hemisphere of the brain is that there are no 'correct answers' to be found there. That being the case, why would anyone ever want to hold a competition in love or music? What would be the point?

We might begin our look at music competition in the ancient world, therefore, by considering the nature of the purpose that the ancient Greeks associated with their own music competitions. Often, it turns out, the purpose had nothing to do with music. For example, there were trumpet contests which began with the 96th Olympiad of 396 BC. But these contests seem to have been more physical than musical. Perhaps the modern Olympic motto, *citius, altius, fortius*, describes well what they were—who could play fastest, highest and loudest. Thus being essentially physical contests, and not musical contests, we are not particularly surprised to find that Heradorus of Megara, one of the winners of the Olympic trumpet playing competition, consumed, in a typical meal, six pints of wheat bread, twenty pounds of meat and six quarts of wine!

Antiphon, a famous fifth century BC speaker and early interpreter of dreams, in a fragment of a speech[1] discussing the fact that pleasure often follows pain, suggests that the purpose of contests in general is to teach men the rewards of greater effort.

> For honors, prizes, the baits which God has given to mankind, bring them to the necessity of great toil and sweat.

---

[1] Quoted in Rosamond Kent Sprague, *The Older Sophists* (Columbia: University of South Carolina Press, 1972), 228.

Xenophon (427–355 BC), an important early historian and, like Plato, a student of Socrates, also tells us that long periods of training and large sums of money were necessary to prepare a chorus for competition and he seems almost perplexed that they do this when the goal is only a 'paltry prize.' In a conversation with a political leader, Hiero, Xenophon speaking through the character of Simonides, one of the lyric poets, observes,

> Think of the large sums that men are induced to spend on horse races, gymnastic and choral competitions, and the long course of training and practice they undergo for the sake of a paltry prize.[2]

He preferred to regard the purpose of competition as being the essential catalyst which brings about the highest levels of performance. He credits Lycurgus, ninth century BC, as having instituted this philosophy.

> He saw that where the spirit of rivalry is the strongest among the people, there the choruses are most worth hearing and the athletic contests afford the finest spectacle.[3]

Xenophon finds a subordinate value in helping to foster civic discipline.

> There is nothing so convenient nor so good for human beings as order. Thus, a chorus is a combination of human beings; but when the members of it do as they choose, it becomes mere confusion, and there is no pleasure in watching it; but when they act and sing in an orderly fashion, then those same men at once seem worth seeing and worth hearing.[4]

Xenophon, now in the voice of Socrates, also tells us that the most successful choruses are those which have as their leaders, 'the best experts.'[5] Although speaking of a battle in another place, he also gives an interesting clue as to how these choruses may have stood when they performed.

> They took position in lines of about a hundred each, like the choral dancers ranged opposite one another.[6]

Aside from such values as discipline and hard work, the important question remains, to what extent was musicality a value or purpose in the ancient Greek music competition? The extant references to this question are somewhat conflicting. Plutarch (45–125 AD) was under the impression that musical skill was indeed the point of the earliest competitions. He writes of the active participation in organizing these festivals by Pericles (495–429 BC).

---

[2] 'Hiero,' IX, in E. C. Marchant, *Scripta Minora* (Cambridge: Harvard University Press, 1956).

[3] 'The Lacedaemonians,' IV, *Ibid*.

[4] 'Oeconomicus,' VIII, trans. E. C. Marchant, *Memorabilia and Oeconomicus* (Cambridge: Harvard University Press, 1953).

[5] 'Memorabilia,' III, in Ibid.

[6] 'The Anabasis of Cyrus,' V, *Anabasis*, trans. Carleton L. Brownson (Cambridge: Harvard University Press, 1947).

> Pericles, also, eager for distinction, then first obtained the decree for a contest in musical skill to be held yearly at the Panathanaea, and he himself, being chosen judge, arranged the order and method in which the competitors should sing and play on the aulos and harp. And both at that time, and at other times also, they sat in this music room to see and hear all such trials of skill.[7]

But, musicality can be affected by the audience and in the case of competition attended by an audience there will always be the temptation to lower the quality of the music in order to gain the enthusiasm of the public. This seems to have been the point in an anecdote by Herodotus (ca. 440 BC) describing an instrumental contest in the context of some ancient Greek festival.

> In early times popularity with the masses was a sign of bad art; hence, when a certain flute player once received loud applause, Asopodorus of Phlius, who was himself still wating in the wings, said, 'What's this? Something awful must have happened!'[8]

This was precisely the concern of Aristotle (384–322 BC) who clearly rejected the introduction of music contests in education because of the consequent impact on the quality of the music.

> Thus then we reject the professional instruments and also the professional mode of education in music (and by professional we mean that which is adopted in contests), for in this the performer practices the art, not for the sake of his own improvement, but in order to give pleasure, and that of a vulgar sort, to his hearers ... The result is that the performers are vulgarized, for the end at which they aim is bad. The vulgarity of the spectator tends to lower the character of the music and therefore of the performers.[9]

The fragments we know from the more recent periods of ancient Greece suggest that perhaps a return to the value of the music itself may have taken place. Such seems to be implied in an epigram by Theocritus, third century BC. It is a memorial poem in honor of one Dionysus, a choral conductor, which read,

> Damomenes the choirmaster put up this tripod,
> Dionysus, and your image, blest and blythest god.
> Measured in all things, he won the victory
> With his male choir, observing beauty and degree.[10]

Polybius (203–120 BC), in writing about music competition specifies that he is talking about 'real music,' which, unfortunately, he does not define further. Nevertheless it is clear that that quality was related to the reason why he found, in retrospect, that competition was a fundamental part of the educational use of music in ancient Greece.

---

7   *Lives*, 'Pericles.'
8   Athenaeus, in *Deipnosophistae*, XIV 631.
9   *Politica*, 1341b.9.
10 Theocritus, 'Epigram XII.' in A. Lang, *Theocritus, Bion and Moschus* (London: Macmillan, 1920).

> For it is a well-known fact, familiar to all, that it is hardly known except in Arcadia, that in the first place the boys from their earliest childhood are trained to sing in measure the hymns and paeans in which by traditional usage they celebrate the heroes and gods of each particular place; later they learn the measures of Philoxenus and Timotheus, and every year in the theater they compete keenly in choral singing to the accompaniment of professional aulos players, the boys in the contest proper to them and the young men in what is called the men's contest. And not only this, but through their whole life they entertain themselves at banquets not by listening to hired musicians but by their own efforts, calling for a song from each in turn. Whereas they are not ashamed of denying acquaintance with other studies, in the case of singing it is neither possible for them to deny a knowledge of it because they all are compelled to learn it, nor, if they confess to such knowledge can they excuse themselves, so great a disgrace is this considered in that country.[11]

The musical competitions of ancient Greece were designed for three mediums, the solo instrumentalist, the lyric singer accompanied by an instrumentalist, or by himself, and choral groups. Most of the poetry of the ancient Greek lyric poets which has survived was associated with the festivals held in connection with the Olympiad. These particular festivals began in 582 BC when the traditional Python festival in honor of Apollo was transformed into one given in the third year of each Olympiad. Two years later the Isthmian festival of Poseidon, in celebration of Spring, began to be held in the second and fourth year of each Olympiad. During these years the festival of the Neiman Zeus was also held. The fourth of these festivals, and the most ancient, dating from 776 BC, was the Olympian festival of Zeus, held each four years according to a lunar cycle. The honoring of the athletes through the music of these lyric poets seems to have preceded somewhat the tradition of their being honored by statues, the earliest sculptors being documented from about 520 BC.[12]

In these public athletic festivals the performance of music centered in competition, called *krisis*, judged by adjudicators called, *kritai*. One fragment by Archilochus responds to some criticism he received.

> Upbraid me not for my songs:
> Catch a cricket instead,
> And shout at him for chirping.[13]

According to comments by Pindar, the greatest of the lyric poets, the choral competitions at these festivals were among professionals.[14] This seems to be the meaning of a fragment of Bacchylides as well.

> The keenly-contested gifts of the Muses are not prizes open to all, which the first comer may win.[15]

---

[11] Polybius, *The Histories*, IV.20.5ff, trans. W. R. Paton (Cambridge: Harvard University Press, 1954).

[12] Richard C. Jebb, *Bacchylides* (Hildesheim, Georg Olms Verlagsbuchhandlung, 1967), 37.

[13] Trans. Guy Davenport, *Archilochos, Sappho, Alkman* (Berkeley: University of California Press, 1980), 76.

[14] Nagy, *Pindar's Homer*, 342.

[15] Jebb, *Bacchylides*, 423.

We know the names of a few of the winners in the instrumental contests. One of the extant Odes of Pindar was written for 'Midas of Acragas, Winner of the Aulos Playing Contest,' and composed for the Pythian festival of 490 BC. Another winner's name is given us by Plutarch.

> As to the form of the lyre, it was such as Cepion, one of Terpander's students first caused to be made, and it was called the Asian lyre, because the Lesbian lyre players bordering on Asia always made use of it. And it is said that Periclitus, a Lesbian by birth, was the last lyre player who won a prize by his skill, which he did at one of the Spartan festivals called Carneius; but he being dead, that succession of skillful musicians which had so long continued among the Lesbians, expired.[16]

The musician mentioned above, Terpander of Lesbos (fl. ca. 710–670 BC), is said to have won the first music contest at the Feast of Carneius, in Sparta, in 676 BC, and to have invented the practice of lyre singing.[17] Plutarch, however, passes on to us the older belief that the invention of this practice belonged to the gods.

> Heraclides in his *Compendium of Music* asserts, that Amphion, the son of Jupiter and Antiope, was the first that invented playing on the lyre and lyric poetry, being first instructed by his father; which is confirmed by a small manuscript, preserved in the city of Sicyon, wherein is set down a catalog of the priests, poets, and musicians of Argos.[18]

Terpander is also said to have broadened the rhythmic practice associated with accompanying poetry, specifically that he 'introduced an elegant manner that gave it much life.'[19] Plutarch also offers the extraordinary comment, in passing, that Terpander, by the power of his music, once appeased a sedition among the Lacedaemonians.[20]

Several early writers, including Strabo and Plutarch, also credit Terpander for being the one who introduced the seven-string lyre, replacing the earlier three- and four-string instruments.[21] Pindar, however, gave credit to Apollo for this instrument.

> Yet for these men the Muses' peerless choir
> Glad welcome sang on Pelion, and with them
> Apollo's seven-stringed lyre and golden quill.[22]

---

[16] Quoted by Plutarch in 'Concerning Music.'

[17] W. Chappell, *The History of Music* (London: Chappell), 32. We can assume this practice was actually much older, in view of the icons we see in the Egyptian tombs. Jebb, *Bacchylides*, 28, says Terpander founded a school of cithara performance in Lesbos which continued for several centuries.

[18] Plutarch, in 'Concerning Music.'

[19] Ibid.

[20] Ibid.

[21] Nagy, *Pindar's Homer*, 89; *The Geography of Strabo*, trans. Horace L. Jones (Cambridge: Harvard University Press, 1960), XIII, 2, 4.

[22] Ode for Pytheas of Aegina, Winner of the Youths' Pankration, Geoffrey S. Conway, *The Odes of Pindar* (London: Dent, 1972), 193.

Some choral performances were accompanied by an aulos player. Socrates, speaking on the subject of imposture, gives us a picture of this aulos player which suggests that some of them must have played the role of the prima donna.

> Suppose a bad aulos player wants to be thought a good one, let us note what he must do. Must he not imitate good players in the accessories of the art? First, as they wear fine clothes and travel with many attendants, he must do the same. Further, seeing that they win the applause of crowds, he must provide himself with a large claque. But, of course, he must never accept an engagement, or he will promptly expose himself to ridicule as an incompetent player and an impostor to boot.[23]

Finally, in another discussion relative to war, Xenophon mentions by analogy the fact that musicians of his experience were both performing older compositions and creating new ones.

> However, my son, since you are desirous of learning all these matters, you must not only utilize what you may learn from others, but you must yourself also be an inventor of stratagems against the enemy, just as musicians render not only those compositions which they have learned but try to compose others also that are new. Now if in music that which is new and fresh wins applause, new stratagems in warfare also win far greater applause, for such can deceive the enemy even more successfully.[24]

Plutarch tells us that Alexander the Great organized aulos contests because he had little interest in the usual boxing and wrestling contests.[25] We have one description of an actual repertoire work played at the contests of this period, and we even know the name of the composer, one Timosthenes (fl. ca. 270 BC). This work, performed by rhapsodists with either aulos or lyre accompanying, told the story of a contest between Apollo and a dragon. It consisted of a prelude, the battle, the triumph following the victory, and the expiration of the dragon—with the aulos player imitating the last hissings of the dragon.[26]

Where there are contests there will be teachers and Athenaeus mentions a number of famous teachers and their (now lost) treatises as well as famous aulos schools at Olypiodorus and Orthagoras.[27]

Before leaving the subject of the instrumental competitions of ancient Greece we should mention three Idylls[28] by Theocritus, each of which stages a musical contest. In 'Idyll Nr. VIII,' for example, we find the shepherd, Menalcas, challenging the cattle boy, Daphnis, to a musical duel. Daphnis responds,

> Herdsman of wool-bearing sheep and performer on Panpipes, Menalcas,
> You'll never beat me, although you may injure yourself in the effort.

---

[23] 'Memorabilia,' I, trans. E. C. Marchant, *Memorabilia and Oeconomicus*.

[24] 'Cyropaedia,' I, trans. Walter Miller, *Cyropaedia* (Cambridge: Harvard University Press, 1960).

[25] Plutarch, *Lives*, 'Alexander,' 4.

[26] *The Geography of Strabo*, IX.3.10.

[27] Athenaeus, *Deipnosophistae*, IV, 184 and XIV, 634.

[28] 'Idylls Nr. V, VI, and VIII.' In the second of these, the contest ended in a tie.

They both agree to the contest and Daphnis proposes they wager an animal from each of their care. Menalcas says he cannot wager a lamb, for it belongs to his father, but instead will put at risk his instrument.

> I have a pipe that I fashioned myself,[29] it's a fine one of nine notes,
> Fastened together with white wax, even on top and on bottom,
> That I am willing to wager, but what is my father's I will not.

Daphnis responds that he, too, has a panpipe he made himself, although he injured himself in the process!

> Well, as it happens, I too have a beautiful panpipe of nine notes
> Fastened together with white wax, even on top and on bottom,
> Which I confected the day before yesterday—and even yet my
> Finger is terribly sore from a reed I was splitting which cut me.

Every contest must have an adjudicator and in this case they saw a goatherd whom they enlisted for this purpose. The contest itself consisted of each poet-musician singing alternate stanzas. They began as follows:

> Both of the children then shouted; the goatherd approached when he heard them.
> Since they were willing to sing, he was equally willing to judge them.
> First, and according to lot, the soprano Menalcas began to
> Sing, and then Daphnis in answer resumed the responsive bucolic
> Song. It is thus that Menalcas as senior began the performance.
>
> *Menalcas*
> Valleys and rivers, divine generation, if ever Menalcas
> Played on his panpipe or sang melody pleasing to you,
> Pasture my flocks with sincere generosity; if ever Daphnis
> Come to this place with his cows, may he obtain nothing less.
>
> *Daphnis*
> Fountains and pasturage, sweet vegetation, if ever your Daphnis
> Made any music that might rival the nightingales, please
> Fatten his flock; if Menalcas bring anything, may he discover
> Everything generous here, grazing and welcome as well.

The contest continued in this manner until the end, when the judge decided in favor of Daphnis.

---

[29] A relatively easy instrument to construct, Bion, in an extant fragment, tells a young person not to depend on expert craftsmen for everything, but to make the instrument himself.

> Dear child, it is not right that you should bring
> Orders to specialists for everything;
> Nor give away what work you have to do.
> Make your own pipes—an easy task for you.

> Daphnis, your diction is pleasant, your voice is extremely attractive.
> I'd sooner listen to you making music than sup upon honey.
> Take as your guerdon the panpipe, for you are the victor in singing.

Daphnis, we are told, celebrated by 'clapping his hands and jumping for joy, as a fawn might have jumped all around its own mother.' But, since one of the problems of all musical contests is that there must of necessity be a loser, Menalcas, 'smoldered and worried his heart with his sorrow.'

With regard to the choral competitions of ancient Greece, we have a great deal of information in Plato's book, *Laws*.[30] First, Plato addresses the importance of festivals to the state and the relationship of the contests to these values.

> As to rhapsodists and the like, and the contests of choruses which are to perform at feasts, all this shall be arranged when the months and days and years have been appointed for gods and demigods, whether every third year, or again every fifth year, or in whatever way or manner the gods may put into men's minds the distribution and order of them. At the same time, we may expect that the musical contests will be celebrated in their turn by the command of the judges and the director of education and the guardians of the law meeting together for this purpose, and themselves becoming legislators of the times and nature and conditions of the choral contests and of dancing in general. What they ought severally to be in language and song, and in the admixture of harmony with rhythm and the dance, has been often declared by the original legislator; and his successors ought to follow him, making the games and sacrifices duly to correspond at fitting times, and appointing public festivals. It is not difficult to determine how these and the like matters may have a regular order; nor, again, will the alteration of them do any great good or harm to the state.[31]

He notes that these festivals have a special value for older folk for 'it reminds them of our former selves; and gladly institute contests for those who are able to awaken in us the memory of our youth.'[32]

Next he discusses the concept of a mixed competition, but explains this never works well because people of different age groups will prefer different kinds of events. It is during this discussion that he pauses to define what he means by the highest kind of music.

> The fairest music is that which delights the best and best educated, and especially that which delights the one man who is preeminent in virtue and education.

Plato next discusses the qualifications of the judges for musical contests and explains why it is not appropriate to allow the public to judge these events.

---

[30] Regarding the dates of festivals, see 653d and following. For general information on the values of festivals, see 828 and following.

[31] *Laws*, 835.

[32] 657d.

And therefore the judges must be men of character, for they will require wisdom and have still greater need of courage; the true judge must not draw his inspiration from the theatre, nor ought he to be unnerved by the clamor of the many and his own incapacity; nor again, knowing the truth, ought he through cowardice and unmanliness carelessly to deliver a lying judgment, with the very same lips which have just appealed to the gods before he judged. He is sitting not as the disciple of the theatre, but, in his proper place, as their instructor, and he ought to be the enemy of all pandering to the pleasure of the spectators. The ancient and common custom of Hellas was the reverse of that which now prevails in Italy and Sicily, where the judgment is left to the body of spectators, who determine the victor by show of hands. But this custom has been the destruction of the poets themselves; for they are now in the habit of composing with a view to please the bad taste of their judges, and the result is that the spectators instruct themselves;—and also it has been the ruin of the theater; they ought to be receiving a higher pleasure, but now by their own act the opposite result follows.[33]

Plato continues his discussion of judges and the wide span of knowledge they must have.

AN ATHENIAN STRANGER. Surely then he who would judge correctly must know what each composition is; for if he does not know what is the character and meaning of the piece, and what it actually represents, he will never discern whether the intention is correct or mistaken.

After discussing some restrictions in musical idioms (men should not sing songs intended for women, one must not mix melodies of freemen and slaves, etc.), Plato makes some comments on the qualifications of the choral groups competing in these festivals.

But we are considering now how our choristers, who are from thirty to fifty years of age, and may be over fifty, are not to use the Muses, but how they are to use them. And the considerations which we have urged seem to show that these fifty-years-old choristers who are to sing, will require something better than a mere choral training. For they need have a quick perception and knowledge of harmonies and rhythms; otherwise, how can they ever know whether a melody would be rightly sung to the Dorian mode, or the the rhythm which the poet has assigned to it?
CLEINIAS. Clearly they cannot.
AN ATHENIAN STRANGER. The many are ridiculous in imagining that they know what is proper harmony and rhythm, and what is not, when they can only be made by force to sing to the aulos and step in rhythm; it never occurs to them that they are ignorant of what they are doing.

......

Then as now, as would appear, we are making the discovery that our newly appointed choristers, whom we hereby invite and, although they are their own masters, compel to sing, must be educated to such an extent as to be able to follow the steps of the rhythm and the notes of the song, that they may review the harmonies and rhythms, and be able to select what are suitable for men of their age and character to sing; and may sing them, and have innocent pleasure from their own performance, and also lead younger men to receive the virtues of character with the welcome which they deserve. Having such training, they will attain a more accurate knowledge than falls to the lot of the common people, or even of the poets themselves.[34]

---

33 *Laws*, 657d.

34 Ibid., 668c.

Finally, Plato also provides some recommendations for the election of conductors for the choral groups.

> First of all, we must choose directors for the choruses of boys, and men, and maidens, whom they shall follow in the amusement of the dance, and for our other musical arrangements;—one director will be enough for the choruses, and he should be not less than forty years of age. One director will also be enough to introduce the solo singers, and to give judgment on the competitors, and he ought to be less than thirty years of age. The director and manager of the choruses shall be elected after the following manner:—Let any persons who commonly take an interest in such matters go to the meeting, and be fined if they do not go, but those who have no interest shall not be compelled. Any elector may propose as director someone who understands music, and he in the scrutiny may be challenged on the one part by those who say he has no skill, and defended on the other hand by those who say that he has. Ten are to be elected by vote, and he of the ten who is chosen by lot shall undergo a scrutiny, and lead the choruses for a year according to law. And in like manner the competitor who wins the lot shall be leader of the solo and concert music for that year; and he who is thus elected shall deliver the award to the judges.[35]

From ancient Rome we do not have nearly as many first-hand reports of music contests as we do from Greece. We have no doubt music competition was going on in ancient Rome, but the writers had something much more vivid to report—the competitions of the coliseum. Thus the music contests now appear in fiction, and usually as mythology. Ovid (43 BC–17 AD), for example, has left a story of an instrumental contest between Pan, the rural musician, and Apollo, the god of music. The adjudicator is a mountain god, Tmolus. Midas is the famous king who came to hate gold by having too much of it.

> But Midas, hating wealth, haunted the woods and fields, worshiping Pan, who has his dwelling in the mountain caves. But stupid his wits still remained, and his foolish mind was destined again as once before to harm its master. For Tmolus, looking far out upon the sea, stands stiff and high, with steep sides extending with one slope to Sardis, and on the other reaches down to little Hypaepae. There, while Pan was singing his songs to the soft nymphs and playing airy interludes upon his reeds close joined with wax, he dared speak slightingly of Apollo's music in comparison with his own, and came into an ill-matched contest with Tmolus as the judge.
> The old judge took his seat upon his own mountain-top, and shook his ears free from the trees. His dark locks were encircled by an oak-wreath only, and acorns hung around his hollow temples. He, looking at the shepherd-god, exclaimed: 'There is no delay on the judge's part.' Then Pan made music on his rustic pipes, and with his rude notes quite charmed King Midas, for he chanced to hear the strains. After Pan was done, venerable Tmolus turned his face toward Phoebus [Apollo]; and his forest turned with his face. Phoebus' golden head was wreathed with laurel of Parnasus, and his mantle, dipped in Tyrian dye, swept the ground. His lyre, inlaid with gems and Indian ivory, he held in his left hand, while his right hand held the plectrum. His very pose was that of an artist. Then with trained thumb he plucked the strings and, charmed by those sweet strains, Tmolus ordered Pan to lower his reeds before the lyre.[36]

---

35 Ibid., 764d.

36 *Metamorphoses*, XI, 147ff. In XIII, 780, Ovid introduces the giant, Cyclops, playing a great panpipes consisting of one hundred pipes. The sound it made was proportionally large:

> All the mountains felt the sound of his rustic pipings; the waves felt it too.

Another musical competition found in Ovid, also in his *Metamorphoses*, recreates for the Roman audience an allegorical version of the ancient Greek art song contests.[37] The contest ensues as the result of nine daughters of Pierus, 'a rich lord in Pella,' who challenge the nine Muses to a musical contest. The daughters issue their challenge and propose both recommendations for adjudicators and the prize.

> 'Quit fooling people,'
> They said, 'Quit fooling silly ignorant people
> With your pretense of music! Hear our challenge!
> We are as many as you are, and our voices,
> Our skill at least as great. If you are beaten,
> Give us Medussa's spring, and Aganippe:
> Or, if we lose, we will cede you all Emathia
> From plains to snow-line; the nymphs shall be the judges.'

The Muses are forced to accept.

> If it was shameful to accept their challenge,
> It would have been more shameful to ignore it.

A representative of the nine daughters is the first to sing, an epic song of battle between gods and giants. Ovid indicates there was little point to the story, nor any more compelling was the music—'if you can call it music.'

> Whoever it was who first proposed the singing
> Never so much as bothered to draw lots,
> Giving herself the first chance; a song of battles
> She sang, that raged between the gods and giants.
> The giants got none the worst of it, the gods,
> As she went warbling on, got none the better …
>   ……
> That was the gist of it, with voice and harp
> attuned together, if you could call it tuneful.

Now it was the Muses' turn and they were represented by Calliope, the goddess who was the mother of the famous mythical musician, Orpheus.

> Our sister, with her flowing hair arrayed
> In ivy wreaths. She tried the plaintive chords,
> Running her thumb across the strings, then, sweeping
> The music soft and low, she sang this song,
> The praise of Ceres:

---

37 Ibid., V, 307ff.

The song itself is a lengthy (320 lines) narration of the myth of Ceres, for which the nymphs awarded the Muses the victory. As for the nine daughters, 'they were bad losers,' and protested the decision. For this, the gods turned them all into birds:

> Magpies, the chatterboxes of the woodland,
> Still loving, as they always did, the sound
> Of their own voices, the appetite for gabble.

The imperial lyric poet, Calpurnius Siculus (fl. first century AD) has left some poetry which is completely in the style and mood of the earlier Greek lyric poets. His *Eclogue VI* centers on boastful youths who challenge each other, but never get around to actually performing in a music contest. One says,

> I'd sooner, I confess, go off condemned unheard
> Than, using half my voice's range, compete with you.

We find something new in the accounts of ancient Rome, something not mentioned in the Greek literature, and that is music contests associated with the theater. During the third century AD a report by the astronomer Firmicus Maternus mentions 'public musicians' who compose music for theatrical plays.[38] Perhaps there was something here which was related to the Greek festivals, for Quintilian refers to the theater as 'a kind of temple for the solemnization of a sacred feast.'[39] Another source tells us that music contests were also introduced on the occasion of public theatrical plays.[40]

Perhaps the most notorious music competitor in history was the emperor Nero. To aid his victories as both a singer and instrumentalist he bribed and even murdered his competitors. Of course the adjudicators, well aware of his reputation, always found him the winner. Not content with a guaranteed victory, Nero rehearsed the audience in their applause and had the exits blocked so no one could leave when he performed. The historian, Suetonius, has left a few clues as to the rules of deportment for contestants.

> In competition he observed the rules most scrupulously, never daring to clear his throat and even wiping the sweat from his brow with his arm. Once indeed, during the performance of a tragedy, when he had dropped his scepter but quickly recovered it, he was terribly afraid that he might be excluded from the competition because of his slip, and his confidence was restored only when his accompanist swore that it had passed unnoticed amid the delight and applause of the people.[41]

---

[38] Alfred Sendrey, in *Music in the Social and Religious Life of Antiquity* (Rutherford: Fairleigh Dickinson University Press, 1974),, 391. The poet, Calpurnius Siculus, in *Eclogue VII*, 23ff., gives an interesting first-hand description of one of the outdoor theaters.

[39] Quintilian, *The Education of an Orator*, III, viii, 30.

[40] Sendrey, *Music in the Social and Religious Life of Antiquity*, 387.

[41] Suetonius, *Lives of the Caesars*, VI, xx.

We want to include a comment about winning made by the famous Spanish writer, Cervantes.

> If it's for a poetry competition, you ought to aim at the second prize, your grace, because the first prize is always awarded as an act of patronage or in recognition of social standing, but second prize strictly on merit, so that third prize really amounts to second, and what's called first prize, if you calculate matters this way, has to be truly the third—much in the fashion that universities award advanced degrees.[42]

The final question which should be raised is, did anyone ever object and declare that contests in music are bad? Only one writer from the ancient world made this point and he is Hesiod (ca. 700 BC), as reported by Plutarch.[43] Hesiod says that when a man sees his wealthy neighbor planting and plowing with zeal, it makes him too 'long for work' and that this form of competition is good. However, artists should not compete, nor create for the market place.

> Then potters eye one another's success and craftsmen, too;
> the beggar's envy is a beggar, the singer's a singer.
> Perses, treasure this thought deep down in your heart,
> do not let malicious [competition] curb your zeal for work [only]
> so you can see and hear the brawls of the market place.[44]

The most enlightened of sixteenth-century Spanish philosophers was Juan Vives (1492–1540). His experience as a student at the University of Paris turned him against Scholasticism and his attacks on this old Church view of philosophy brought him to the attention of Erasmus and Henry VIII, who invited him to England.

In his *Introduction to Wisdom*, an early treatise on education, Vives discourages the spirit of competition, which he says leads to 'quarrels, wrangling and dissensions.'[45]

The great philosopher of the early Baroque in England, Roger North, accepted the importance of aristocratic money in supporting music but he was much opposed to a current trend in London whereby nobles contribute money to a 'pot' to be given to the performer who pleases them best in a concert. Competition in music, he says, has largely negative results.

---

[42] Miguel de Cervantes, *Don Quijote*, trans. Burton Raffel (New York: Norton, 1995), II, xviii.

[43] Plutarch in 'How to Profit by our Enemies,' notes, 'Neither doth Hesiod approve of one potter or one singer's envying another.'

[44] *Works and Days*, 25–29. Aethenaeus, in *Deipnosophistae*, VII, 310, mentions a singing contest at this time in which the prize was 'a lad with the fair bloom of youth,' for the enjoyment of the winner!

[45] *Vives: On Education,* trans. Foster Watson (Cambridge: University Press, 1913), II, i.

> Instead of encouraging the endeavors of all, the happy victor only was pleased, and all the rest were discontented and some who thought they deserved better, were almost ready to [give up music] … So much a mistake it is to force artists upon a competition, for all but one are sure to be malcontents.[46]

Of the great composers, the most outspoken against the idea of competition in music was Mendelssohn. In 1838 the English publisher, Novello, sent him some text asking him to join a competition among composers in setting this text to music. Mendelssohn answered,

> It is altogether impossible for me to do anything in the way of prize composition; I cannot do it … When I was compelled to do so, when a boy, in competition with my sister and fellow-students, my works were always wonders of stupidity … I think that is the reason why I felt afterwards such an antipathy to prize-fighting in music.[47]

In our introduction to this topic we pointed out that there are no 'correct answers' in the experiential side of our personality. As we also noted, this makes the very idea of competition in music (or love) questionable, for everyone's opinion is valid for them, but them only. Mendelssohn, in a letter to his mother, brings us full-circle by making this same point.

> I made a resolution … never again to participate in any way in the awarding of prizes at a musical competition … I should be the last person to set myself up as a criterion and my taste as incontrovertible, and, in an idle hour passing in review all the assembled competitors, criticizing them, and—God knows—possibly being guilty of the most glaring injustice towards them. So I have renounced such activity once and for all.[48]

---

46 Roger North, *Memoirs of Music*, ed. Edward Rimbault (London: Bell, 1846), 118ff. An advertisement in the London Gazette for March 21, 1699, reads,

> Several persons of quality having, for the encouragement of musick advanced 200 guineas, to be distributed in 4 prizes, the first of 100, the second of 50, the third of 30 and the four of 20 guineas shall be adjudged to compose the best …

47 Letter to Alfred Novello, April 7, 1838.

48 Letter to his mother, March 30, 1840.

PART 2
FUNCTIONAL MUSIC IN ANCIENT SOCIETIES

Entertainment Music in the Ancient World

> *Most people assert that the value of music consists in its power of affording pleasure to the soul. But such an assertion is quite intolerable, and it is blasphemy even to utter it.*[1]
>
> Plato

Theodorus, a fifth century BC actor of tragedies, supposedly said to Satyrus, a comedian, that it takes greater art to move an audience to tears than to make it laugh. Plutarch (46–127 AD), who mentions this, answers for the comedian that perhaps it is a more noble aim to free them from their sorrows.[2] Some what later, Thucydides (455–400 BC), in his only reference to entertainment, quotes a speech by Pericles in which the latter gives another rather high definition of public entertainment.

> We, moreover, provide the greatest variety of recreation for the public mind, by the exhibition of games and sacrifices throughout the whole year, and by the use of those private and handsomely furnished entertainments and spectacles, the daily delight of which dispels all weariness.[3]

Favorable views such as the two above are very rare among ancient philosophers. More typical is the one quoted by Plato, a statement which reflects Plato's moral perspective of music. Since he believes the highest value of music is in promoting the highest virtue, he regards any reference to mere pleasure as 'intolerable.' Indeed, the most positive recognition which he could give to entertainment in general is that it is amusing and provides neither harm nor good.

> An Athenian Stranger. That only can be rightly judged by the standard of pleasure, which makes or furnishes no utility or truth or likeness, nor on the other hand is productive of any hurtful quality, but exists solely for the sake of the accompanying charm; and the term 'pleasure' is most appropriately applied to it when these other qualities are absent.
> Cleinias. You are speaking of harmless pleasure, are you not?
> An Athenian Stranger. Yes; and this I term amusement, when doing neither harm nor good in any degree worth speaking of.[4]

The principal concern was that amusement in any form, aside from the immediate pleasure, had a potential for harming the soul.

---

[1] *Laws*, 655d. We remind the reader that the works of Plato are thought to be the teachings of Socrates.
[2] 'How a Man may Praise Himself without being Envied.'
[3] S. T. Bloomfield, *The History of Thucydides* (London: Longman, Rees, Orme, Brown, and Green, 1829), Book II, xxxviii.
[4] Ibid., 667e.

> SOCRATES. I would have you consider ... whether there are not other similar activities which have to do with the soul—some of them activities of art, making a provision for the soul's highest interest; others despising the interest, and as in the parallel case considering only the pleasure, of the soul, and how this may be acquired, but not considering what pleasures are good or bad, and having no other aim but to afford gratification, whether good or bad. In my opinion, Callicles, there are such activities, and this is the sort of thing which I term flattery, whether concerned with the body or the soul or anything else on which it is employed with a view to pleasure and without any consideration of good and evil.[5]

Another concern of Plato was that in sampling entertainment one tends to become like the gourmand who, 'snatches a taste of every dish which is successively brought to the table, without having allowed himself time to enjoy the one before.'[6] And, of course, he was especially concerned over the potential for harm of entertainment within the educational environment.

> Then, I said, our guardians must lay the foundations of their fortress in music?
> Yes, he said; the lawlessness of which you speak too easily steals in.
> Yes, I replied, in the form of amusement, and as though it were harmless.
> Why, yes, he said, and harmless it would be; were it not that little by little this spirit of license, finding a home, imperceptibly penetrates into manners and customs; whence issuing with greater force it invades contracts between man and man, and from contracts goes on to laws and constitutions, in utter recklessness, ending at last, Socrates, by an overthrow of all rights, private as well as public.
> Is that true? I said.
> That is my belief, he replied.
> Then, as I was saying, our boys should be trained from the first in a stricter system, for if childish amusement becomes lawless, it will produce lawless children, who can never grow up into well-conducted and virtuous citizens.[7]

Plato correctly recognized that the artist makes a Faustian compromise when he decides to create or perform according to dictates of the masses. How, he wondered, can the artist 'allow himself to be dazzled by the foolish applause of the world, and heap up riches to his own infinite harm?'[8]

> And in what way does he who thinks that wisdom is the discernment of the tempers and tastes of the motley multitude, whether in painting or music, or, finally, in politics, differ from him whom I have been describing? For when a man consorts with the many, and exhibits to them his poem or other work of art or the service which he has done the State, making them his judges when he is not

---

5   *Gorgias*, 501b.
6   *Republic*, I, 354b.
7   Ibid., IV, 424d.
8   Ibid., IX, 591d.

obliged, the so-called necessity of Diomede will oblige him to produce whatever they praise. And yet the reasons are utterly ludicrous which they give in confirmation of their own notions about the honorable and good.[9]

There are some interesting references to entertainment music in ancient Greece. Athenaeus mentions songs which *all* the guests sung during banquets,[10] as well as a very interesting reference to the women of Corcyra who, 'to this very day sing as they play ball.'[11]

The most common references to entertainment music are those relative to the prostitute 'flute-girls.' This was no doubt what Plutarch was thinking of when he mentions 'light music and wanton songs and discourses which suggest to men obscene fancies debauch their manners, and incline them to an unmanly way of living in luxury and wantonness.'[12] Such was the case with the Lydians at this time, according to Athenaeus.

> So dissolute did they become in unseasonable carousing that some of them never saw the sun either rising or setting. And so they passed a law, which was still in force in our day, that the flute-girls and harp-girls and all such entertainers should receive wages from early in the morning until midday, and from then until lamplight; and from this time on they were immersed in drinking for the rest of the night.[13]

The satirist, Lucian (120–180 AD), describes the philosopher Aristippus of Cyrene as one who enjoyed flute-girls in the spirit of the previous description.

> Well, in brief, he's handy to have as a constant companion, and good to crack a bottle with and sing and dance with the flute-girl—in fact, just the fellow for a master who is fond of favorites and given to riotous living. As for the rest, he knows how to make pastry, and is skilled in fine cookery—in short, an expert in the art of luxurious living. At all events, he got his education at Athens, and was also at one time in the service of the tyrants of Sicily, and held in high esteem among them. His course of life may be summed up as follows—to think slightly of everything, make use of everything, and lay every form of pleasure under contribution.[14]

As the reader might expect, there is much more discussion of entertainment in general in the extant literature of the Roman Empire. Cicero (106–43 BC), who rarely mentions music at all in his works, does so usually in connection with some, often rather low, forms of entertainment. In one case, for example, he joins in the same category, 'debauch, love affairs, nocturnal

---

9 Ibid., VI, 493d.

10 Athenaeus, *Deipnosophistae*, XV, 694.

11 Ibid., I, 24.

12 'How a Young Man Ought to hear Poems.'

13 Athenaeus, *Deipnosophistae*, XII, 526. In XIII, 571, Athenaeus suggests that some of these girls were quite young, 'just beginning to ripe.'

14 'The Auction of Philosophers.'

revels with music, lechery, and ruinous spending.'[15] For the ever serious Cicero, in Homer's remarkable story about the Sirens he refused to believe it was the *music* that captured the sailors, but rather their *knowledge*!

> For my part I believe Homer had something of this sort [delight in knowledge] in view in his imaginary account of the songs of the Sirens. Apparently it was not the sweetness of their voices or the novelty and diversity of their songs, but their professions of knowledge that used to attract the passing voyagers; it was the passion for learning that kept men rooted to the Sirens' rocky shores … Homer was aware that his story would not sound plausible if the magic that held his hero immeshed was merely an idle song! It is knowledge that the Sirens offer, and it was no marvel if a lover of wisdom held this dearer than his home.[16]

Given the associations above of debauchery, lechery, and revels with music, not to mention his moral approach to everything, it will come as no surprise that Cicero had a very poor view of the entire range of amusement. As he considered amusement to be something primarily 'for the untutored masses,'[17] he particularly objected to the money wasted on amusements. Here he was not only thinking of economy of money, but of the fact that amusements are so fleeting in nature.

> In the case of the enormous expenditures and limitless outlays on shows, we do not feel any great amazement. Yet they do not relieve any need, they do not increase anyone's importance, the crowd itself gets amusement only for a brief and limited time, only the most thoughtless elements feel amused, and what is more, their memory of being amused starts fading the moment they have had enough of it.[18]

Better to spend public money on city walls, dockyards, port facilities, and aqueducts, not theaters.[19]

> Charity belongs to men of dignity and greatness; but public spectacles seem to be the mark of those who fawn on the people, those, it seems, who use pleasure to encourage the frivolity of the crowd.[20]

As for himself, 'I did not devote myself to trivial amusements unworthy of an educated man.'[21] This strict old philosopher made the ridiculous suggestion that a better form of entertainment might be a discussion of philosophy! 'If we must have amusement,' Cicero asks, 'why not the study of philosophy?'

---

15 Cicero, *In Defense of Murena*, 6.
16 Cicero, *De Finibus*, V, xviii, 49.
17 Cicero, 'In Defense of Murena,' 19.
18 Cicero, *De Officiis*, II, 56.
19 Ibid., II, 60.
20 Ibid., II 63.
21 Ibid., II, 2.

> If you want intellectual amusement and relaxation from cares, what can be compared with the studies of men who are always trying to find a relevant and effective way to live well and happily?[22]

As the Roman Empire grew in wealth and power there seems to have been a corresponding trend among many of the aristocratic class to look to lower forms of entertainment for amusement rather than the arts. Pliny the Elder (23–79 AD) outlines this decay and mourns its impact on society.

> The fact is that other customs have come into vogue, and the minds of men are occupied about other matters: the only arts cultivated are the arts of avarice. Previously a nation's sovereignty was self-contained, and consequently the people's genius was also circumscribed; and so a certain barrenness of fortune made it a necessity to exercise the gifts of the mind, and kings innumerable received the homage of the arts, and put these riches in the front place when displaying their resources, believing that by the arts they could prolong their immortality. This was the reason why the rewards of life and also its achievements were then so abundant. But later generations have been positively handicapped by the expansion of the world and by our multiplicity of resources. After senators began to be selected and judges appointed on the score of wealth, and wealth became the sole adornment of magistrate and military commander, after lack of children to succeed one began to occupy the place of highest influence and power, and the legacy-hunting ranked as the most profitable profession, and the only delights consisted in ownership, the true prizes of life went to ruin, and all the arts that derived their name 'liberal' from liberty, the supreme good, fell into the opposite class, and servility began to be the sole means of advancement ... The consequence is, I protest, that pleasure has begun to live and life itself has ceased.[23]

The kinds of public entertainment which had become popular at this time are described by Pliny the Younger (63–113 AD) in a letter to a correspondent in which he also makes a point of maintaining his complete indifference to these amusements.

> I have spent these several days past, in reading and writing, with the most pleasing tranquility imaginable. You will ask, 'How that can possibly be in the midst of Rome?' It was the time of celebrating the Circensian games; an entertainment for which I have not the least taste. They have no novelty, no variety to recommend them, nothing, in short, one would wish to see twice. It does the more surprise me therefore that so many thousand people should be possessed with the childish passion of desiring so often to see a parcel of horses gallop, and men standing upright in their chariots. If, indeed, it were the swiftness of the horses, or the skill of the men that attracted them, there might be some pretense of reason for it. But it is the *dress* they like; it is the dress that takes their fancy. And if, in the midst of the course and contest, the different parties were to change colors, their different partisans would change sides, and instantly desert the very same men and horses whom just before they were eagerly following with their eyes, as far as they could see, and shouting out their names with all their might. Such mighty charms, such wondrous power reside in the color of a paltry tunic! And this not only with the common crowd (more contemptible than the dress they espouse), but even with serious-thinking people. When I observe such men thus insatiably fond of so silly, so low, so uninteresting, so common an entertainment, I congratulate myself on my indifference to these pleasures.[24]

---

[22] Ibid., II, 6.

[23] Pliny the Elder, *Natural History*, XIV, i, 5.

[24] Letter XCVII, to Calvisius.

For Pliny, the ideal form of entertainment was something quite different, something much more enlightening. He had in mind short and 'sprightly' poems which he called, 'poetical amusements.'

> It is surprising how much the mind is enlivened and refreshed by these little poetical compositions, as they turn upon love, hatred, satire, tenderness, politeness, and everything, in short, that concerns life and the affairs of the world.[25]

Aristocratic entertainment designed for larger numbers of participants must have been quite extravagant during the Empire Period. One given by the Emperor Nero (37–68 AD), as described by Tacitus (56–117 AD), is particularly interesting as it reveals many of the characteristics of the allegoric entertainments of the later middle ages.

> Nero, to win credit for himself of enjoying nothing so much as the capital, prepared banquets in the public places, and used the whole city, so to say, as his private house. Of these entertainments the most famous for their notorious profligacy were those furnished by Tigellinus, which I will describe as an illustration, that I may not have again and again to narrate similar extravagance. He had a raft constructed on Agrippa's lake, put the guests on board and set it in motion by other vessels towing it. These vessels glittered with gold and ivory; the crews were arranged according to age and experience in vice. Birds and beasts had been procured from remote countries, and sea monsters from the ocean. On the edge of the lake were set up brothels crowded with noble ladies, and on the opposite bank were seen naked prostitutes with obscene gestures and movements. As darkness approached, all the adjacent grove and surrounding buildings resounded with song, and shone brilliantly with lights.[26]

During the reign of the emperors, Carus, Carinus and Numerian, large-scale public entertainments were also organized in Rome. An account of one of these shows includes hundreds of musicians!

> For there was exhibited a rope-walker, who in his buskins seemed to be walking on the winds, also a wall-climber, who, eluding a bear, ran up a wall, also some bears which acted a farce, and, besides, one hundred trumpeters who blew one single blast together, one hundred horn-blowers, one hundred flute-players, also one hundred flute-players who accompanied songs, one thousand pantomimists and gymnasts, moreover, a mechanical scaffold, which, however, burst into flames and burned up the stage ...[27]

Gibbon describes an entertainment of a similar scale, namely a nine-hour long procession throughout Rome, during the reign of Aurelian.[28]

---

[25] Letter LXXVI, to Tuscus.

[26] Tacitus, *Annals*, XV, 37.

[27] *The Scriptores Historiae Augustae*, trans. David Magie (London: Heinemann, 1924),, 447. Gibbon, *Op. cit.*, I, 249, refers to a similar celebration in 248 AD.

[28] Edward Gibbon, *The History of the Decline and Fall of the Roman Empire* (Philadelphia: Coates), I, 374. An unusually enthusiastic warrior, Aurelian, according to an ancient writer, in one battle killed forty-eight of the enemy by his own hand [Gibbon, Ibid., 354, fn. 17].

Some private entertainment at the aristocratic level was no doubt more elegant. One of the extant letters of Pliny the Younger is written to a friend who failed to appear for a private dinner. After gently scolding his friend, Pliny tells him what he missed that evening and in so doing provides us with a brief view of a more refined private entertainment.

> I had prepared, you must know, a lettuce apiece, three snails, two eggs, and a barley cake, with some sweet wine and snow (the snow most certainly I shall charge to your account, as a rarity that will not keep). Olives, beet-root, gourds, onions, and a thousand other dainties equally sumptuous. You should likewise have been entertained either with an interlude, the rehearsal of a poem, or a piece of music, whichever you preferred; or (such was my liberality) with all three.[29]

Another private dinner with music is reflected in this charming invitation by Valerius Martial (86–103 AD):

> It's a poor sort of dinner; yet, if you deign to grace it,
> You'll neither say nor hear
> One word that's not sincere,
> You can lounge at ease in your place,
> Wearing your own face,
> You won't have to listen while your host reads aloud from some thick book
> Or be forced to look
> At girls from that sink, Cadiz, prancing
> Through the interminable writhings of professional belly-dancing.
> Instead, Condylus, my little slave,
> Will pipe to us—something not too rustic, nor yet too grave.[30]

There was also music used for entertainment in the games in the arena. A first-century mosaic in the amphitheater at Zliten shows a trumpet player and two cornu players performing while two gladiators engage in combat. After the beginning of the Christian Era, the Church fathers denounced these great public entertainments of the circus and forbid the Christian to attend. It appears, however, that it was not easy to take away these pleasures from the faithful and that many preferred to go to the circus rather than to church. St. John Chrysostom complains,

> Again there are chariot races and satanic spectacles in the hippodrome, and our congregation is shrinking ... See how some who heard my previous instruction have today rushed away. They gave up the chance to hear this spiritual discourse and have run off to the hippodrome.[31]

The Church father who wrote most extensively about the evils of public entertainment was Salvian, in his book, *On the Government of God*. Here one finds that even in the fifth century the worst examples of the 'games' still continued.

---

[29] Letter XI, to Septitius Clarus.

[30] Valerius Martial, *Epigrams*, Nr. 78.

[31] St. John Chrysostom, *Baptismal Instructions*, trans. Paul W. Harkins (Westminster, MD: The Newman Press, 1963), 93.

> There is almost no crime or vice that does not accompany the games. In these the greatest pleasure is to have men die, or, what is worse and more cruel than death, to have them torn in pieces, to have the bellies of wild beasts gorged with human flesh; to have men eaten, to the great joy of the bystanders and the delight of onlookers, so that the victims seem devoured almost as much by the eyes of the audience as by the teeth of beasts.[32]

And, in spite of five centuries of admonitions, the Christians themselves were still enjoying these public entertainments and, according to Salvian, attending in greater numbers than those found in church.

> Whenever it happens, as it does only too often, that on the same day we are celebrating a feast of the church and the public games, I ask it of everyone's conscience, which is it that collects greater crowds of Christians, the rows of seats at the public games or the court of God?[33]

Finally, it is interesting that Salvian notes that these kinds of entertainments are no longer given in other cities of the empire with the frequency of earlier times. The reason for this was that many cities outside Rome had been destroyed, whereas in Rome it was because of the worsening economy.

> I shall even go so far as to say that they are not now being done in all places where they have been hitherto. For instance, no shows are given now in Mayence, but this is because the city has been destroyed and blotted out; nor at Cologne, for it is overrun by the enemy. They are not being performed in the most noble city of Treves, which has been laid low by a destruction four times repeated, nor finally in many other cities of Gaul or Spain ...
>
> Moreover, the only reason for the cessation of the games themselves [in Rome] is that they cannot be given at the present time because of the misery and poverty in which we live ... For the collapse of the imperial fiscus and the beggary of the Roman treasury do not permit money to be lavished on trifling matters that make no return.[34]

Horse shows were also a popular form of entertainment in the arena and these productions developed into the horse ballets of later European tradition. Pliny the Elder remarks with astonishment,

> [The horses] docility is so great that we learn that the entire cavalry of the army of Sybaris used to perform a sort of ballet to instrumental music [*symphoniae*].[35]

---

[32] Salvian, *On the Government of God*, trans. Eva Sanford (New York: Columbia University Press, 1930), 160.
[33] Ibid., 169.
[34] Ibid., 170ff.
[35] Pliny the Elder, *Natural History*, VIII, lxiv, 157.

Finally we have an interesting description of some sort of mechanical trumpet which played during an entertainment featuring a 'sea battle,' given by the Emperor Claudius (41–54 AD). Claudius, who according to Suetonius would 'foam at the mouth and trickle at the nose; he stammered besides and his head was very shaky at all times, but especially when he made the least exertion,'[36] is further described as,

> leaping from his throne and running along the edge of the lake with his ridiculous tottering gait, he induced them to fight, partly by threats and partly by promises. At this performance a Sicilian and a Rhodian fleet engaged, each numbering twelve triremes, and the signal was sounded on a horn by a silver Triton, which was raised from the middle of the lake by a mechanical device.[37]

The spectrum of Roman entertainment was a wide one, including private aristocratic entertainment of a much lower order. As one representative, we mention the entertainment sought by bored wives.

> The playhouses closed and empty, in those summer
> Dogdays when only the lawcourts go droning on,
> Some women relieve their boredom by taking in
> Low-down vaudeville farces—and their performers.
> Look at that fellow who scored such a hit in the late-night
> Show as Actaeon's mother, camping it up like mad—
> Poor Aelia's crazy about him. There are the women
> Who'll pay out fancy prices for the chance to defibulate
>
> A counter-tenor, to ruin a concert performer's voice.[38]
> One as a kink for ham actors. Are you surprised? What else
> Do you expect them to do? Go ape on a good book?
> Marry a wife, and she'll make some flute-player
> Or guitarist a father, not you.[39]

An account by the famous second-century medical doctor and philosopher, Galen, describes music used by children at play. Interestingly enough, one can still see this very same activity in Spain today.

> Children take the bladders of pigs, fill them with air, and then rub them on ashes near the fire, so as to warm, but not to injure them. This is a common game in the district of Iona, and among not a few other nations. As they rub, they sing songs, to a certain measure, time, and rhythm, and all their words are an exhortation to the bladder to increase in size.[40]

---

[36] Suetonius, *Lives of the Caesars*, V, xxx.

[37] Ibid., V, xxi.

[38] Peter Green, translator of this passage, in *Roman Poets of the Early Empire* (London: Penguin Group, 1991), 344, provides the following explanation for this passage:

> To remove the metal wire inserted through the prepuce to inhibit copulation, which was regarded as detrimental to the singing voice.

[39] Juvenal, *Satire VI*, 67ff.

[40] Galen, *On the Natural Faculties*, trans. Arthur John Brock (Cambridge: Harvard University Press, 1979), I, vii.

There is a famous letter of Cassiodorus (490–583 AD) to Boethius which praises the many virtues of music. One passage in this letter discusses the ancient modes and begins by correctly pointing out that their origin was in geography, and not in music theory. He singles out the Lydians as particularly associated with entertainment music.

> Among men all this is achieved by means of five modes, each of which is called by the name of the region where it was discovered … The Dorian mode bestows wise self-restraint and establishes chastity; the Phrygian arouses strife, and inflames the will to anger; the Aeolian calms the storms of the soul, and gives sleep to those who are already at peace; the Ionian sharpens the wits of the dull, and, as a worker of good, gratifies the longing for heavenly things among those who are burdened by earthly desire. The Lydian was discovered as a remedy for excessive cares and weariness of the spirit: it restores it by relaxation, and refreshes it by pleasure. This one a corrupt age perverted to cabaret performances, making an immoral invention out of a decent remedy.[41]

The Christian Church fathers, from the very beginning, were opposed to entertainment in almost all its forms primarily because of the proximity of emotions, which the early Christians were frequently told was the first step toward sin. St. Basil (329–379) reveals that even some of the monks themselves were even participating in musical performances. In criticizing one such monk for abandoning 'your common sense,' he adds,

> Moreover, you will also separate yourself from God with your songs and your robes, by which you are leading young maidens, not to God, but to the pit.[42]

St. John Chrysostom (347–407) even condemns music and dance in the celebration of private occasions in the home. He tells of Herod who had his wife dance as part of his celebration of his birthday. But this was wrong!

> He ought to have honored the day with hymns and thankfulness to the Master, but he honored it with dishonor. For what is more dishonorable than dancing?
> Listen, you men and women who celebrate your own greatest days with such dances and songs. There are no small evils, even though they seem to be neither good nor bad; it is because they seem to be neither good nor bad that they are great evils … Does someone have the boldness to bring dancing into the house of one of the faithful, and is he not afraid that a thunderbolt will sweep down from above to consume all things with its flames? I say this also to the women, that they may also correct the men and lead them away from such pleasure.[43]

What are the entertainments of the Devil, this writer asks?

> Every form of sin, spectacles of indecency, horse racing, gatherings filled with laughter and abusive language.[44]

---

[41] *Variae*, trans. Thomas Hodgkin (London: Frowde, 1886).

[42] St. Basil, 'Letter to Glycerius,' in *Letters of Saint Basil*, trans. Sister Agnes Way (New York: Fathers of the Church, 1951), I, 333.

[43] St. John Chrysostom, *Baptismal Instructions*, 157.

[44] Ibid., 168.

Having in mind the evils he associated with music at festive banquets, St. John Chrysostom recommends as an alternative that the Christian teach his family to sing sacred music instead at the table.

> This I say, not only that you may yourselves sing praises, but also that you may teach your wives and children to do so ... especially at the table. For since Satan, seeking to ensnare us at feasts, for the most part employs as allies drunkenness, gluttony, immoderate laughter, and an inactive mind; at this time, both before and after table, it is especially necessary to fortify oneself with the protection of the psalms and, rising from the feast together with one's wife and children, to sing sacred hymns to God ...
>
> What if drunkenness or gluttony does make our minds dull and foolish? Where psalmody has entered, all these evil and depraved counsels retreat.
>
> And just as not as a few wealthy persons wipe off their tables with a sponge filled with balsam, so that if any stain remain from the food, they may remove it and show a clean table; so should we also, filling our mouths with spiritual melody instead of balsam, so that if any stain remain in our mind from the abundance, we may thereby wipe it away ...
>
> And as those who bring comedians, dancers, and harlots into their feasts call in demons and Satan himself and fill their homes with innumerable contentions (among them jealousy, adultery, debauchery, and countless evils); so those who invoke David with his lyre call inwardly on Christ.[45]

A thousand years later the objections of the Church fathers remained much the same, as we can see in comments by Bernard of Clairvaux (1090–1153 AD), known to us as 'St. Bernard.' In a letter to a canon, Oger, he describes the theater as a place, 'where lust is excited by the effeminate and indecent contortions of the actors.'[46] In another letter Bernard points to the fact that money spent on amusement is money that could be spent on more pressing needs.

> The walls of the church are aglow, but the poor of the Church go hungry. The stones of the church are covered with gold, while its children are left naked. The food of the poor is taken to feed the eyes of the rich, and amusement is provided for the curious, while the needy have not even the necessities of life.[47]

A church philosopher of the following generation, John of Salisbury (1115–1180 AD) was not only outspoken, but angry on the subject of entertainment.

> Concerning actors and mimes, buffoons and harlots, panders and other like human monsters, which the prince ought rather to exterminate entirely than to foster, there needed no mention to be made in the law; which indeed not only excludes all such abominations from the court of the prince, but totally banishes them from among the people of God.[48]

---

[45] St. John Chrysostom, 'Exposition of Psalm XLI,' quoted in Oliver Strunk, *Source Readings in Music History* (New York: Norton, 1950), 68ff.

[46] *The Letters of St. Bernard of Clairvaux*, trans. Bruno James (Chicago: Regnery, 1953), 135.

[47] 'An Apologia to Abbot William,' in Ibid.

[48] *Policraticus*, IV, 4, in *The Stateman's Book of John of Salisbury,* trans. John Dickinson, (New York: Russell & Russell, 1963), 16.

In spite of the objections by the Church fathers, entertainment continued without a pause. We have some interesting descriptions of entertainment music by the thirteenth-century German Romance writers. Gottfried von Strassburg describes what many days in palace life must have been like in the thirteenth century: during the day hunting and 'at night here at home we shall sustain ourselves with courtly pursuits, such as harping, fiddling, and singing.'[49] On special occasions, such as the visit of a noble from a distant country, there must have been a much broader range of entertainment. We have a glimpse of an elaborate outdoor entertainment in the anonymous Romance, *Laurin*.

> The noble guests saw many beautiful things and were treated very well. They were seated on golden benches that sparkled with precious stones, and the best of wine and mead was poured for them. There was much entertainment of different kinds for them to watch. On one side there was singing; on the other men were jumping and engaged in tests of strength; then came the spear throwing and stone throwing, with several events going on at the same time; riders charged into each other right in front of them, and many spears were broken in jousts; they heard a large number of skillful musicians: fiddlers, harpers, and pipers.
>
> Later two short fiddlers, delightful dwarfs in rich and elegant clothing, came before the princes. The fiddles they carried were of red gold, glittered with jewels, and were worth more than a country. Their strings made sweet music. The princes enjoyed the fiddling, and time passed quickly ...
>
> Afterwards two fine singers and narrators appeared and sang many courtly tales to amuse and charm the guests ... Anyone who was well-versed in song would have forgotten all his sorrow.[50]

This same writer makes a clear aesthetic distinction in entertainment between musicians and entertainers such as magicians and story tellers. This last type of entertainer offers nothing to delight the heart, they are, he says, like a tree without leaves.

> Inventors of wild tales, hired hunters after stories, who cheat with chains and dupe dull minds, who turn rubbish into gold for children and from magic boxes pour pearls of dust!—these give us shade with a bare staff, not with the green leaves and twigs and boughs of May. Their shade never soothes a stranger's eyes. To speak the truth, no pleasurable emotion comes from it, there is nothing in it to delight the heart. Their poetry is not such that a noble heart can laugh with it.[51]

In one of the examples of the Minnesinger repertoire, *Parzival,* we read of some of the squires playing fiddle after dinner. But apparently their level of performance was not satisfactory, 'their mastery did not go beyond playing old-fashioned dances,' so a call goes out for any visiting minstrels who may be in court.[52] Accounts of court festivities often mention that such visiting minstrels were well paid. The anonymous Romance, *Duke Ernst*, describes a wedding banquet for the emperor and the lavish gifts he gave his knights and ladies in attendance. The visiting musicians were included in this largess.

---

49 Gottfried von Strassburg, *Tristan*, trans. Arthus Hatto (Harmondsworth: Penguin Books, 1960), 92.

50 Trans. J. W. Thomas, in *The Best Novellas of Medieval Germany* (Columbia, S.C.: Camden House, 1984), 71ff.

51 *Tristan*, 105.

52 Book XIII, 639.

> The host of wandering minstrels there also received plenty of gifts, so they too were joyous.[53]

In the *Nibelungenlied* we read of a minstrel who was not so fortunate. Playing for a banquet, he was caught in a scene of slaughter.

> He saw a minstrel sitting at Etzel's table, and sprang at him in wrath, and lopped off his right hand on his viol: 'Take that for the message thou broughtest to the Burgundians.'
> 'Woe is me for my hand!' cried Werbel. 'Sir Hagen of Trony, what have I done to thee? I rode with true heart to thy master's land. How shall I make my music now?'
> Little recked Hagen if he never fiddled more.[54]

Another work in the Minnesinger repertoire, *Tannhauser,* one finds dance with singing.

> Come, young folks, taste it, life is sweet!
> And since God gave us voice and feet,
> We'll seize this chance to sing and dance.[55]

Many of the songs with dance were seasonal and outdoors, such as for May-day. But there is also some indication that they were performed during any festivity. Such a dance occurs after jousting, for example, in Wernher der Gartenaere's Romance, *Meier Helmbrecht*.

> When they had finished with the lance
> They trod the measures of a dance
> Accompanied by dashing song.
> To no one did the time seem long.[56]

We might also mention that among the accounts of the Holy Roman Emperor at this time, Frederick II (1194–1250), is one which speaks of the entertainment offered a visitor, which included two Saracen girls, whom Frederick had brought back with him from his Crusade.

> Two Saracen girls of handsome form, mounted upon four round balls placed upon the floor, namely, one of the two on two balls, and the other on the other two. They walked backwards and forwards, clapping their hands, moving at pleasure on these revolving globes, gesticulating with their arms, singing various tunes, and twisting their bodies according to the tune, beating cymbals or castanets together with their hands.[57]

---

53 *Duke Ernst*, trans. J. W. Thomas and Carolyn Dussere, in *Medieval Tales* (New York: Continuum, 1983), 27.

54 'Thirty-Third Adventure.'

55 'Uns kvmt ein wunneklichu zit,' in *Tannhauser: Poet and Legend,* trans. J. W. Thomas (Chapel Hill: University of North Carolina Press, 1974), 103.

56 Clair Bell, trans., *Peasant Life in Old German Epics* (New York: Octagon Books, 1965), 62.

57 Matthew Paris, *English History*, trans. J. A. Giles (London: Bohn, 1852, I, 369ff.

Banquet Music in the Ancient World

> *Old age lacks the heavy banquet, the loaded table, and the oft-filled cup;*
> *therefore it also lacks drunkenness, indigestion, and loss of sleep.*[1]
>
> Cicero

THE BANQUET WITH MUSIC AND DANCE was the primary form of indoor entertainment in the ancient world and this chapter will focus on the entertainment music heard on such occasions. But we must also point out that ancient literature often mentions a special moment at the end of banquets when music was performed which was expected to be listened to. These moments, always described in the literature as occurring 'after the table was cleared,' were the earliest performances which had the characteristics of art music concerts as we know them.

There exists a two thousand year old papyrus contract from Egypt which calls for a musician to play for the delight of those who cried, 'Let there be music and singing!'[2] Perhaps this contract was for the kind of banquet scene represented in a fresco now in the British Museum, which is described as follows:

> A number of guests, men and women, are seated on chairs, while women servants are handing wine to them, and female musicians, sitting on the ground, play to them, and women dance before them. Many of the guests hold a lotus flower, and one man a handkerchief as a mark of refinement. The servants and dancers are unclothed with the exception of a slight band.[3]

Such banquet scenes with music are frequently seen in the paintings made for the tombs of ancient Egypt. The distinguished scholar of Egyptian life, Lise Manniche, summarizes the elements seen in these paintings.

> Although the banquet scenes in which the ensembles are depicted appear to be secular—feasts like those which must have taken place in real life—they represent the 'idea' of a feast rather than any specific event. Right up to the New Kingdom the basic components change little: men and women in their finest outfits; food and drink; music, song and sometimes dance. In the New Kingdom, and in the eighteenth Dynasty in particular, there is a marked change of character in these scenes, which begin to show a wealth of detail with a distinctly erotic significance: lotus flowers, mandrake fruits, wigs, unguent cones, semi-transparent garments, and the gestures of the participants. It is clear that the underlying intention is to create a climate propitious to the rebirth of the tomb owner. Music

---

[1] *De Officiis*, xiii.

[2] Henry G. Farmer, 'The Music of Ancient Egypt,' *New Oxford History of Music* (London: Oxford University Press, 1966), 266.

[3] Samuel Sharpe, *Egyptian Antiquities in the British Museum* (London, 1862), 49.

played a vital part in this process: in the New Kingdom it accompanied songs which expressed the possibility of renewed life explicitly; in the Old Kingdom we can trace a similar message in the gestures of dancing girls moving to the music.[4]

The few texts which survive together in tomb paintings with the singing pictured in these banquet scenes clearly identify the entertainment nature of the music. Two examples will suffice.

> Can it be the goddess Maat
> in whose face there is a desire for getting drunk?
> ......
> The beauty of your face shines, you appear, you come in peace.
> One gets drunk by looking at you,
> You who are as beautiful as gold, O Hathor.
> May I be given a fresh mouth with the water you have provided.[5]

As one would expect, there is little attention given in the Old Testament to banquet music, but here and there are hints that the ancient Semitic aristocracy may have enjoyed the same kinds of entertainments found in Egypt, Greece and Rome. One of the passages they never read in church, for example, has the wise King Solomon admitting,

> I also gathered for myself silver and gold and the treasure of kings and provinces; I got singers, both men and women, and many concubines, man's delight.[6]

We may be sure these are the same kinds of singers referred to when we read such scriptures as,

> Use not much the company of a woman that is a singer, lest thou be taken with her attempts,[7]
> ......
> ... and one rises up at the voice of a bird, and all the daughters of song are brought low.[8]

Psalm 149 also has an unmistakable reference to the couches that we usually associate with ancient Rome, upon which the guests reclined during banquets.

> Sing to the Lord a new song ...
> Let them praise his name with dancing,
>   making melody to him with timbrel and lyre! ...
> Let them sing for joy on their couches.[9]

---

4 In Lise Manniche, *Music and Musicians in Ancient Egypt* (London: British Museum Press, 1991), 24.

5 Ibid., 50.

6 Ecclesiastes 2:8.

7 Ecclesiasticus 9:4.

8 Ecclesiastes 12:4.

9 A similar scene of music and dancing is found in the New Testament in Luke 15:25.

One interesting Old Testament reference to banquet music describes a scene similar to a Greek *symposium*.[10]

> The mirth of the timbrels is stilled, the noise of the jubilant has ceased, the mirth of the lyre is stilled. No more do they drink wine with singing.[11]

And speaking of the similarity with Greek life, there is a very interesting passage in one of the books left out by the redactors of the Old Testament which reminds us of Aristotle's complaint that the musical entertainers at banquets prevented good conversation. Here we are told: don't talk while the music is being performed for the music is the highpoint of a good banquet.

> If thou be made the master of a feast, lift not thyself up, but be among them as one of the rest, take diligent care for them, and so sit down.
> And when thou hast done all thy office, take thy place, that thou mayest be merry with them, and receive a crown for thy well-ordering of the feast.
> Speak, thou that art the elder, for it becometh thee, but with sound judgment; and hinder not the music.
> Pour not out words where there is a musician, and [thus] show not forth wisdom out of time.
> A concert of music in a banquet of wine is as a signet of carbuncle set in gold.
> As a signet of an emerald set in a work of gold, so is the melody of music with pleasant wine.[12]

A final Old Testament reference to banquet music is found in the course of a warning:

> Woe to those ... who tarry late into the evening till wine inflames them!
> They have lyre and harp, timbrel and flute and wine at their feasts; but they do not regard the deeds of the Lord.[13]

In the extant literature of ancient Greece we have a description of banquet music in one of the very oldest books of that language, *The Odyssey* by Homer, which pre-dates the modern written form of the language. This is a very important passage, for the descriptions here of the listeners crying as they listened to this singer with his lyre made a significant impression on musical thinkers of the sixteenth century in Italy and France. They said, in effect, 'Why doesn't our music have this effect on listeners?' By 'their music' they meant the medieval heritage of Church created mathematical music. The rediscovery of the literature of the ancient writers, which the Church had attempted to burn, led to Humanism in music, which means, basically, putting the emotions back into music. And that was why opera was created, to create a new medium of theater in which music communicated the emotions of the plot.

---

[10] In Greek this word meant 'drinking-party.'
[11] Isaiah 24:8ff.
[12] Ecclesiasticus 32:1ff.
[13] Isaiah 5:12.

In *The Odyssey* the setting is a banquet, but, as this extraordinary passage makes clear, this is not the usual banquet music—this is music to be *listened* to. Indeed, we are told that only when everyone stopped eating and drinking did the singer begin to play and sing. In this case the singer is the blind Demodocus, 'to whom above all others has the god granted skill in song.' He is requested to 'give delight in whatever way his spirit prompts him to sing.'

> For him, the herald, set a silver-studded chair in the midst of the banqueters, leaning it against a tall pillar, and he hung the clear-toned lyre from a peg close above [the singer's] head, and showed him how to reach it with his hands. And beside him he placed a basket and a beautiful table [of food], and a cup of wine, to drink when his heart should bid him. So they put forth their hands to the good cheer lying ready before them. But when they had put from them the desire of food and drink, the Muse moved the minstrel to sing of the glorious deeds of warriors.[14]

A listener, Odysseus [Ulysses], is moved to tears.

> This song the famous minstrel sang; but Odysseus grasped his great purple cloak with his stout hands, and drew it down over his head, and his his comely face; for he had shame [that his guests, the Phaeacians, should see him] as he let fall tears from beneath his eyebrows. Yea, and as often as the divine minstrel ceased his singing, Odysseus would wipe away his tears and draw the cloak from off his head ... But as often as he began again, and the nobles of the Phaeacians bade him sing, because they took pleasure in his lay [song], Odysseus would again cover his head and moan. Now from all the rest he concealed the tears that he shed.

Later, Demodocus is sent for again, for the purpose of having him play music for a dance. When the artist arrives however, he 'struck the chords in prelude to his sweet lay and sang of the love of Ares and Aphrodite,' forcing the guests to listen rather than dance.[15]

A third time[16] Demodocus is brought before the guests to perform and again Homer notes that the performance waited until the eating had stopped. Because of the impact Odysseus received from the first performance, he now begs the singer to 'change thy theme' and sing no more of the fate of the Achaeans, but rather of the 'building of the horse of wood.' This request the singer complies with, but apparently in such a way that Odysseus was again moved to tears.

> This song the famous minstrel sang. But the heart of Odysseus was melted and tears wet his cheeks beneath his eyelids. And as a woman wails and flings herself about her dear husband, who has fallen in front of his city and his people, seeking to ward off from his city and his children the pitiless day; and as she beholds him dying and gasping for breath, she clings to him and shrieks aloud, while the foe behind her smite her back and shoulders with their spears, and lead her away to captivity to bear toil and woe, while with most pitiful grief her cheeks are wasted: even so did Odysseus let fall pitiful tears from beneath his brows. Now from all the rest he concealed the tears that he shed, but Alcinous alone marked him and took heed, for he sat by him and heard him groaning heavily.

---

14 *The Odyssey,* trans. A. T. Murray (London: Heinemann, 1960), VIII, 60ff.

15 Ibid., 250ff.

16 Ibid., 470ff.

Finally this Alcinous says, 'Let the minstrel cease, that we may all make merry.'

Historians call this singer an 'epic poet,' one who sang of great epic, or historical events. Musicians call this singer by a name found in *Ion*, by Plato, which consists of a conversation with one of them. We call them 'Rhapsodists' and when they sang for banquets there was also a certain educational purpose in their performance. According to Athenaeus (fl. ca. 200 AD), the noble guests depended on these singers to restore balance in their character.

> It is plain that Homer observes the ancient Greek system when he says, 'We have satisfied our souls with the equal feast and with the lyre, which the gods have made the companion of the feast,' evidently because the art is beneficial also to those who feast. And this was the accepted custom, it is plain, first in order that every one who felt impelled to get drunk and stuff himself might have music to cure his violence and intemperance, and secondly, because music appeases surliness; for, by stripping off a man's gloominess, it produces good-temper and gladness becoming to a gentleman ... It is plain, therefore, that while most persons devote this art to social gatherings for the sake of correcting conduct and of general usefulness, the ancients went further and included in their customs and laws the singing of praises to the gods by all who attended feasts, in order that our dignity and sobriety might be retained through their help. For, since the songs are sung in concert, if discourse on the gods has been added it dignifies the mood of every one ... It is plain, therefore, in the light of what we have said, that music did not, at the beginning, make its way into feasts merely for the sake of shallow and ordinary pleasure, as some persons think.[17]

There are several other descriptions of banquet music in Homer which are lacking only the emphasis on the *attentive* audience, thus we presume these to be characterizations of entertainment music. One such scene, at the beginning of *The Odyssey*, also gives us the name of another poet-musician.

> Now after the wooers had put from them the desire of food and drink, their hearts turned to other things, to song and to dance; for these things are the crown of a feast. And a herald put the beautiful lyre in the hands of Phemius, who sang perforce among the wooers; and he struck the chords in prelude to his sweet tale.[18]

In *The Iliad* there are two banquet scenes of the gods. In one Apollo plays the lyre while the Muses sang, 'replying one to the other with sweet voices,'[19] and in the other they sing and dance.[20] Hesiod, a poet of the same general time as Homer, in his *Theogony*, also has a banquet of the gods with 'enchanting song.'[21]

Pindar (522–443 BC), perhaps the greatest of the lyric poets, gives us an example of a private dinner during which the guests sing light music.

---

[17] Athenaeus, *Deipnosophistae*, XIV, 627ff.

[18] *The Odyssey*, I, 148ff. Similar banquet scenes with music in *The Odyssey* are found in XIII, 25ff (where Demodocus appears again) and in XXI, 432.

[19] *The Iliad*, I, 600.

[20] Ibid., XVI, 182.

[21] 917.

> In Sicily, land of rich flocks, and culls
> Of all things excellent the noblest fruit;
> Made glorious too by the fine flower
> Of music's utterance—
> Such strains as men will often blithely sing
> Where we sit round the table of a friend.
> Come then, take from its peg the Dorian lyre.[22]

Plato (427–347) also makes a passing reference to the lowest forms of the use of music in entertainment, drinking songs[23] and the infamous prostitute 'flute-girl,' who played for male banquets.[24] Regarding the latter, he could not understand why a group of cultivated men would not find greater pleasure merely in intelligent discussion among themselves.

> To talk about poetry would make our gathering like the symposia of common and vulgar men. For being unable, through lack of cultivation, to amuse one another in company at a symposium, by their own resources or through their own voices and conversation, they raise high the market-price of flute-girls, hiring for a large sum an alien voice—that of the flutes—and for this they come together. But wherever men of gentle breeding and culture are gathered at a symposium, you will see neither flute-girls nor dancing-girls nor harp-girls; on the contrary, they are quite capable of entertaining themselves without such nonsense and child's play, but with their own voices, talking and listening in their turn, and always decently, even when they have drunk much wine.[25]

Athenaeus attributes much of the idea of having entertainment music at banquets to Epicurus (who indeed said, 'The beginning and the root of all good is the pleasure of the stomach'[26]) and his followers, 'those who walk with eyebrows uplifted,' whom he says believed that 'pleasure is the highest Good.'[27] Certainly we may take as an illustration of the Alexandrian Epicurean, Athenaeus' account of one, Caranus of Macedonia (d. 329 BC), and the banquet he gave for twenty of his friends to celebrate his marriage.[28]

We are told that as the guests arrived they received as gifts gold tiaras and silver cups. The first course included duck, ringdove, chicken, and a goose; the second course featured rabbit, more geese, young goats, pigeons, turtle-doves, partridge, and other fowl. The custom was for the guest to merely sample this and then pass the rest back to their servants behind a curtain. More gifts followed and then drinks.

---

[22] Ode for Hieron of Syracuse, Winner of the Horse Race.
[23] *Gorgias*, 451e.
[24] *Symposium*, 176e. Socrates said, 'Send her away so we can have a good conversation!'
[25] 'Protagoras,' 347c, here as quoted by Athenaeus, *Deipnosophistae*, III, 97.
[26] *Epicurus*, trans. Cyril Bailey (Oxford: Clarendon Press, 1926), 135.
[27] Athenaeus, *Deipnosophistae*, VII, 279.
[28] Ibid., IV, 128ff.

Now the single-pipe girls entered, together with other entertainers. 'To me,' goes the account, 'these girls looked quite naked, but some said that they had on tunics. After a prelude they withdrew.' Another round of gifts followed: jars of gold and silver, perfume, and a great silver platter with a roast pig, filled with a variety of small fowl. Again gifts were distributed: more perfume, more gold and silver, and breadbaskets made of ivory.

Next more entertainers appeared, including naked female jugglers who performed tumbling acts among swords and blew fire from their mouths. This was followed by more gifts: a large gold cup for each guest, a large silver platter filled with baked fish, a double jar of perfume and gold tiaras twice the size of the first ones.

After a round of drinking a chorus of one hundred men entered, 'singing tunefully a wedding hymn; then came in dancing girls, some attired as Nereids, others as Nymphs.' Now a curtain was drawn back revealing statues of Cupids, Dianas, Pans, and Hermae holding torches in silver brackets. While they were admiring this, 'veritable Erymanthian boars' were served to each guest, on square platters rimmed with gold and skewered with silver spears.

The sounding of a trumpet announced the end of the banquet and the enriched guests all, we are told, went out to look for real estate agents!

As the reader might expect, the accounts of banquets in ancient Rome include many references to entertainment music. Two extant poems by the first century poet, Lucilius (180–130 BC), suggest that banquet music ranged from solo lyre singers to choral-dance ensembles. In his case, he was not favorably disposed to either.

> You know the rule of my little banquets. Today, Aulus, I invite you under new convivial laws. No lyric poet shall sit there and sing, and you yourself shall neither trouble us nor be troubled with literary discussions.
>
> ......
>
> I never knew, Epicrates, that you were a tragedian or a choral aulos player or any other sort of person whose business it is to have a chorus with them. But I invited you alone; you, however, came bringing with you from home a chorus of dancing slaves, to whom you hand all the dishes over your shoulder as a gift. If this is to be so, make the slaves sit down at the table and we will come and stand at their feet to serve.[29]

In the smaller, private banquets, the solo performer was often invited to join the guests in a round of drinking before the music began. One such performer, Antipater of Thessalonica (first century BC), sent his host a song as a thank-you note for his generosity.

> A little dew is enough to make the cicadas tipsy, but when they have drunk they sing louder than swans. So can the singer who has received hospitality repay his benefactors with song for their little gifts. Therefore first I send thee these lines of thanks, and if the Fates consent thou shalt be often written in my pages.[30]

---

[29] Ibid., IV, 10, 11.

[30] Antipater of Thessalonica, in *The Greek Anthology*, IX, 92.

We may imagine that the banquets of the emperors had lavish entertainment, including music. Suetonius wrote of the banquets of the Emperor Augustus.

> He served a dinner of three courses or of six when he was most lavish, without needless extravagance but with the greatest good fellowship. For he drew into the general conversation those who were silent or chatted under their breath, and introduced music and actors, or even strolling players from the circus, and especially story tellers.[31]

A banquet given by another emperor, Nero (37–68 AD), as described by Tacitus (56–117 AD), is particularly interesting because we see here already many of the characteristics of the allegoric entertainments of the later Middle Ages.

> Nero, to win credit for himself of enjoying nothing so much as the capital, prepared banquets in the public places, and used the whole city, so to say, as his private house. Of these entertainments the most famous for their notorious profligacy were those furnished by Tigellinus, which I will describe as an illustration, that I may not have again and again to narrate similar extravagance. He had a raft constructed on Agrippa's lake, put the guests on board and set it in motion by other vessels towing it. These vessels glittered with gold and ivory; the crews were arranged according to age and experience in vice. Birds and beasts had been procured from remote countries, and sea monsters from the ocean. On the edge of the lake were set up brothels crowded with noble ladies, and on the opposite bank were seen naked prostitutes with obscene gestures and movements. As darkness approached, all the adjacent grove and surrounding buildings resounded with song, and shone brilliantly with lights.[32]

Even private banquets might have extensive music, as is perhaps the point of a satire, 'The Banquet of Trimalchio,' by Petronius (27–66 AD), which describes the use of music for bringing in the food, carving it, and even to provide rhythm for the cleaning of the tables. He felt he was in a theater, not a private home!

Some private entertainments at the aristocratic level were no doubt more elegant. One of the extant letters of Pliny the Younger is written to a friend who failed to appear for a private dinner. After gently scolding his friend, Pliny tells him what he missed that evening and in so doing provides us with a brief view of a more refined private entertainment.

> I had prepared, you must know, a lettuce apiece, three snails, two eggs, and a barley cake, with some sweet wine and snow (the snow most certainly I shall charge to your account, as a rarity that will not keep). Olives, beet-root, gourds, onions, and a thousand other dainties equally sumptuous. You should likewise have been entertained either with an interlude, the rehearsal of a poem, or a piece of music, whichever you preferred; or (such was my liberality) with all three.[33]

There are also a few surviving objections to the music at banquets during the first century in Rome. The continuous banquet music so annoyed the writer, Martial (86–103 AD), that he said the best way to arrange a good banquet was to eliminate the singing of the choir and its

---

[31] Suetonius, *Lives of the Caesars*, II, lxxiv.
[32] Tacitus, *Annals*, XV, 37.
[33] Letter XI, to Septitius Clarus.

accompaniment!³⁴ Judging by Quintilian (35–95 AD), perhaps part of Martial's objection lay in the low quality of the music as well. Quintilian, speaking of the bad influence of their environment on the education of children, observes,

> We have no right to be surprised. It was we that taught them: they hear us use [profane] words, they see our mistresses and minions; every dinner party is loud with foul songs, and things are presented to their eyes of which we should blush to speak.³⁵

Needless to say, objections to the banquets and their entertainment become much stronger in the commentary by the early Church fathers. Clement of Alexandria (ca. 50–216 AD) believed it was the music which inspired most of the evils he saw in banquets. Therefore, in an extraordinary attack on music entitled, 'How to Conduct Ourselves at Feasts,' he urges the Christians to have 'rational entertainment' and rid themselves of the music.

> Let revelry keep away from our rational entertainments, and foolish vigils, too, that revel in intemperance. For revelry is an inebriating pipe, the chain of an amatory bridge, that is, of sorrow. And let love, and intoxication, and senseless passions, be removed from our choir. Burlesque singing is the boon companion of drunkenness. A night spent over drink invites drunkenness, rouses lust, and is audacious in deeds of shame. For if people occupy their time with pipes, and psalteries, and choirs, and dances, and Egyptian clapping of hands, and such disorderly frivolities, they become quite immodest and intractable, beat on cymbals and drums, and make a noise on the instruments of delusion; for plainly such a banquet, as seems to me, is a theater of drunkenness ... Let the pipe be resigned to the shepherds, and the flute to the superstitious who are engrossed in idolatry. For, in truth, such instruments are to be banished from a temperate banquet, being more suitable to beasts than men, and the more irrational portion of mankind.³⁶

It is obvious that it was the character of the banquet music which Clement objected to. One regrets that he did not go into more specific detail regarding both this music and the music which he recommended for the Christian banquet, hymns and 'temperate harmonies.'

> Among the ancient Greeks, in their banquets over the brimming cups, a song was sung called a skolion, after the manner of the Hebrew psalms, all together raising the paean with the voice, and sometimes also taking turns in the song while they drank healths round; while those that were more musical than the rest sang to the lyre. But let amatory songs be banished far away, and let our songs be hymns to God ... For temperate harmonies are to be admitted; but we are to banish as far as possible from our robust mind those liquid harmonies, which, through pernicious arts in the modulations of tones, train to effeminacy and scurrility. But grave and modes strains say farewell to the turbulence of drunkenness. Chromatic harmonies are therefore to be abandoned to immodest revels, and to florid and meretricious music.

---

34 Alfred Sendrey, in *Music in the Social and Religious Life of Antiquity* (Rutherford: Fairleigh Dickinson University Press, 1974), 409.

35 Quintilian, *The Education of an Orator*, I, ii, 8.

36 Clement of Alexandria, 'The Instructor,' trans. William Wilson (Edinburgh: T. & T. Clark, 1884), 215ff.

St. John Chrysostom (347–407 AD) makes a similar recommendation that the Christian teach his family to sing sacred music instead at the table.

> This I say, not only that you may yourselves sing praises, but also that you may teach your wives and children to do so ... especially at the table. For since Satan, seeking to ensnare us at feasts, for the most part employs as allies drunkenness, gluttony, immoderate laughter, and an inactive mind; at this time, both before and after table, it is especially necessary to fortify oneself with the protection of the psalms and, rising from the feast together with one's wife and children, to sing sacred hymns to God ...
>
> What if drunkenness or gluttony does make our minds dull and foolish? Where psalmody has entered, all these evil and depraved counsels retreat.
>
> And just as not as a few wealthy persons wipe off their tables with a sponge filled with balsam, so that if any stain remain from the food, they may remove it and show a clean table; so should we also, filling our mouths with spiritual melody instead of balsam, so that if any stain remain in our mind from the abundance, we may thereby wipe it away ...
>
> And as those who bring comedians, dancers, and harlots into their feasts call in demons and Satan himself and fill their homes with innumerable contentions (among them jealousy, adultery, debauchery, and countless evils); so those who invoke David with his lyre call inwardly on Christ.[37]

Apparently among the nobles there was a popular tradition during banquets to pass a lyre around the table for each guest to sing in turn. Bede (672–735 AD) mentions this custom in reference to the poet, Caedmon, whose serious approach to poetry prevented him from participating.

> Others after him attempted, in the English nation, to compose religious poems, but none could ever compare with him, for he did not learn the art of poetry from men, but from God; for which reason he never could compose any trivial or vain poem, but only those which relate to religion suited his religious tongue; for having lived in a secular habit till he was well advanced in years, he had never learned anything of versifying; for which reason being sometimes at entertainments, when it was agreed for the sake of mirth that all present should sing in their turns, when he saw the instrument come towards him, he rose from the table and returned home.[38]

We have only a few secular accounts of banquet music which was contemporary with the early Christian church, because of the latter's control of books. One of the most extraordinary accounts of an early banquet with music was described by Marcellinus (ca. 325–391 AD). Here the guest of honor, a young king, is actually murdered while the musicians played!

> The king came, fearing no hostility, and took his place in the seat of honor granted him. And when choice dainties were set before him, and the great building rang with the music of strings, songs, and wind instruments, the host himself, already heated with wine, went out, under pretense of a call of nature. Then a rude barbarian, fiercely glaring with savage eyes and brandishing a drawn sword, one of the class called scurrae, was sent in to kill the young man, who had already been cut off from any possibility of escape.

---

[37] St. John Chrysostom, 'Exposition of Psalm XLI,' quoted in Oliver Strunk, *Source Readings in Music History* (New York: Norton, 1950), 68ff.

[38] The Venerable Bede, *Ecclesiastical History of England*, trans. J. A. Giles (London: Bohn, 1849), XXIV.

> At this sight the young king, who, as it happened, was leaning forward beyond his couch, drew his
> dagger and was rising to defend his life by every possible means, but fell disfigured, pierced through
> the breast like some victim at the alter, foully slain by repeated strokes.[39]

Another secular account, by Sidonius, a French born writer of the fifth century, describes the dinner music of Theodoric, a contemporary king of the Goths. While Roman literature always refers to the Goths as 'barbarians,' here we have the descriptions of a highly discerning taste in music.

> Withal there is no noise of hydraulic organ, or choir with its conductor intoning a set piece; you will
> hear no players of lyre or flute, no master of the music, no girls with cithara or tabor; the king cares
> for no strains but those which no less charm the mind with virtue than the ear with melody.[40]

On the other hand, in chronicling the fall of Rome, Gibbon paints a rather grim scene in describing banquets ca. 590 AD.

> The restoration of Chosroes was celebrated with feasts and executions; and the music of the royal
> banquet was often disturbed by the groans of dying or mutilated criminals.[41]

In one reference to a court banquet given for Louis I of France (814–840), we find the later medieval custom of serving food with music already clearly established.

> Of the service there must be no question; All of the possible meats to be found were in abundance,
> and served between trumpets and clarions; and minstrels, lutes, psalterons and followers were many.[42]

As one comes to accounts from the end of the Middle Ages, the range of stories told of banquets and music is quite broad. One passing reference to dinner music, in Wolfram von Eschenbach's (d. 1216 AD) *Parzival*, does mention, 'At the foot of his table sat his minstrels.'[43] In the case of art music, we may assume that a performance at such a banquet was given 'after the tables were cleared,' a common description indicating music to be listened to, rather than to eat by. Indeed, such a phrase is used in the account of an outdoor banquet in the anonymous thirteenth-century Romance, 'Laurin.'

> After they had eaten and drunk and the tables had been cleared, the princes sat there and listened to
> the singing and recitation that was performed before them. This was followed by music from so many
> stringed instruments that the entire mountain resounded.[44]

---

39 Ammianus Marcellinus, *Constantius et Gallus*, trans. John C. Rolfe (London: Heinemann, 1935), III, 305.

40 *Sidonius Poems and Letters*, trans. W. B. Anderson (Cambridge: Harvard University Press, 1965), I, 6.

41 Edward Gibbon, *The History of the Decline and Fall of the Roman Empire* (Philadelphia: Coates), IV, 62.

42 Chronicle of St-Denis.

43 Wolfram von Eschenbach, *Parzival*, trans. Helen Mustard and Charles Passage (New York: Vintage Books, 1961), Book I, page 20.

44 *Laurin*, trans. J. W. Thomas, in *The Best Novellas of Medieval Germany* (Columbia, S.C.: Camden House, 1984), 72.

In the early thirteenth-century German heroic epic poem, *Nibelungenlied,* we repeat the story of a minstrel who was most unfortunate. Playing for a banquet, he was caught in a scene of slaughter.

> He saw a minstrel sitting at Etzel's table, and sprang at him in wrath, and lopped off his right hand on his viol: 'Take that for the message thou broughtest to the Burgundians.'
>
> 'Woe is me for my hand!' cried Werbel. 'Sir Hagen of Trony, what have I done to thee? I rode with true heart to thy master's land. How shall I make my music now?'
>
> Little recked Hagen if he never fiddled more.[45]

---

45 'Thirty-Third Adventure.'

Wedding Music in the Ancient World

Rejoice with the wife of thy youth ...
Let her breasts satisfy thee at all times; and be thou ravished always with her love.
Proverbs V: 18–19

Rejoice in the wife of your youth ...
Let her affection fill you at all times with delight, be infatuated always with her love.
Revised Standard Version

NOT WISHING TO MAKE THE MODERN CHRISTIAN at all uncomfortable, the *Revised Standard Version* translation of the biblical passage above turns ravishing sex into the pale and pulse-less 'affection' and 'infatuation.' In some ways it is also symbolic of the fact that weddings themselves which are now a sacrament had in ancient times been an eagerly anticipated form of entertainment. Further, since the weddings worthy of reporting by the ancient writers were aristocratic ones, the entertainment was often a hallmark of the cost of the celebration. In *The Odyssey*, for example, Homer (eighth to ninth century BC) even describes acrobats performing during the wedding music.

> ... and among them a divine minstrel was singing to the lyre, and two tumblers whirled up and down through the midst of them, as he began his song.[1]

A central feature of ancient wedding celebrations was the procession through the town. Homer describes such a marriage procession, with aulos and lyres in *The Iliad*.

> By the light of the blazing torches they were leading the brides from their bowers through the city, and loud rose the bridal song. And young men were whirling in the dance, and in their midst aulos and lyres sounded continually; and there the women stood each before her door and marveled.[2]

A similar description is given by Hesiod (eighth century BC).

> And far in the distance
> the light of bright torches
> in the hands of serving maids
> danced in the night,
> and the maids themselves,
> brimming with festive verve,
> pressed on,
> trailed by bands of minstrels and singers.

---

[1] IV, 18.

[2] XVIII, 490.

> And all about there echoed
> the men's smooth song
> to the sound of the shrill pipes,
> while the girls' voices,
> filled with longing,
> took up the lead.
> On the other side young men
> reveled to the sound of the aulos,
> some playfully dancing and singing,
> while others ran ahead,
> and their laughter rang
> in unison with the trills of the aulos.[3]

In an Ode by the greatest of the lyric poets, Pindar (522–443 BC), we have another early reference to a bridal hymn. Later writers often mention this[4] and it was perhaps a traditional text, if not traditional music.

> She waited not to see the marriage feast,
> Nor stayed to hear
> The sound of swelling bridal hymns,
> Such notes as maiden friends of a like age are wont
> To spread in soothing songs upon the evening air.[5]

The great ancient Greek playwright, Euripides (480–406 BC), presents an allegorical wedding scene in one of his plays. We quote it because an allegorical scene usually contained elements familiar to the observer or otherwise it would not work dramatically.

> Who knows the marriage-song that once so proudly rang
> To the flute and the pipe and the dancer's lyre,
> The song the Muses sang?
> Up Pelion's glades they danced,
> The bright Pierian choir:
> Their golden sandals glanced,
> Their tresses gleamed as they made their way,
> Chanting the names, the names of bride and bridegroom,
> Through woods where Centaurs lay
> To the god-given feast
> For Thetis and her lover.
> Page Ganymede, the Phrygian boy,
> Darling of Zeus, his luxury's toy,
> Poured wine in golden beakers.
> Far down on white-lit sand

---

3   *Theogony, Works and Days, Shield*, trans. Apostolos N. Athanassakis (Baltimore: Johns Hopkins University Press, 1983), 274–284.

4   Including Plato in his *Laws*, 775b.

5   Ode for Hieron of Syracuse. Several of Sappho's poems seem to be for weddings, but they do not describe music.

> Beside Aegaean waters
> Danced, circling hand-in-hand,
> The Nereid maids,
> The Sea-king's fifty daughters.[6]

Another wedding scene seems to reflect mortal men:

> Come, greet ye Hymen, greet
> Hymen with songs of pride:
> Sing to him loud and long,
> Cry, cry, when the song
> Faileth, for joy of the bride![7]

In other references to marriage celebrations, Euripides mentions, 'the glad music of lutes at her wedding,'[8] and 'the sound of aulos and dancing feet.'[9] We might also mention that the later playwright, Menander (155–130 BC), a representative of so-called 'New Comedy,' provides an interesting account of the preparations necessary for an evening wedding procession.

> All that remains is to fetch the ritual water. Chrysis, send out the women, the water-carrier and the musician. And someone bring us out a torch and garlands, so that we can form a proper procession.[10]

Toward the end of the ancient Greek period we find two unusually interesting descriptions of wedding music. One, a poem by Bion (fl. 105 BC), called 'The Dirge for Adonis,' commemorates a marriage which did *not* take place, due to the death of Adonis. Thus, here the usual marriage hymns turn to dirges.

> Now Hymen all the torches round the door
> Quenches; on earth he scatters all the flowers
> The bride and groom for bridal garlands wore;
> No longer he sings 'Hymen' to the hours.
>
> No longer Hymen sings his wonted song;
> But 'Out! alas, Adonis!' now he cries;
> His lamentation rises loud and long;
> No bridal, but a dirge for one who dies.[11]

Nearly all Greek philosophers comment on the general decline in Greek culture after the fourth and fifth centuries BC. Athenaeus (ca. 200 AD) documents a general decline in the decorum of wedding celebrations as well, even in the case of the most distinguished hosts.

---

6   *Iphigenia in Aulis*, 1041ff.
7   *The Trojan Women*, 365ff.
8   *Heracles*, 8.
9   *Iphigenia in Aulis*, 432.
10 *The Girl from Samos*, 729ff., trans. Norma Miller, Menander Plays and Fragments (London: Penguin Books, 1987).
11 Henry H. Chamberlin, *Last Flowers* (Cambridge: Harvard University Press, 1937), 35.

> Today we are serving a wedding feast; the animal to be slaughtered is an ox. The father of the bride is distinguished, distinguished too is the groom. The women of this company are priestesses to goddess and to god; there will be drunken revelers, aulos playing, all-night vigils, a riot.[12]

The Roman Empire adapted much from the Greek culture and so it is no surprise to find similar descriptions of the wedding tradition. In the Etruscan period, a sort of pre-Roman Empire period, we see the traditional wedding procession in a stone sarcophagus from Nefro, from the fourth century BC. Here we see a wedding procession in which the bride and groom are followed by musicians playing the harp, cornu, and aulos.[13]

In accounts from the Roman Empire the references to the singing of the wedding hymn seem to point to one that has become traditional. Gibbon, for example, mentions that the Roman wedding humn was known and sung in other, 'barbarian,' countries, citing a wedding of the Goth, Adolphus.[14] And Psellus mentions, in passing, the singing of traditional 'wedding songs' as late as the eleventh century.[15]

In Plautus's (254–184 BC) *Casina*,[16] we are actually provided with some words of the hymn, when Olympio says to a musician on the stage,

> Come, piper, make the entire street resound with a sweet wedding song, as they bring out the new bride.
>
> *Lysidamus and Olympio* (singing)
> Hymen hymenaee o hymen![17]

In another early play, *The Brothers*, by Terence (190–158 BC), there is a reference to the musicians who sing the wedding hymn, as well as 'Guests, torches, music, hymn singing....'[18] On some occasions such music must have been sung by professional singers, for in Poem 62 of Catullus we find,

> Worthy of these rites, which none will mar
> Who sing the sacred marriage hymn before your eyes.
> Companions listen: how their voices rise
> In practiced song.

---

[12] Athenaeus, *The Deipnosophists*, I, 19, trans., Charles Burton Gulick (Cambridge: Harvard University Press, 1951), IX, 377.
[13] A fifth century urn (Chiusi, Museo Civico, Nr. 2260) shows an aulos player leading a wedding procession.
[14] Edward Gibbon, *The History of the Decline and Fall of the Roman Empire* (Philadelphia: Coates), III, 62.
[15] Michael Psellus, *Chronographia*, trans. E. R. A. Sewter (Baltimore: Penguin Books, 1966), VII, 9.
[16] Act IV, Scene iii.
[17] This phrase, 'Hymen, god of marriage,' must have been a traditional one for it also appears as a refrain in Poem 61 of Catullus.
[18] Act V, Scene vii.

We have mentioned above the poem by Bion (fl. 105 BC) which describes the tragic occasion of a wedding celebration cancelled at the last moment because the groom died. In the Roman literature there are two more such tales which represent the irony of death occurring at the moment which should be the happiest in one's life. In the following second century AD example by Philippus, we again read of the usual wedding hymns, as well as 'sweet' aulos music.

> But now the sweet flute was echoing in the bridal chamber of Nikippis, and the house rejoiced in the clapping of hands at her wedding. But the voice of wailing burst in upon the bridal hymn, and we saw her dead, the poor child, not yet quite a wife. O tearful Hades, why didst thou divorce the bridegroom and bride, thou who thyself takest delight in ravishment?[19]

The second of these tales of a wedding marred by death is found in the fifth century AD poem, 'Hero and Leander,' by Musaeus, which bemoans in particular the absence of music.

> Wedding it was, but without a dance; bedding, but hymnless.
> None glorified in song Hera the union-maker,
> Nor did the attendant gleam of torches flash on the bed
> Nor was there any who gamboled and sprang in leaping dance,
> Nor father nor lady-mother intoned the hymenael;
> But laying ready the couch in the hour of consummation
> Silence made fast the bed; Gloom was the bride's attendant,
> And it was a marriage afar from the singing of hymenaeals.[20]

In spite of the advance of Christianity, there was still a strong tradition of 'pagan' festivals enjoyed by the people of the Roman Empire. In the older cities, such as Athens, Alexandria and Rome the ancient pagan religious-cults continued until the end of the fourth century, with more than seven hundred pagan temples still standing in Rome alone by the end of that century.[21] But by the fifth century there are very few remaining descriptions of these ceremonies, although we read of various attempts to revive them, including efforts by the emperor Julian. He even composed a hymn for the worship of the Sun.

In Martianus Capella, of whom little is known, we can see this older pagan festival tradition. He composed in the middle of the fifth century a remarkable allegorical work describing a heavenly wedding called 'The Marriage of Mercury and Philology,' or the Marriage of Eloquence and Learning, in which the seven bridegrooms were the seven disciplines of the liberal arts and the guests were various Greek gods, together with a dozen famous earlier philosophers.

---

[19] *The Greek Anthology*, VII, 186.

[20] Musaeus, 'Hero and Leander,' trans. Cedric Whitman (Cambridge: Harvard University Press, 1975), 381. Musaeus is called 'Grammaticus' in the manuscripts.

[21] Will Durant, *Caesar and Christ* (New York: Simon and Schuster, 1944), 33.

In one chapter, 'The Marriage,' Capella describes wedding music of extensive size, which we would like to think reflects performances he may have heard at some extravagant Roman wedding. If that were the case, then it is important to note here the mention of the well-trained choir and the concerted ensemble of a number of instruments playing together.

> Before the door, sweet music with manifold charms was raised, the chorus of assembled Muses singing in well-trained harmony to honor the marriage ceremony. Flutes, lyres, the grand swell of the water organ blended in tuneful song and with melodious ending as they became silent for an appropriate interval of unaccompanied singing by the Muses. Then the entire chorus with melodious voices and sweet harmony outstripped the beauty of all the instrumental music.[22]

In a poem by Ausonius (310–395 AD) we also see a wedding ceremony more in the ancient tradition, reflecting as yet no Christian influence.

> Hymns do they chant, they beat the ground in dances, and songs repeat. Withal, a long-robed Thracian priest accompanies on his seven strings their various tones. But on another side the flute [aulos] breathes song from its twin mouths.[23]

Needless to say, if there were not yet Christian influences it was not because the Church fathers failed to cry out against the ancient customs. St. John Chrysostom (347–407 AD), for example, referring to the marriage of Rebecca and Isaac, pleads,

> Consider, I ask you, dearly beloved, how there was no sign of superfluities and inanities, no sign of devilish rites, no sign of cymbals and pipes and dances, nor those dreadful satanic orgies and the utter obscenity that marks their screaming—instead, complete dignity, complete wisdom, complete restraint.[24]

And again, regarding the wedding of Jacob:

> Surely there's no place for flutes? Surely there's no place for cymbals? Surely there's no place for satanic dances? Why is it, tell me, that you introduce such a nuisance into the house and call in people from the stage and the theater so as to undermine the girl's chastity with this regrettable expenditure and make the young person shameless?[25]

Because the Church won the fight against the Roman Empire, and the consequent control of the Church over literature, we find little on this subject until the thirteenth century, the period we think of as the pre-Renaissance. We particularly like a passage by the philosopher, Bartholomew Anglicus, which speaks of the need not for just entertainment music, but for

---

[22] *Martianus Capella and the Seven Liberal Arts*, trans. William Harris Stahl and Richard Johnson (New York: Columbia University Press, 1977), 40.

[23] *Ausonius*, trans. Hugh G. Evelyn White (London: Heinemann, 1961), I, 379.

[24] St. John Chrysostom, 'Homilies on Genesis 46–67,' trans. Robert C. Hill (Washington, D.C.: The Catholic University of America Press), 40.

[25] Ibid., 119.

more traditional values. In a discussion of the needs in planning a proper wedding feast, he recommends that in addition to food, drink, and gifts, one must, 'comforteth and gladeth his guests with songs and pipes and other minstrelsy of music.'[26]

This was also a wonderful new moment for literature and in the Romances of the various countries we have some of the most enjoyable reading of the Middle Ages. In these stories we read of a character not found in the literature of the ancient period, the minstrel. One of the traditions frequently mentioned is that the minstrels were richly rewarded by the host when they appeared in town to help celebrate great aristocratic weddings. A fine example is found in the French Romance, 'Erec and Enide,' by Chretien de Troyes. In this case the wedding was hosted by none other than King Arthur. The celebrations lasted fifteen days and the musicians were richly rewarded, even by today's standards!

> All the minstrels were pleased with their excellent wages that day. Whatever had been due them was paid, and many beautiful gifts were presented to them: clothes of spotted fur and ermine, of rabbit and of purple cloth, and of rich gray wool or silk. Each man received his desire, whether a horse or money, according to his skill.[27]

A similar rewarding of the minstrels is mentioned in the anonymous German Romance, *Duke Ernst*, which describes a wedding banquet for the emperor and the lavish gifts he gave his knights and ladies in attendance. The visiting musicians were included in this largess.

> The host of wandering minstrels there also received plenty of gifts, so they too were joyous.[28]

Another German romance, by Hartmann von Aue (d. 1215), tells of a similar wedding festivity in which he assures us there were no fewer than three thousand visiting musicians!

> A dance began as soon as the meal was finished and lasted until nightfall. Sadness vanished. If they had been unhappy, their joy was now as great. They went to the ladies who received them warmly. There the entertainment was good. In addition they were delighted by sweet string music and other pastimes—storytelling and singing, and lively dancing. All types of skills were presented, and each by a master in his field. There were easily three thousand or more of the very best minstrels in the world there, who were called masters. Never was there greater splendor neither before nor since than at this celebration.[29]

---

[26] 'Medieval Manners,' in *Medieval Lore*, trans. Robert Steele (London: Stock, 1893), 48.

[27] David Staines, *The Complete Romances of Chretien de Troyes* (Bloomington: Indiana University Press, 1993), 27.

[28] *Duke Ernst*, trans. J. W. Thomas and Carolyn Dussere, in *Medieval Tales* (New York: Continuum, 1983), 27.

[29] Hartmann von Aue, *Erec*, trans. Thomas Keller (New York: Garland, 1987), lines 2142ff.

Funeral Music in the Ancient World

> *And when Jesus came to the ruler's house and saw the aulos[1] players and...said, 'Depart, for the girl is not dead ...*
> Matthew 9:23

THERE IS MORE THAN MEETS THE EYE in this occasion when Jesus throws out the aulos players before he performs one of his earliest miracles. There was an ancient and influential Greek myth regarding dying, two divisions of Hell and the role music played in one's destiny. The earliest explanation of this myth which we know of is found in Philetaerus (fourth century BC) who explains this myth relating to the two divisions of Hell. If one goes to Hell, but is a recognized lover of good music, one is permitted 'to revel in love affairs,' whereas 'those whose manners are sordid, having no knowledge of music,' are condemned to spend eternity carrying water in a fruitless effort to fill 'the leaky jar.'[2] Thus Philetaerus exclaims, 'Zeus, it is indeed a fine thing to die to the music of the aulos!' By this he meant arranging to have these musicians playing around one's bed as one dies so as to demonstrate to the gods that one truly appreciated good music, thereby insuring his transportation to the more attractive of the two divisions of Hell.

It is in this context that the aulos is called for to aid in the mourning of a recent death in an earlier play by Euripides (480–406 BC).

> Ah me! what piteous dirge shall I strive to utter, now that I am beginning my melody of bitter lamentation? What Muse shall I approach with tears or songs of death or woe? Ah me! ye Sirens, Earth's virgin daughters, winged maids, come, oh! come to aid my mourning, bringing with you the Libyan flute or pipe, to waft to Persephone's ear a tearful plaint, the echo of my sorrow, with grief for grief, and mournful chant for chant, with songs of death and doom to match my lamentation.[3]

We assume the 'Libyan flute' to be an aulos not only from numerous references to it in the literature, but from a definition by Isidore, Bishop of Seville (560–636 AD), in his encyclopedia, *Etymologiarum*, which specifically associates it with funerals.

> They were long used only in funerals, and afterward in the sacred rites of the heathen. It is thought that they are called tibiae because they were first made from the leg bones of deer and fawns.

---

[1] The *Revised Standard Version* here, as is the case with almost all later English literature, incorrectly translates aulos into 'flute' in English. The aulos and panpipes were common in ancient Greece, but the true flute was almost non-existant.

[2] Philetaerus, *The Aulos Lover*, quoted in Athenaeus, *The Deipnosophists*, trans. Charles Burton Gulick (Cambridge: Harvard University Press, 1951), XIV, 633.

[3] *Helen*, 219.

It is also this ancient myth that gives meaning to a line in Menander's (342–291 BC) play, *Old Cantankerous*. The character, Getas, enters the stage from a shrine as an aulos player begins to play for him. Getas tells the aulos player to stop playing, 'I'm not ready for you yet!' And this is precisely the meaning of the passage, Matthew 9:2. When Jesus confronts the aulos players at the house of the aristocrat he tells the players the girl is not dead yet.

The committee in the fourth century AD who put together the New Testament hurried by this passage without elaboration because they had made the decision to eliminate all references to instrumental music in the service. Unlike the Old Testament, with its rich discussion of instrumental music in the service, in the New Testament there is not a single reference. Vocal music they had to permit, due to the tradition of the angels singing at the birth of Jesus and the one account of Jesus himself singing. Consequently, with respect to the ancient Greek myth, we wonder if among the early Christians vocal music replaced the aulos as the music of choice to perform as one was dying (just in case the old myth was true!). We notice, for example, that Pope Gregory the Great (540–604 AD), who was a contemporary of the quotation by Isidore of Seville, writes of the brothers singing psalms as one of their own was actually dying.[4]

One might assume that the faithful of Europe were hesitant to give up the old traditions of using instruments as part of their funerals. Indeed, in 1237 a group of the faithful in Eichstadt rebelled against an interdict by bishop Friedrich III which forbad them to continue to bury their dead with the accompaniment of instruments.[5]

The music most often mentioned in ancient accounts of funerals was the dirge. This is the music one finds in the ancient dramatic literature in funeral scenes. Aeschylus (525–456 BC) speaks of the profound emotions associated with the dirge when the Chorus in *The Supplices* sings,

> As I speak there comes a crying
> From within that checks my breath:
> Tis a music full of tears
> For some terror that it hears,
> As a dirge over the dying;
> For this life I count as death.[6]

One finds a similar passage in Euipides (480–406 BC) when the Chorus in *Iphigenia in Tauris* sings,

> To thee thy faithful train
> The Asiatic hymn will raise,
> A doleful, a barbaric melody,
> Responsive to thy lays,

---

4 Gregory the Great, 'Dialogue Four,' trans. Odo Zimmerman (New York: Fathers of the Church, 1959).

5 *The New Grove Dictionary of Music and Musicians*, ed. Stanley Sadie (London: Macmillan, 1980), VII, 810.

6 *The Supplices*, 112ff.

> And steep in tears the mournful song,—
> Notes, which to the dead belong;
> Dismal notes, attuned to woe.[7]

There are also two quite unusual passages in Euripides which fall in the context of the dirge. One is a reference to dancing as part of the mourning ceremony[8] and the other is a curious appeal to a bird to accompany the dirge.

> Thee let me invoke, tearful Philomel, lurking 'neath the leafy covert in thy place of song, most tuneful of all feathered songsters, oh! come to aid me in my dirge, trilling through thy tawny throat, as I sing the piteous woes of Helen.[9]

Later references to the dirge range from Seneca's (4 BC–65 AD) *Trojan Women* (I, 77) to the late medieval poems known as the 'Elder Edda,' where we find,

> Din arose from the benches,
> Dread song of men was there
> Noise 'mid the fair hangings,
> As all Hun's children wept.[10]

The procession also had an ancient association with funerals. Cornu and lituus players can also be seen in funeral processions in the tombs of Bruschi and Tifone, near Tarquinia. Professional aulos players also performed during the lying-in-state,[11] an excellent example of which is an aulos player we see performing for the lying-in-state in the fragment of a tomb stone from Chiusi, now in the Museo Barracco in Rome.

The use of the aulos in funeral processions in ancient Rome was so popular during the Republic period of Rome (240–27 BC) that the city issued an edict in the fifth century BC limiting such processions to only five players.[12] There were also professional mourners, called *Praefica* ('praise-leader') who were hired to sing the praises of the deceased in front of his house. In mentioning this, Varro also quotes a fragment from Claudius.

> A woman who *praeficeretur* 'was to be put in charge' of the maids as to how they should perform their lamentations, was called a *praefica*.[13]

---

7   *Iphigenia in Tauris*, 178.
8   *The Suppliants*, 77.
9   *Helen*, 1113ff.
10 'Song of Atli,' in *Songs from the Elder Edda*, vol. 49, *The Harvard Classics* (New York: Collier, 1910), 442.
11 *Grove*, VI, 289.
12 Alfred Sendrey, in *Music in the Social and Religious Life of Antiquity* (Rutherford: Fairleigh Dickinson University Press, 1974), 410.
13 Varro, *On the Latin Language*, VII, 70.

The above mentioned edict limiting the number of aulos players to five seems to have been ignored, for during the Augustan Age (27 BC–14 AD) Ovid tells us that a government regulation at this time limited the number of aulos players for such occasions at ten.[14] The principal funeral song was the *Nenia*, which praised the deceased in song with aulos accompaniment.

The Christian church again substituted vocal music for the funeral procession. The seventh-century writer, Adomnan, recalls the service for St. Columba in Ireland:

> After the departure of the holy soul, when the matin hymns were ended, the sacred body was carried back from the church, with the brothers' tuneful psalmody, to the lodging from which alive, he had come a little while before.[15]

We conclude the subject of the funeral procession, and our brief look at ancient funeral music, with a perfectly reasonable plan which we recommend to our academic colleagues. The 1412 will of Ludovico Cortusi, a professor of canon law at the University of Padua, stipulated that his funeral procession should include fifty musicians, performing on trumpets, string instruments and organs, together with twelve virgins singing and rejoicing.[16]

---

[14] *Fasti*, VI, 663–664.

[15] *Life of Columba*, trans. Alan Anderson and Marjorie Anderson (London: Nelson, 1961), 133a.

[16] Nan Cooke Carpenter, *Music in the Medieval and Renaissance Universities* (Norman: University of Oklahoma Press, 1958), 38.

On Music of the Ancient Military

The armies of the Persian Empire (600–330 BC) began their battles by lifting their trumpets and playing a 'war hymn.'[1]

FOR THE ABOVE REFERENCE, Kastner did not give further detail or provide any examples of such military hymns played before battle by the Persian military trumpeters. The references in ancient Greek literature to the role of trumpets associated with the beginning of battle seem more like descriptions of functional signals. One account of a fourth century BC battle involving one of Alexander the Great's most trusted generals, Ptolemy, reads,

> At approximately the fourth watch the Indians, just as Alexander's informants had said they would do, opened the town gates which led to the lake and made their way with all speed towards it. Ptolemy and his guards were ready for them. At once the trumpeters sounded the alarm, and Ptolemy led his men fully armed and in good order against the enemy; their way of escape was already blocked by the carts and the new section of palisade, and when the trumpets sounded and they found Ptolemy's troops on top of them, cutting down every man who managed to struggle through between the carts.[2]

In reading of Alexander's armies going into battle we were struck by descriptions of the coordinated swinging movements of the soldier's spears just like we have all seen in modern marching bands with their trombones and sousaphones movements, not to mention the 'intricate movements' of the army as a whole.

> Then Alexander gave the order for the heavy infantry first to erect their spears, and afterwards, at the word of command, to lower the massed points as for attack, swinging them, again at the word of command, now to the right, now to the left. The whole phalanx he then moved smartly forward, and, wheeling it this way and that, caused it to execute various intricate movements. Having thus put his troops with great rapidity through a number of different formations, he ordered … the attack.[3]

As curious as it may seem to our eyes, these 'intricate movements' of the armies included geometric figures, as we see in Machiavelli's discussion of battle technique or in the case of the ancient Persians going into battle in the formation of a giant figure of a crescent![4]

To begin with, the ancient Greek armies used music and dance as a basic form of physical training. One of these dances, for example, was the *pyrrhiche*, danced to the aulos. The first part consisted of very fast feet movement, needed to chase the enemy, or escape its pursuit.

---

[1] Georges Kastner, *Manuel General de Musique Militaire* (Paris, 1848), 23, 30.

[2] Arrian, *The Campaigns of Alexander* (New York: Penguin, 1978), 289.

[3] Ibid., 52.

[4] Herodotus, *The Histories* (New York: Penguin, 1977), 530.

The second part was a simulated combat and the third part consisted of leaping movements, as might be needed to leap over walls and ditches.[5] It is no doubt for this reason that Socrates is quoted as having said, 'The best dancer makes the best warrior.'[6] One of the earliest historians, Xenophon (427–355 BC), provides a more complete picture of how dancing and music would have been of benefit to the soldier. While only his first example is specifically military, the rest have a certain martial arts quality about them.

> After they had made libations and sung the paean, two Thracians rose up first and began a dance in full armor to the music of an aulos, leaping high and lightly and using their sabers; finally, one struck the other, as everybody thought, and the second man fell, in a rather skillful way. And the Paphlagonians set up a cry. Then the first man despoiled the other of his arms and marched out singing the Sitalcas, while other Thracians carried off the fallen dancer, as though he were dead; in fact, he had not been hurt at all.
>
> After this some Aenianians and Magnesians arose and danced under arms the so-called carpaea. The manner of the dance was this: a man is sowing and driving a yoke of oxen, his arms laid at one side, and he turns about frequently as one in fear; a robber approaches; as soon as the sower sees him coming, he snatches up his arms, goes to meet him, and fights with him to save his oxen. The two men do all this in rhythm to the music of the aulos. Finally, the robber binds the man and drives off the oxen; or sometimes the master of the oxen binds the robber, and then he yokes him alongside the oxen, his hands tied behind him, and drives off.
>
> After this a Mysian came in carrying a light shield in each hand, and at one moment in the dance he would go through a pantomime as though two men were arrayed against him, again he would use his shields as though against one antagonist, and again he would whirl and throw somersaults while holding the shields in his hands, so that the spectacle was a fine one. Lastly, he danced the Persian dance, clashing his shields together and crouching down and then rising up again; and all this he did, keeping time to the music of the aulos.
>
> After him the Mantineans and some of the other Arcadians arose, arrayed in the finest arms and accouterments they could command, and marched in time to the accompaniment of an aulos playing the martial rhythm and sang the paean and danced, just as the Arcadians do in their festal processions in honor of the gods.[7]

The aulos is described in the earliest accounts of the Greek armies, as for example in the twelfth century BC battle when the Heracleidae defeated Eurystheus of Argos, claiming the Peloponnesus Island. Tradition says it was the aulos players marching in front of the troops, playing a 'rhythmic chant,' which enabled the soldiers to keep their ranks and defeat the enemy.[8] The aulos was probably nearly as loud as the narrow bore trumpet, but its great advantage, of course, was its ability to play melodies. Exactly as Xenophon wrote in his last paragraph, above, an eyewitness of the troops of Lycurgus (ninth century BC) marveled,

---

5   Kastner, *Manuel General de Musique Militaire*, 9ff.

6   Athenaeus, in *Deipnosophistae*, XIV, 628. Athenaeus, in I, 20, says Socrates himself was a dancer.

> Even the wise Socrates was fond of the 'Memphis' dance, and was often surprised in the act of dancing it, according to Xenophon. He used to say to his acquaintances that dancing was exercise for every limb.

7   'The Anabasis of Cyrus,' VI, *Anabasis,* trans. Carleton L. Brownson (Cambridge: Harvard University Press, 1947).

8   Georges Kastner, *Manuel General de Musique Militaire*, 26.

> It was a magnificent and terrible sight to see them marching to the tune of the aulos, with no gap in their lines and no terror in their souls, but calmly and gaily led by music into the perilous fight. Such men were not likely to be either panic stricken or over-reckless, but steady and assured, as if the gods were with them.[9]

Indeed the gods *were* with them, or at least so an oracle informed the Spartans—so long as they marched to the sound of the aulos. In their famous battle of Leuctra, in 371 BC, against the Thebans, they failed to use the aulos, for they had traditionally recruited these players from Thebes itself. They lost this battle and while modern historians speak only of the greater tactics of the Thebes, for the ancient historians the failure to use the aulos was sufficient reason to explain the defeat.[10]

More rare are references to the troops singing at the moment of battle. Thucydides (460–400 BC) describes a military engagement involving the Spartans during which their foes, the Argives, 'marched on with vehement impetuosity':

> The Lacedaemonians meanwhile, man to man, and with their war-songs in the ranks, exhorted each braver comrade to remember what he had learnt before; well aware that the long training of action was of more saving virtue than any brief verbal exhortation, though never so well delivered.
>
> After this ... the Lacedaemonians slowly, and to the music of many aulos players stationed in the ranks by military law, and not for any religious reason, but in order that, stepping in time [to the music], they may advance evenly, and their ranks not be disordered, as is usually the case in large armies, in their approaches.[11]

With regard to this use of music, Plutarch adds,

> If one studies the poetry of Sparta, of which some specimens were still extant in my time, and makes himself familiar with the marching songs which they used, to the accompaniment of the aulos, when charging upon their foes, he will conclude that Terpander and Pindar were right in associating valor with music. The former writes thus of the Lacedaemonians:
>
>> Flourish there both the spear of the brave and the
>> Muse's clear message,
>> Justice, too, walks the broad streets ...
>
> And Pindar says:
>
>> There are councils of Elders,
>> And young men's conquering spears,
>> And dances, the Muse, and joyousness.
>
> The Spartans are thus shown to be at the same time most musical and most warlike;
>
>> In equal poise to match the sword hangs the sweet art of the harpist, as their poet says.[12]

---

9   Plutarch, *Lives*, 'Lycurgus,' 22.
10 Kastner, *Manuel General de Musique Militaire*.
11 *The History of the Peloponnesian War*, Book 322.
12 *Lives*, 'Lycurgus,' xxi.

Although we have very little musical description, there are additional references to the Greek soldiers singing. One form they sang seems to have been a traditional 'Paean,' which is mentioned by Thucydides in a description of the use of music in a religious-cult ceremony involving the blessing of ships before they sail.

> When the ships were manned, and every thing was put on board which was to be taken with them, silence was ordered by the sound of the trumpet, and the usual prayers directed by law were recited, not by each ship separately, but all together, the whole multitude responding to the voice of the heralds; cups of wine, too, were mixed throughout the whole armament, and the officers and soldiers made libations out of golden and silver goblets ... And after the singing of the Paean, and completing the libations, they put to sea.[13]

Xenophon mentions on two occasions the military troops singing 'the paean' just before the commencement of battle.[14]

In an account of Alexander in India we read of his trumpets signaling for the departure of the fleet after another ceremonial blessing.

> After a libation to Heracles his ancestor and to Ammon and the other gods it was his custom to honor, Alexander ordered the trumpets to sound the signal for departure and the whole fleet, each vessel in her proper station, began to move down-river.[15]

In a world where one very rarely heard music of other cultures, foreign music was always considered strange. We find such an example in this same account. As Alexander's fleet moves down the river they heard the music of the Indians:

> The natives ... followed [the fleet] down the banks for miles ... singing their barbaric songs. For the Indians, be it said, are an extremely musical race and have loved dancing ever since the days when Dionysus came with his wild revelers to their country.

Ancient literature also suggests that during lulls in battle, music was used as a form of entertainment while the soldiers rested. We believe this is what is implied at the beginning of Book X of *The Iliad* by Homer.

> So often as [Agamemnon] gazed toward the Trojan plain, he marveled at the many fires that burned before the face of Ilios, and at the sound of aulos and pipes, and the din of men.

In one of the plays by Euripides we find what appears to be an account based on the Homer reference above.

> A very weariness of joy
> Fell with the evening over Troy:

---

13 Thucydides, *The Peloponnesian War* (New York: Modern Library, 1951), 356.
14 'The Anabasis of Cyrus,' Book IV, 16 and Book V, 14.
15 Arrian, *The Campaigns of Alexander*, Book 6, 304.

> And lutes of Afric mingled there
> With Phrygian songs: and many a maiden,
> With white feet glancing light as air,
> Made happy music through the gloom:
> And fires on many an inward room
> All night broad-flashing, flung their glare
> On laughing eyes and slumber-laden.[16]

A similar description by the early lyric poet, Alkman, of soldiers at rest gives a hint of the nature of the music.

> Eating and singing and the soldiers
> Nearby begin a hymn to Apollo.

Most references of a military nature in the Old Testament only mention the use of trumpet signals. There are, however, two attractive stories which are familiar to all readers. The first tells of blowing down the walls of Jericho.

> And seven priests shall bear seven trumpets of ram's horns before the ark; and on the seventh day you shall march around the city seven times, the priests blowing the trumpets. And when they make a long blast with the ram's horn, as soon as you hear the sound of the trumpet, then all the people shall shout with a great shout; and the wall of the city will fall down flat.[17]

The second is the story of Gideon's famous surprise attack when, at night, he surrounded the enemy and gave them the impression that a much greater army was accompanying him. As it was, he had three hundred trumpet players.

> So Gideon and the hundred men who were with him came to the outskirts of the camp at the beginning of the middle watch, when they had just set the watch; and they blew the trumpets and smashed the jars that were in their hands. And the three companies blew the trumpets and broke the jars, holding in their left hands the torches, and in their right hands the trumpets to blow; and they cried, 'A sword for the Lord and for Gideon!' They stood every man in his place around about the camp, and all the army ran; they cried out and fled. When they blew the three hundred trumpets, the Lord set every man's sword against his fellow and against all the army; and the army fled.[18]

Aside from the functional use of trumpets for signal purposes during battle, we can assume the effect of this music also instilled in the soldiers a raised sense of excitement, as the story of Gideon suggests. We also get an indirect allusion to this heightened state of readiness in a description of the effect the trumpet had on the horses.

---

[16] *The Trojan Women*, 543.

[17] Joshua 6:4ff.

[18] Judges 6:34ff. Other examples of the use of military trumpet signals can be found in Numbers 31:6, 2 Samuel 2:28, 2 Chronicles 13:12, Jeremiah 4: 19ff, Jeremiah 6, Jeremiah 42:14, Hosea 8, Joel 2:1 and 15, Amos 3:6, and Zephanian 1:16.

> His majestic snorting is terrible.
> He paws in the valley, and exults in his strength; he goes out to meet the weapons.
> He laughs at fear, and is not dismayed; he does not turn back from the sword.
> Upon him rattle the quiver, the flashing spear and the javelin.
> With fierceness and rage he swallows the ground; he cannot stand still at the sound of the trumpet.
> When the trumpet sounds, he says 'Aha!'
> He smells the battle from afar, the thunder of the captains, and the shouting.[19]

For the period before the Republic Period of Rome (before 240 BC) our knowledge of military matters comes primarily from the extant portions of the *History of Rome* by Titus Livius, known as Livy. Writing in the first century BC, Livy was concerned mostly with political events and only rarely does he mention music. However, his first reference to music is quite revealing. The king Servius Tullius (ca. sixth century BC) created a formal organization of society, based on wealth, which would be used for the assessment of taxes and military obligation. In this social order we can see that the only represented musicians, trumpeters, were valued rather low, in the fifth of six classes. What this meant, at least in human terms, can be seen in how the various levels were equipped for defense. The first class was equipped with helmet, round shield, greaves, breast-plate and armed with sword and spear. The fourth class had only spear and javelin and the fifth class, which included the musicians, had only slings and stones.[20]

His most interesting references to music and the military involve the songs sung by soldiers. His descriptions, however, always seem to carry an uncomplimentary tone, as in the case of the 'rough soldiers' songs,' sung by the troops who entered Rome in a procession with Quintus Fabius.[21]

His most colorful descriptions are of the songs of the enemy, the Gauls. A very intriguing reference, for the period ca. 403–390 BC, only makes us wish we could hear the music itself.

> All too soon cries like the howling of wolves and barbaric songs could be heard, as the Gallic squadrons rode hither and thither close outside the walls.[22]

Perhaps his choice of language here only reflects his feelings for the enemy, whom in another place he pictures in one of their moments of victory.

> Some Gallic horsemen came in sight, carrying heads hanging from their horses' breasts and fixed on their spears, singing their customary song of triumph.[23]

Another reference to Roman soldiers singing is found in Virgil, who mentions the songs of soldiers.

---

[19] Job 39:20ff.

[20] Livy, *A History of Rome*, I, 43.

[21] Ibid., X, 30.

[22] Ibid., V, 39.

[23] Ibid., X, 26.

> They marched to even rhythms and they sang
> To praise their king.[24]

Suetonius also mentions the fact that soldiers sang songs while marching and also relates an extraordinary tale of a ghost trumpeter.

> On a sudden there appeared hard by a being of wondrous stature and beauty, who sat and played upon a reed instrument; and when not only the shepherds flocked to hear him, but many of the soldiers left their posts, and among them some of the trumpeters, the apparition snatched a trumpet from one of them, rushed to the river, and sounding a war-note with mighty blast, strode to the opposite bank.[25]

This ghost story reminds us that the common people were never far from the primitive and superstitious origins of their quasi religious cults. Tacitus, for example, tells of an occasion when, upon the occurrence of a lunar eclipse, the soldiers in the field became frightened and immediately lapsed into a cult ceremony directed at the god in question.

> Suddenly in a clear sky the moon's radiance seemed to die away. This the soldiers in their ignorance of the cause regarded as an omen of their condition, comparing the failure of her light to their own efforts, and imagining that their attempts would end prosperously should her brightness and splendor be restored to the goddess. And so they raised a din with brazen instruments and the combined notes of trumpets and horns, with joy or sorrow, as she brightened or grew dark. When clouds arose and obstructed their sight, and it was thought she was buried in the gloom, with that proneness to superstition which steals over minds once thoroughly cowed, they lamented that this was a portent of never ending hardship, and that heaven frowned on their deeds.[26]

The early Roman military strategists were very much aware of the effective use made by music by the ancient Greeks. This is clear in a reference by the historian Polybius (203–120 BC). He departs from his description of the internal wars of the period 220–216 BC to give a fervent testimonial to the role music plays in shaping the character of entire peoples and a plea that the Cynaetheans return to this use of music to save themselves. In the course of his argument he mentions the military music of the Greeks.

> We should not think that the ancient Cretans and Lacedaemonians acted at haphazard in substituting the aulos and rhythmic movement for the bugle in war, or that the early Arcadians had no good reason for incorporating music in their whole public life to such an extent that not only boys, but young men up to the age of thirty were compelled to study it constantly, although in other matters their lives were most austere.[27]

---

[24] Virgil, *Aenei*, VII, 731.
[25] Suetonius, *Lives of the Caesars*, I, xlix and xxxii.
[26] Tacitus, *Annals*, I, 28.
[27] Polybius, *The Histories*, IV.20.5ff, trans. W. R. Paton (Cambridge: Harvard University Press, 1954).

Cicero also seems to have known of and admired the discipline supplied by music among the Greeks.

> As for military affairs—I mean ours, not the Spartans', whose line advances to a musical measure and the aulos, and every cry of encouragement is expressed in the anapaestic meter.[28]

We do not know if the Romans were as active as the Greeks in the use of music and dance for the physical training of their soldiers, but one reference to these military musicians, during the Jugurthine War, suggests that the military musicians were in pretty good shape. When Marius needed a small group to climb a rock wall to spy on an enemy fortress, he turned to 'five of the most agile men he could find among his trumpeters and hornblowers, and four centurions.'[29]

In the Roman literature of this period there are frequent references to the use of the trumpet for playing military signals. They must always have been heard at the beginning of battle and in one such case[30] Livy captures the quality of their sounds when he writes of the seventh century BC, 'The trumpet s blared.' Tacitus recounts trumpets signaling during a surprise night attack.

> Day dawned, and with the sound of trumpets and fierce shouts, they were on the half-asleep barbarians ... The enemy utterly surprised, without arms, order, or plan, were seized slaughtered, or captured like cattle.[31]

It is likely that there were some trumpet signals used in battle which were in common usage and would have been recognized by the enemy. Livy, in his account of the war with Hannibal, mentions an occasion during the siege of a city when upon hearing the trumpets the defenders concluded the city was lost and gave up.[32] This same presumption of the common understanding of the trumpet signals would have been the background in a case where the trumpet playing made no sense.

> A further cause of confusion was a trumpet-blast from the theater: it was a Roman trumpet, furnished by the traitors for the purpose, and the fact that it was blown by a Greek who was naturally unfamiliar with the instrument made it impossible to tell clearer knowledge.[33]

Polybius, apparently referring to this same incident, suggests the confusion was deliberate and with more dramatic results.

---

[28] Cicero, *Tusculan Disputations*, II, 37.
[29] Sallust, *The Jugurthine War*, 94, 1ff.
[30] Livy, *History*, I.25.
[31] *The Complete Works of Tacitus* (New York: Modern Library, 1942), 158.
[32] Livy, XXV, 24 in *The War with Hannibal* (New York: Penguin classics, 1980), 328.
[33] Ibid., 306.

> Meanwhile Philemenus and his companions had provided themselves with some Roman trumpets and some men who had learned how to blow them, and stood in the theater and sounded the call to arms. The Romans rallied to the summons carrying their weapons, and according to their usual custom ran towards the citadel, which was exactly what the Carthaginians had intended. They came on to the streets in groups that were scattered and too small to take up a formation. There they encountered the Carthaginians and the Celts, and in this way many of them were killed.[34]

In one case the blare of the Roman trumpets frightened Hannibal's famous elephants:

> Hannibal was still addressing his Carthaginian contingent, and the various national leaders of their own countrymen—mainly through interpreters because of the admixture of foreign troops—when from the Roman side the horns and trumpets blared out and so tremendous a cheer was raised that the elephants panicked and turned against their own men, especially against the Moors and Numidians on the left wing.[35]

No doubt in the confusion of battle perhaps one heard trumpets from all sides, as in a conflict of 190 BC described Livy in which, 'a hubbub of indistinguishable shouts, almost drowned by the blare of trumpets.'[36]

Livy also wrote of trumpets playing to assemble the troops and in one case they were up very early for this purpose.

> Next morning when the trumpets began to sound, these men were the first to assemble, all prepared and in formation, at headquarters. After sunrise Gracchus drew up his battle-line.[37]

We also find accounts of the trumpets giving the signal to begin a march,[38] to call for a retreat,[39] to begin an assault,[40] to signal the time to sail after the blessing ritual[41] and even to 'blare' for silence so a leader can speak.[42]

Trumpet signals were also used in the navy, sometimes for the purpose of establishing rhythm for the oarsmen.[43] The musicians of the army were noncommissioned officers, while the musicians of the navy were slaves.[44]

---

34 Polybius, *The Rise of the Roman Empire* (New York: Penguin, 1981), 381.

35 Ibid., 661.

36 Livy, *History*, XXXVII, 29.

37 Livy, *Hannibal*, 248.

38 Ibid., 623

39 Livy, *History*, V, 36, and Polybius, *The Rise of the Roman Empire* (New York: Penguin, 1981), 91.

40 Polybius, Ibid., 412, 414.

41 Livy, *Hannibal*, 602, where he also gives the text of the prayer before sailing.

42 Livy, *History*, II, 45.

43 Polybius, *The Rise of the Roman Empire*, 63, describes the rehearsal process for teaching new slaves the art of coordinated rowing in time.

44 Alfred Sendrey, in *Music in the Social and Religious Life of Antiquity* (Rutherford: Fairleigh Dickinson University Press, 1974), 421.

Pollux mentions specific signals for attack, for encouragement during the battle, for retreat and for setting up camp.[45] Josephus writes that in camp the Roman trumpets gave the signal to wake, a second to prepare to march, and a third for departure.[46] There are accounts of having some trumpet players placed far behind the troops for the purpose of misleading the enemy regarding the location of the Roman armies.

The Greek writer, Aristides Quintilianus (third century AD), provides very interesting detail regarding these musical signals.

> As to war, in which Rome was and is outstandingly glorious (and, let me add, may it so remain), the fact that drill exercises 'in pyrrhic style' are done to music hardly needs mentioning, since everyone knows it quite well. What most people do not know is that in the perils of battle itself they often avoid the use of verbal commands, since damage would be done if they were understood by those of the enemy who speak the same language. Instead they signal by musical means, using that martial and rousing instrument the trumpet [*salpinx*], and each command is assigned a specific tune. Thus frontal attacks and flanking advances, for instance, have each been given their own particular melodies; another sounds the retreat; there are special calls for wheeling to left or to right. Thus they can go through all these maneuvers one after another, using signals which are incomprehensible to the enemy but perfectly clear to their own side, and which are understood the moment they are given. The signals are not heard first by one section, then the next; the whole army acts at a single sound.[47]

Aristides suggestion here that every soldier knew these signals seems to be confirmed by an occasion when Hannibal attempted to confuse the Roman soldiers by having his trumpeters play false signals, but was unable to confuse them.[48] But Athenaeus gives some extraordinary instances where an enemy was defeated by a spy learning the aulos melodies to which the enemy's *horses* responded.[49]

Such a system of signals being so vital to the progress of the battle, it was important, of course, that the correct signals be played at the correct time. In one famous instance when this failed to happen, Hirtius, in his *History of the War of Africa*, reported hearing the cornus pass on the order for attack, while Julius Caesar was still making up his mind to attack or not![50]

Polybius, in his account of the musical signals heard during a battle between the Romans and the Celts, speaks of 'the dreadful din, for there were innumerable cornu blowers and trumpeters.'[51]

---

45 Ibid., 405.

46 *The Jewish Wars*, III, 89ff.

47 *De Musica*, quoted in Andrew Barker, *Greek Musical Writings* (Cambridge: Cambridge University Press, 1989), II, 466. References to the military trumpet of this period can also be found in Seneca's *Thyestes*, 189; Pliny the Younger, Letter XX, to Macrinus; Tacitus, *Annals*, IV, 25 and XV, 30; and in Valerius Flaccus (d. ca. 94 AD), *Argonautica*, VII, 629.

48 Georges Kastner, *Manuel General de Musique Militaire* (Paris, 1848), 35.

49 Athenaeus, *Deipnosophistae*, XII, 520.

50 Quoted in Kastner, *Manuel General de Musique Militaire*, 34.

51 *Histories*, II, 29, 6–7.

Less frequently mentioned are the letter 'J' shaped instrument, the *lituus*,[52] which was apparently assigned to the cavalry, and the letter 'G' shaped instrument similar to the cornui, the *buccina*. This last instrument, made from an animal horn, was used for giving signals during the night, when the louder trumpet might prevent sleep entirely.[53]

There is not sufficient extant information to know how many trumpet and cornu players were used with a Roman army of a particular size. There is one extant listing of players in the third Augustan Legion in Lambaesis (Numidia) which gives a surprisingly large contingent of thirty-nine trumpet players and thirty-six cornu players.[54] Plutarch, speaking of the sounds of the trumpets, 'coming from every direction,' also seems to confirm such large numbers of players.

> Moving stealthily over the ground between, they charged the camp about midnight, and with loud shouts and blasts of trumpets from every direction, by their din threw the Gauls ... into complete confusion.[55]

---

[52] Livy, *Histories*, 1.18, gives this word for the 'smooth, crook-handed staff' carried by a priest. The instrument, in an unknown descendant, appears again in Cantata 118 by Bach.

[53] Kastner, *Manuel General de Musique Militaire*, 33.

[54] G. Wilmanns, ed., *Corpus inscriptionum latinarum* (Berlin, 1881), VIII, Nr. 2557, 295.

[55] *Lives*, 'Camillus,' 23.

PART 3
SECULAR MUSIC PERFORMANCE IN THE MIDDLE AGES

On Medieval Military Music

OF THE VARIOUS ACCOUNTS of the music of the Roman armies, the most interesting are those by the historian, Marcellinus, because his descriptions often have the character of an eyewitness. He mentions specific musical signals, including calling the ranks together,[1] to attack ('having ordered the horns to sound the war-note'[2]) and reveille ('the day had ended and the trumpet sounded'[3]). One can almost hear the trumpets when he writes of the style of the trumpet music, as in a mention of the trumpets of the Batavians, which 'pealed savagely,'[4] in another place, the 'blare' of the trumpets,[5] and an interesting reference to 'slow' notes by the trumpets.

> And day was now dawning, when mail-clad siege-works veiled almost the entire sky, and the dense forces moved forward, not as before in disorder, but led by the slow notes of the trumpets and with no one running forward.[6]

He is less complimentary of the enemy trumpets, once referring to them as,

> The bands of raging savages, blaring some ferocious tune on their barbaric trumpets.[7]

It is with this prejudice, that on one occasion he gives us a direct comparison of the military songs of the Roman and barbarians (Goths).

> The light of day had hardly appeared, when the trumpets on both sides sounded the call to take up arms …
> So, when both armies after advancing cautiously remained unmoved, the opposing warriors stared at each other with savage and sidelong glances. The Romans in unison sounded their war-cry, as usual rising from a low to a louder tone, of which the national name is *barritus*, and thus roused themselves to mighty strength. But the barbarians sounded the glories of their forefathers with wild shouts, and amid this discordant clamor of different languages skirmishes were first tried.[8]

---

[1] Ammianus Marcellinus, *Constantius et Gallus*, trans. John C. Rolfe (London: Heinemann, 1935), II, 475.
[2] Ibid., I, 265, and II, 75..
[3] Ibid., I, 299.
[4] Ibid., I, 289.
[5] Ibid., III, 71
[6] Ibid., I, 503.
[7] Ibid., III, 269.
[8] Ibid., III, 431.

Marcellinus makes two brief references to military entertainment, the first to the dancing of the 'pyrrhic dance,' in which music accompanied the gestures of the performers.[9] He also mentions, in uncomplimentary language, soldiers singing popular songs.

> To these conditions, shameful as they were, were added serious defects in military discipline. In place of the war-song the soldiers practiced effeminate ditties.[10]

Gibbon also mentions that during the winter, when not engaged in battle, the Roman troops maintained their skills by practicing the Pyrrhic dance.

> They repeated each day their military exercise on foot and on horseback, accustomed their ear to obey the sound of the trumpet, and practiced the steps and evolutions of the Pyrrhic dance.[11]

Procopius provides an interesting description of Roman army music during the early sixth century. From this account one would have to believe there had been a decline in the organization of military signals, the number of recognizable signals, and in the instruments used. In the case of the latter, only the trumpet and lituus are mentioned, with no reference to the most important military instrument of earlier Roman armies, the cornu. In this account, Procopius himself is speaking to the famous Roman general, Belisarius.

> The men, General, who blew the trumpets in the Roman army in ancient times knew two different strains, one of which seemed unmistakably to urge the soldiers on and impel them to battle, while the other used to call the men who were fighting back to the camp, whenever this seemed to the general to be for the best. And by such means the generals could always give the appropriate commands to the soldiers, and they on their part were able to execute the commands thus communicated to them. For during actual combat the human voice is in no way adapted to give any clear instructions, since it obviously has to contend with the clash of arms on every side, and fear paralyzes the senses of those fighting. But since at the present time such skill has become obsolete through ignorance and it is impossible to express both commands by one trumpet, do you adopt the following course hereafter. With the cavalry trumpets urge on the soldiers to continue fighting with the enemy, but with those of the infantry call the men back to the retreat. For it is impossible for them to fail to recognize the sound of either one, for in the one case the sound comes forth from leather and very thin wood, and in the other from rather thick brass.[12]

By the eleventh century in England we read of well-organized military music, including established repertoire, relative to the siege of Rochester in 1088.

---

9   Ibid., I, 453.

10 Ibid., II, 199.

11 Edward Gibbon, *The History of the Decline and Fall of the Roman Empire* (Philadelphia: Coates), III, 626.

12 *Variae*, trans. Thomas Hodgkin (London: Frowde, 1886)., VI, xxiii. Gregory of Tours, in *The History of the Franks*, 243, mentions a certain Sigulf, who, in 573 AD, chased Clovis, son of King Chilperic, 'as if he were chasing a hunted deer,' with these same two instruments.

> When Bishop Eudes was forced to surrender, he obtained the king's permission to quit the city with all arms and horses. Not satisfied with this, he further endeavored to seek the favor, that the king's military music should not sound their triumphant fanfares during the capitulation. But William [the Conqueror] angrily refused, saying that he would not make the concession for a thousand gold marks. So, when the rebellious Normans marched out of Rochester, they did so with colors lowered, and to the sound of the king's trumpets.[13]

In terms of military music, the most interesting accounts of the Middle Ages are all associated with the Crusades. The Crusades were also a major contributor to the great step forward which occurs during the twelfth and thirteenth centuries when European culture clearly was moving away from the 'Dark Ages' and toward the Renaissance. Literature also came back to life during this 'Pre-Renaissance' and among the many European Romances and poems we find some colorful references to military music. Often these tales seem greatly exaggerated, a trait common to early literature. But, if we feel we can't trust the numbers, on the other hand these accounts had to have been based on something and often they seem very vivid.

Of these twelfth and thirteenth century tales the most complete account of military music is found in the French Romance, 'The Song of Roland,' an account of the ambush of Charlemagne's nephew, Roland, at Roncesuals. First we find Charlemagne's army preparing to return to France, with Roland bringing up the rear.

> Throughout the host a thousand trumpets sound;
> The Franks break camp and get their pack-mules loaded;
> They all are on their way now to sweet France.[14]

Next comes a description of the enemy, Marsilla, which includes reference to his four hundred thousand soldiers,

> Marsilla summons up his Spanish barons
> And counts, viscounts, and dukes and almacors
> And chieftains, and the sons of his contors;
> In three days' time he has four hundred thousand.
> He lets his drums resound through Saragossa;
> They raise Mohammed to the highest tower ...
> ......
>
> A thousand trumpets sing, to add more splendor;
> So deafening their noise, the Frenchmen hear it.
> 'My lord companion,' says Olivier,
> 'I think we'll have some Saracens to fight.'[15]

---

[13] Henry G. Farmer, *The Rise and Development of Military Music* (London, 1912), 8.

[14] Robert Harrison, trans., *Of the Digby 23 mss in the Bodleian Library, Oxford* (New York: New American Library, 1970), lines 700ff.

[15] Lines 848ff and 1004ff.

Here follows a description of the battle, which begins with a request of Roland that he blow on his ivory trumpet-type instrument, called an oliphant, to alert Charlemagne who is miles away at the head of the long line of soldiers. Curiously, Roland refused to blow the alarm:

> 'Companion Roland, sound your oliphant,
> so Charles, who's going through the pass, will hear;
> I promise you, the Franks will soon return.'
> 'May God forbid,' flung Roland back at him,
> 'that it be said by any man alive
> I ever blew my horn because of pagans.'[16]

Now the enemy approaches with seven thousand trumpets sounding. The battle itself begins,

> Marsilla is advancing through a valley,
> Together with the great host he assembled;
> The King has numbered them in twenty columns.
> Light flashes from those golden-studded casques
> And from those shields and saffron-yellow byrnies.
> Now seven thousand trumpets sound the charge;
> The din is great throughout the countryside.
> ......
>
> Marsilla sees the slaughter of his men
> And orders horns and trumpets to be sounded.[17]

Now, in one of the most striking passages in instrumental music literature, Roland finally decides to blow his oliphant.

> Then Roland says: 'Our fight is getting rough;
> I'll sound my horn—King Charles is sure to hear it.'
> ......
>
> Count Roland brought the horn up to his mouth:
> He sets it firmly, blows with all his might.
> The peaks are high, the horn's voice carries far;
> They hear it echo thirty leagues away.
> Charles hears it, too, and all his company:
> The King says then: 'Our men are in a fight.'
> ......
>
> Count Roland, racked with agony and pain
> And great chagrin, now sounds his ivory horn:
> Bright blood leaps in a torrent from his mouth:

---

[16] Line 1070ff.

[17] Lines 1449ff and 1467.

> And a temple has been ruptured in his brain.
> The horn he holds emits a piercing blast:
> Charles hears it as he crosses through the pass.
>
> ......
>
> Count Roland's mouth is filling up with blood;
> The temple has been ruptured in his brain.
> In grief and pain he sounds the oliphant;
> Charles hears it, and his Frenchmen listen, too.
> The King says then, 'That horn is long of wind.'[18]

Now Charlemagne's troops have turned and travel back to join the battle. Meanwhile, Roland continues to fight while the 'pagans' hear the sixty thousand (!) trumpets of Charlemagne and become alarmed.

> Count Roland keeps on fighting skillfully,
> Although his body's hot and drenched with sweat:
> He feels great pain and torment in his head,
> Since, when he blew his horn, his temple burst.
> Yet he has to know if Charles is coming back:
> He draws the ivory horn and sounds it feebly.
> The emperor pulled up so he might listen:
> 'My lords,' he says, 'it's very bad for us;
> today my nephew Roland will be lost.
> From his horn blast I can tell he's barely living;
> Whoever wants to get there must ride fast.
> So sound your trumpets, all this army has!'
> And sixty thousand of them blare so loud,
> The mountains ring, the valleys echo back.
>
> ......
>
> The pagans cry out: 'We were doomed at birth;
> A bitter day has dawned for us today!
> We've been bereft of all our lords and peers,
> The gallant Charles is coming with his host,
> We hear the clear-voiced trumpets of the French.'[19]

Now we have the description of the death of Roland, but not before he rises up once more and hits an enemy over the head with his oliphant horn. The blow cracks his horn.[20]

> Now Roland feels his sword is being taken
> And, opening his eyes, he says to him:
> 'I know for certain you're not one of us!'

---

[18] Lines 1712, 1754, 1761 and 1784.

[19] Lines 2099ff and 2146ff.

[20] Tradition has long held that this ivory horn, with its famous crack, could be seen hanging high on a column in the Prague cathedral. When we looked for it in 1968 it was not there.

> He takes the horn he didn't want to leave
> And strikes him on his jeweled golden casque;
> He smashes through the steel and skull and bones,
> And bursting both his eyeballs from his head,
> He tumbles him down lifeless at his feet
> And says to him: 'How dared you, heathen coward,
> Lay hands on me, by fair means or by foul?
> Whoever hears of this will think you mad.
> My ivory horn is split across the bell,
> And the crystals and the gold are broken off.'
> ......
>
> Now Roland feels death coming over him,
> Descending from his head down to his heart.
> He goes beneath a pine tree at a run
> And on the green grass stretches out, face down.
> He puts his sword and ivory horn beneath him
> And turns his head to face the pagan host.
> He did these things in order to be sure
> That Charles, as well as all his men, would say:
> 'This noble count has died a conqueror.'[21]

Now Charlemagne has returned, together with 335,000 soldiers. One of his officers suggests that they separate the dead and bury their own men in a common grave. Charlemagne indicates that a trumpet signal specific to this be played.[22]

Charlemagne orders his trumpets to sound to signal the resumption of the battle. The 'pagans' also sound their drums, horns and clarions. Apparently someone has picked up the oliphant for it too is blown. The leader of the Eastern 'pagans,' the emir, also personally blows a trumpet to call his troops to resume the battle.

> A Syrian delivers his report:
> 'We've had a look at arrogant King Charles.
> His men are bold, they have no heart to fail him,
> So arm yourself—you'll have a battle soon!'
> 'That's gallantry I hear!' says Baligant.
> 'To let my pagans know this, sound your trumpets.'
> Throughout the host they beat upon the drums
> And sound those horns and brilliant clarions:
> ......
>
> Undoubtedly the emperor's returning:
> The Syrian, my messenger, reported
> The he has made up ten immense battalions.
> The man who sounds the oliphant is brave—
> His comrade's clear-voiced trumpet rackets back—
> And thus they ride as leaders, up ahead.
> ......

---

[21] Lines 2284ff and 2355ff.

[22] Line 2950.

> The Frankish geste counts thirty battle corps,
> A mighty force amassed where trumpet's sound.
>
> ......
>
> The emperor gives word to sound his trumpets
> And the oliphant, which heartens all the rest.
>
> ......
>
> The trumpets sound, their tones are very clear;
> the oliphant's high note sings out the charge.
>
> ......
>
> The emir has now put out his flowing beard:
> It's just as white as blossoms of the hawthorn.
> Whatever happens, he will not take cover.
> He sets a clear-voiced trumpet to his mouth
> And sounds it clearly, so his pagans, hearing,
> Will rally his supporters in the field.[23]

Singing on the battle field is also mentioned and it is understandable prejudice that the allies *sing* their battle cry, while the pagans *bellow* theirs.[24] We wish we had more information in the two references to the victors singing 'mocking' songs to the defeated.[25]

From the Minnesinger repertoire of the same period, Wolfram von Eschenbach's epic poem, *Willehalm*, is a Romance of chivalry also dealing with the campaigns against the Saracens. It too includes some extraordinary descriptions of actual battle music and many musical instruments. In one place he describes the 'heathen's' use of eight hundred of the modern-type metal trumpet, which we know the Western armies brought back from the crusades.

> Eight hundred trumpets the king ordered to blow 'Advance at the gallop!' It is still a known fact that trumpets were invented in his country; they were brought from Thusi.[26]

In another place he mentions the roll of a thousand drums![27]

In *Parzival*, it is the sound, rather than the numbers, of these same heathen musicians, which is meant to impress us.

> He rode up with six banners, in front of which fighting began in early dawn. Trumpeters sounded ringing blasts, like thunder rousing fear and dread, and drummers beat a lively accompaniment to the noise of the trumpets.[28]

---

23   Lines 3132ff, 3190ff, 3263, 3301, 3309 and 3520ff.

24   Lines 1793 and 1921.

25   Lines 1014 and 1517.

26   Wolfram von Eschenbach, *Willehalm*, trans. Charles Passage (New York: Ungar, 1977), 202.

27   Ibid., 231.

28   Wolfram von Eschenbach, *Parzival*, trans. Helen Mustard and Charles Passage (New York: Vintage Books, 1961), Book I, 203.

A typical passage, found in the Volsung and Niblung literature, speaks of the primitive trumpet-types made from animal horns.

> Now the Vikings rushed from their ships in numbers not to be borne up against, but Sigmund the King, and Eylimi, set up their banners, and the horns blew up to battle; but King Sigmund let blow the horn his father first had had, and cheered on his men to the fight.[29]

A similar instrument is described in another poem in this North German literature, where we read, 'their great horn winded.'[30]

Another reference to war music is found in 'Da Derga's Hostel,' where an unusually large number of nine pipers are said to 'sally forth.'[31]

---

[29] 'The Story of the Volsungs and Niblungs,' trans. Eir'kr Magnœsson and William Morris in *Epic and Saga*, vol. 49, *The Harvard Classics* (New York: Collier, 1910), 298.

[30] 'The Lay of Hamdir,' in *Songs from the Elder Edda*, vol. 49, *The Harvard Classics* (New York: Collier, 1910), 454.

[31] 'The Destruction of Da Derga's Hostel,' trans. Whitley Stokes, in *Epic and Saga*, vol. 49, *The Harvard Classics* (New York: Collier, 1910), 261.

On Music of the Medieval Courts

THE FIRST THREE CENTURIES OF THE CHRISTIAN ERA, from which we date the Middle Ages, was still a period when Europe was governed by the Roman Empire. In previous essays we have mentioned many details of musical practice during these years. Here we will suffice with one representative, an eye-witness to one of the large-scare public entertainments organized under the emperors, Carus, Carinus and Numerian:

> For there was exhibited a rope-walker, who in his buskins seemed to be walking on the winds, also a wall-climber, who, eluding a bear, ran up a wall, also some bears which acted a farce, and, besides, one hundred trumpeters who blew one single blast together, one hundred horn-blowers, one hundred aulos-players, also one hundred aulos-players who accompanied songs, one thousand pantomimists and gymnasts, moreover, a mechanical scaffold, which, however, burst into flames and burned up the stage.[1]

Great public processions by the emperors were common and Gibbon describes a nine-hour long procession throughout Rome, during the reign of Aurelian.[2]

The fourth and fifth centuries saw the effective demise of the Roman Empire, as every reader knows. The long period of economic decline and the constant battles to preserve a continually shrinking empire produced an environment which was hardly conducive to art. It might be of interest to the reader to review again Gibbon's summary of the climate of civilization at this time.

> It is almost unnecessary to remark that the civil distractions of the empire, the license of the soldiers, the inroads of the barbarians, and the progress of despotism, had proved very unfavorable to genius, and even to learning. The succession of Illyrian princes restored the empire without restoring the sciences. Their military education was not calculated to inspire them with the love of letters; and even the mind of Diocletian, however active and capacious in business, was totally uninformed by study or speculation. The professions of law and [medicine] are of such common use and certain profit that they will always secure a sufficient number of practitioners endowed with a reasonable degree of abilities and knowledge; but it does not appear that the students in those two faculties appeal to any celebrated masters who have flourished within that period. The voice of poetry was silent. History was reduced to dry and confused abridgments, alike destitute of amusement and instruction. A languid and affected eloquence was still retained in the pay and service of the emperors, who encouraged not any arts except those which contributed to the gratification of their pride or the defense of their power.[3]

---

1. *The Scriptores Historiae Augustae*, trans. David Magie (London: Heinemann, 1924), 447. Edward Gibbon, *The History of the Decline and Fall of the Roman Empire* (Philadelphia: Coates), I, 249, refers to a similar celebration in 248 AD.
2. Gibbon, *The History of the Decline and Fall of the Roman Empire*, I, 374. An unusually enthusiastic warrior, Aurelian, according to an ancient writer, in one battle killed forty-eight of the enemy by his own hand [Gibbon, Ibid., 354, fn. 17].
3. Ibid., I, 455.

In another place, Gibbon cites a dramatic symbol of the decline of the arts by the early fourth century.

> The triumphal arch of Constantine still remains a melancholy proof of the decline of the arts....as it was not possible to find in the capital of the empire a sculptor who was capable of adorning that public monument, the arch of Trajan.[4]

One fourth-century emperor, Julian (331–363 AD), stands out as a more cultured man. Marcellinus, the last great historian of the ancient Latin world, writes of the self-education of the Emperor Julian:

> It is unbelievable with what great eagerness he sought out the sublime knowledge of all [the best] things, and as if in search of some sort of sustenance for a soul soaring to loftier levels, ran through all the departments of philosophy in his learned discussions. But yet, though he gained full and exhaustive knowledge in this sphere, he did not neglect more humble subjects, studying poetry to a moderate degree.[5]

Julian was also evidently trained in music, for he composed a hymn for the Festival of Cybele and the worship of the Sun as part of his attempt to reestablish the ancient pagan cults.[6] We also are indebted to Julian for an eye-witness account of the fourth-century waterorgan. Judging by his reference to 'swift fingers,' virtuoso repertoire pieces must also have been heard on this instrument at this time.

> I see a new kind of reeds. Are they, perchance, the wild product of some strange brazen soil? They are not even moved by our winds, but from a cave of bull's hide issues a blast and passes into these hollow reeds at their root. And a valiant man with swift fingers stands touching the notes which play in concert with the pipes, and they, gently leaping, press the music out of the pipes.[7]

While Roman literature always refers to the Goths as 'barbarians,' an account by Sidonius, a French writer of the fifth century, describes the dinner music of Theodoric, the king of the Goths, which implies a taste in music higher than most of the Romans.

> Withal there is no noise of hydraulic organ, or choir with its conductor intoning a set piece; you will hear no players of lyre or flute, no master of the music, no girls with cithara or tabor; the king cares for no strains but those which no less charm the mind with virtue than the ear with melody.[8]

---

[4] Ibid., 488.
[5] Ammianus Marcellinus, *Constantius et Gallus*, trans. John C. Rolfe (London: Heinemann, 1935), I, 219.
[6] Gibbon, *The History of the Decline and Fall of the Roman Empire*, III, 239ff.
[7] Julian, in *The Greek Anthology* (London: Heinemann, 1925), III, 365.
[8] *The Letters of Sidonius*, trans. O. M. Dalton (Oxford: Clarendon Press, 1915), I, 6.

Another early eye-witness account of the visit of the Greek exarch, Longinus, to Venice in 568 recalls a welcoming by 'bells, flutes, and other instruments.' It was said the total effect was such that one could not have heard the thunder of heaven.[9]

After the fall of the Roman Empire, and the consequent recall of the Roman armies, Europe entered a period of violence during which the nomadic tribes of the East pillaged villages everywhere. Consider, for example, that Paris was pillaged in 856, 861, and burned in 865. Tours was pillaged in 853, 856, 862, 872, 886, 903, and 919. It is no wonder that Gregory of Tours, in his *History of the Franks*, wrote,

> In fact in the towns of Gaul the writing of literature has declined to the point where it has virtually disappeared altogether. Many people have complained about this, not once but time and time again. 'What a poor period this is!' they have been heard to say. 'If among all our people there is not one man to be found who can write a book about what is happening today, the pursuit of letters really is dead in us!'[10]

Another writer described Europe in the year 909 AD.

> The cities are depopulated ... the country reduced to solitude ... As the first men lived without law ... so now every man does what seems good in his own eyes, despising laws human and divine ... The strong oppress the weak; the world is full of violence against the poor ... Men devour one another like the fishes in the sea.[11]

This was the 'Dark Ages,' the spoils of the victory of the Church over Rome. The Church's further actions of closing the schools and burning the books of the ancient Greek and Romans gave further meaning to the term, 'Dark Ages.'

The first break in the subsequent chain of illiteracy came with the court of the greatest of medieval kings, Charlemagne (768–814), who learned to read but never quite mastered writing. A naturally brilliant man, Charlemagne, observing the appalling illiteracy of his age, called leading scholars to his court for the purpose of restoring the schools of France. In 787 he issued an historic document, *Capitulare de litteris colendis*, urging the Church to establish schools. In another document of 789, he urged these schools to,

> take care to make no difference between the sons of serfs and of freemen, so that they might come and sit on the same benches to study grammar, music, and arithmetic.[12]

---

[9] W. C. Hazlitt, *The Venetian Republic* (New York, 1915), I, 15.

[10] Gregory of Tours, *The History of the Franks*, trans. Lewis Thorpe (Harmondsworth: Penguin Books, 1974), 63.

[11] H. W. C. Davis, *Medieval England* (Oxford, 1928), 266.

[12] Quoted in Will Durant, *The Age of Faith* (New York: Simon and Schuster, 1950), 466.

The result of his efforts saw the founding of numerous schools in France and Western Germany.[13] Among these were the first examples in history of free public education.[14]

As a consequence of Charlemagne attracting so many scholars to his court, we are fortunate to have historical portraits of this man and the music of his immediate circle. One of these scholars, Einhard, writes of Charlemagne's personal interest in the liberal arts.

> He paid the greatest attention to the liberal arts; and he had great respect for men who taught them, bestowing high honors upon them. When he was learning the rules of grammar he studied with Peter the Deacon of Pisa ... but for all other subjects he was taught by Alcuin ... a man of the Saxon race who came from Britain and was the most learned man anywhere to be found.[15]

Another member of the court tells of Greek envoys who came to visit the court and brought a number of musical instruments. His account includes some of the most interesting details extant regarding the early organ.

> These Greek envoys brought with them every kind of organ, as well as all sorts of other instruments. These were all examined by the craftsmen of the most sagacious Charlemagne to see just what was new about them. Then the craftsmen reproduced them with the greatest possible accuracy. The chief of these was that most remarkable of organs ever possessed by musicians which, when its bronze wind chests were filled and its bellows of ox-hide blew through its pipes of bronze, equaled with its deep note the roar of thunder, and yet which, for very sweetness, could resemble the soft tinkle of a lyre or a cymbal.[16]

A description of music heard at a banquet suggests that even on such occasions this court heard a high level of aesthetic music.

> The bishop ordered skilled choristers to advance: they were accompanied by every musical instrument one could think of, and by the sound of their singing they could have softened the hardest hearts or turned to ice the limpid waters of the Rhine.[17]

Charlemagne also took an interest in jongleurs, the first of the wandering minstrels, and even rewarded them with gifts of land in Provence. According to another source, Charlemagne even had prepared a collection of his hunting signals, called *Fröhliche Jagd*.[18] While this music is not extant, iconographic clues suggest it was performed by various animal horns, trumpet-types, flute-types, drums and bells.

---

13 Quoted in Nan Cooke Carpenter, *Music in the Medieval and Renaissance Universities* (Norman: University of Oklahoma Press, 1958), 17ff.

14 Einhard and Notker the Stammerer, *Two Lives of Charlemagne*, trans. Lewis Thorpe (Harmondsworth: Penguin Books, 1981), 95.

15 Ibid., 79.

16 Ibid., 143.

17 Ibid., 112.

18 Gottfried Veit, *Die Blasmusik* (Innsbruck, 1972), 20.

Charlemagne also took an active interest in Church music. Einhard describes his actual singing.

> He made careful reforms in the way in which the psalms were chanted and the lessons read. He was himself quite an expert at both of these exercises, but he never read the lesson in public and he would sing only with the rest of the congregation and then in a low voice.[19]

It was in this regard that Charlemagne once requested that the pope send him two singers who were expert in the approved style of singing to instruct the various churches of his realm. These two came, but deviously instructed each congregation in a separate style. When Charlemagne discovered this he sent them back to Rome, where they were punished with life imprisonment. Thereupon, the pope wrote Charlemagne,

> If I send you some more they will be just as blind with envy as the first ones, and they will cheat you in their turn ... Send me two of the most intelligent monks whom you have in your own entourage ... With God's help they will acquire the proficiency in this art which you are looking for.[20]

Finally, there are two interesting anecdotes regarding Charlemagne and his Church music. In the first,[21] a choir member appeared at an important feast somewhat drunk and intoned the final response instead of the first. This monk was fired on the spot. The monk in the second anecdote was considerably more fortunate.

> One day when Charlemagne was on a journey he came to a great cathedral. A certain wandering monk, who was unaware of the Emperor's attention to small detail, came into the choir and, since he had never learned to do anything of the sort himself, stood silent and confused in the middle of those who were chanting. Thereupon the choir-master raised his baton and threatened to hit him, if he did not sing. The monk, not knowing what to do or where to turn, and not daring to go out, twisted and contorted his throat, opened his mouth wide, moved his bottom jaw up and down, and did all that he could to imitate the appearance of someone singing. The others present had not the self-control to stop laughing. Our valiant Emperor, who was not to be moved from his serenity by even the greatest events, sat solemnly waiting until the end of the Mass, just as if he had not noticed this pretense at singing. When it was all over, he called the poor wretch to him and, taking pity on his struggles and the strain he had gone through, consoled with with these words: 'My good monk, thank you very much for your singing and your efforts.' Then he ordered him to be given a pound of silver to relieve his poverty.[22]

We don't have many accounts such as this for court music during the Dark Ages, but we believe the problem is a lack of literature, than a lack of art. Only an occasional reference to functional court music can be found, such as an eye-witness account of the marriage of Louis I of France (814–840),

---

[19] Einhard and Notker, *Two Lives of Charlemagne*, 80.

[20] Ibid., 103ff.

[21] Ibid., 98ff.

[22] Gibbon, *The History of the Decline and Fall of the Roman Empire*, 100ff.

> Of the service there must be no question; All of the possible meats to be found were in abundance, and served between trumpets and clarions; and minstrels, lutes, psalterons and followers were many.[23]

From the very same period, Leo V, who reigned 813–820, emperor of the Eastern (Byzantine) Church, was murdered as he sang during a church festival service.

> On the great festivals, a chosen band of priests and singers was admitted into the palace by a private gate to sing matins in the chapel; and Leo, who regulated with the same strictness the discipline of the choir and of the camp, was seldom absent from these early devotions. In the ecclesiastical habit, but with swords under their robes, the conspirators mingled with the procession, lurked in the angles of the chapel, and expected, as the signal of murder, the intonation of the first psalm by the emperor himself. The imperfect light, and the uniformity of dress, might have favored his escape, whilst their assault was pointed against a harmless priest; but they soon discovered their mistake, and encompassed on all sides the royal victim. Without a weapon and without a friend, he grasped a weighty cross, and stood at bay against the hunters of his life; but as he asked for mercy, 'This is the hour, not of mercy, but of vengeance,' was the inexorable reply. The stroke of a well-aimed sword separated from his body the right arm and the cross, and Leo the Armenian was slain at the foot of the altar.[24]

Gibbon describes the music heard in a procession honoring a tenth century emperor in Constantinople.

> From either side they echoed in a responsive melody the praises of the emperor; their poets and musicians directed the choir, and long life and victory were the burden of every song.[25]

Another account of a king singing is found in the twelfth-century North German body of poems known as the 'Elder Edda,' which deals with the Volsungs. The king sings at a banquet, but the nature of his song, of 'sore trouble,' suggests music to be listened to and not mere entertainment music.

> There the king, the wise-hearted,
> Swept his harp-strings,
> For the mighty king
> Had ever mind
> That I to his helping
> Soon should come.
> But now was I gone
> Yet once again
> Unto Geirmund,
> Good feast to make;
> Yet had I hearing,
> E'en out of Hlesey,
> How of sore trouble
> The harp-strings sang.[26]

---

23 *Chronicle of St-Denis.*

24 Gibbon, *The History of the Decline and Fall of the Roman Empire*, IV, 201.

25 Ibid., IV, 569.

26 'The Lament of Oddrun,' in *Songs from the Elder Edda*, vol. 49, *The Harvard Classics* (New York: Collier, 1910), 463.

With the twelfth and thirteenth centuries the dark cloud of the Middle Ages began to lift and was replaced by the beginnings of Humanism, a final burst of freedom from the dogma of the Dark Ages. The virtual explosion of confidence in man and his works is both the hallmark of these two centuries and the harbinger of the Renaissance. What greater display of this new confidence can there be than the huge cathedrals which began to spring up everywhere. Built in cities which had only a fraction of the population they have today, they remain not only as symbols of faith, but of man himself and of the glorious final two centuries of the Middle Ages.

Many factors contributed to this period of enthusiastic renewal of society, in particular the growing awareness of the writings of the ancient Greek philosophers which were assumed to have been lost and were now being rediscovered in Arabic translations. Reading these works, the Christian could never again let the Church do all his thinking for him. Certainly the great Crusades introduced to the West the more advanced and more cultured civilizations of the East. International trade followed the Crusades and through it not only a dramatic expansion of the general economy, but a great stimulus to all the arts.

Literature as well comes back to life and suddenly we have numerous accounts of music in the courts. The optimistic new spirit is evident in a passage from a thirteenth-century Romance which tells of a noble who took two string players with him on his trip to a tournament. Tournaments were not only a great form of outdoor entertainment for the nobles but also the primary form of training for war.

> Gerars Malfillastres, noble, valiant, courteous
> and forbearing, went in this magnificent way to
> the tournament. He took six companions with him
> in whom he put the deepest trust; and he had two
> fiddlers with him who sang a *son d'amours* between
> themselves, one Sunday morning. They rode straight
> along on the first day of May, when the grass is
> green, the gladioli are in flower, and everything
> takes on a verdant hue. The fiddlers, with loud and
> clear voices, sang a *son d'amour*, according themselves
> with their fiddles.[27]

The musicians employed by private nobles also performed a wide variety of indoor services, the most frequent were centered on dining. The musicians made musical announcement telling the guests that it was time to wash their hands, then time to enter the dining hall. Descriptions of the performance of music while people are actually eating, such as in the following instance, are fairly rare in early literature.

---

[27] Gautier de Tournai, *Gille de Chyn*, quoted in Christopher Page, *Voices and Instruments of the Middle Ages* (London: Dent, 1987), 181.

> While the king and queen were eating, minstrels went to and fro in the hall singing and playing their instruments.[28]

A more frequent description is of the performance of music while the food is paraded in from the kitchen. A contemporary describes Richard I, Coeur de Lion (1189–1199) of England sitting on a platform, surrounded by his nobles, with the music playing as the food is brought in from the kitchen.

> To Westemenstre they wente in fere,
> Lordyngs and ladys that ther were
> Trumpes begonne for to blowe,
> To mete they went in a throwe.
> King Richard was set on des
> With dukes and eerles, prowde in pres,
> Fro keehene com the fyrste cours,
> With pypes and trumpes and tabours.[29]

On occasion these brief references by contemporary scribes will contain a comment in their reports that we wish had been given much more discussion. A case in point is an eyewitness to the marriage of Henry III of England, in 1236, which mentions the royal musicians in a performance which the scribe regarded as musically unusual.

> … preceded by the king's trumpeters and with horns sounding, so that such a wonderful novelty struck all who beheld it with astonishment.[30]

This same writer describes the wedding celebration of Earl Richard of England in 1243, for which the elaborate banquet included thirty thousand dishes! Among the entertainers were apparently separate ensembles of jongleurs, here called 'gleemen.'

> Worldly pomp, and every kind of vanity and glory, was displayed in the different bodies of gleemen, the variety of their garments …[31]

We have an unusual account of an aristocratic dinner, this one describing Hereward the Wake, an eleventh-century English leader who led the resistance to the Norman Conquest. In a twelfth-century biography of this man we find him to be a nobleman unusually skilled in performance. We note here, as well, attentive listeners, even though in an entertainment atmosphere.

---

[28] Ramon Lull, *Libre de Meravelles*, quoted in Ibid., 183.

[29] *Der mittelenglische Versroman über Richard Löwenherz*, ed. K. Bruner (Vienna and Leipzig, 1913), 88, 268.

[30] Paris, *English History*, I, 8.

[31] Ibid., I, 461.

> One of the girls offered Hereward a goblet full of wine while the man with the harp was standing by. But he refused to take it from the woman's hand because he and the Irish king's son had just taken a vow to accept nothing until they had received something they had long wanted from the hand of the prince's daughter. The guests immediately condemned him for this severe slight to the cupbearer, and the jongleur described the affair disapprovingly to his mistress ... Directing that he should be excused this time since he was unfamiliar with their customs, she promptly conveyed a ring from her hand into a fold of his clothing. But the jongleur, strolling about everywhere, wouldn't keep quiet, and as often as he passed by declared that a man who at a feast would slight the cup-bearer with her cup simply wasn't fit to pluck the harp. Eventually stirred to anger by his conduct, Hereward gave him an answer—which the jongleur stupidly spread about—that given the chance, he could better perform that duty than him. Indignantly, as if he alone were skilled in the art, the jongleur pushed the harp into Hereward's arms. Taking it, he touched the strings most adroitly, and for a while produced sounds and strains to the admiration of all, while the other was quite shamefaced at the business, and kept trying to snatch the harp from his hands. But in fact the guests reckoned him well worthy of a reward, and said that he should be allowed to keep the harp for the time being. Since they persisted in plying him with drink he acquiesced singing to the harp in a variety of ways. And he sang in different styles, now by himself now in a trio with his friends in the manner of the Fenland people. Whereupon everyone was greatly delighted.[32]

The processions of the nobles usually resulted in contemporary comments about the music. In France an eye-witness describes a royal welcome Philip III (1270–1285) gave for his brother, Charles of Anjou, who came to visit him in Tunis.

> If one commands to know what passed, the sound of trumpets, buisines and araines.[33]

In Italy the Popes followed the style of their secular brothers. One reads that during the coronation procession of Gregory IX, in 1227, 'the crowds were taken by the sound of the trumpets.'[34] The coronation procession of Boniface VIII in 1295 included a much broader use of instruments, including shawms, several trumpet-types, timpani, cymbals and horns.[35]

We have an interesting eyewitness account of the Doge leaving Venice to accompany the Fourth Crusade. Pictured here are both the personal musicians of the Doge, together with those of the city itself.

> The Doge of Venice had with him fifteen galleys, all at his own cost. The galley wherein he himself was, was all vermilion-colored, and it had a pavilion stretched above it of vermilion samite, and there were four silver trumpets which sounded before him, and timbrels that made a most joyful noise ...

---

32 Richard of Ely, 'The Life of Hereward the Wake,' in *Three Lives of the Last Englishmen*, trans. Michael Swanton (New York: Garland Publishing, 1984), 53.

33 Bowles, 'Haut and Bas: The Grouping of Musical Instruments in the Middle Ages,' in *Musica Disciplina* (1954), 149.

34 Alessandro Vessella, *La Banda* (Milan, 1935), 35.

35 Francesco Cancellieri, *Storia di solenni possessi de' Sommi Pontefici* (Rome, 1802), 33.

> And when the fleet set forth from the haven of Venice ... it was the goodliest thing to behold that ever hath been since the beginning of the world. For there were full an hundred pair of trumpets, both silver and brass, which all sounded for the departure, and so many timbrels and tabors and other instruments that it was a fair marvel to hear.[36]

Pedro III (1276–1285) of Aragon maintained an ensemble of trumpets and percussion (*atabale*) and a separate group of minstrels under the leadership of Cerveri de Girona.[37] His son, Jaime II (1291–1327) hosted musicians from England, Portugal, Castile, Navarre, France, Venice, Sicily, Majorca as well as Muslim minstrels.[38] The historian, Angles, gave Jaime's own personal ensemble as, 'trompes, trumpets, tambor, viula, xebela [flute], and meocanon der Araber.'[39] Jaime's son, the 'Infant of Catalonia-Aragon,' once entered Toledo on a state visit accompanied by one hundred Moorish trumpeters.[40]

In a contemporary picture of a procession in the German-speaking countries we see the medieval trumpet-type instrument used in the West before the metallic trumpet was discovered in the East during the crusades. The icon from the late twelfth century pictures Henry VI, Emperor of the Holy Roman Empire (1190–1197) entering Palermo preceded by three busine players.[41]

Frederick II (1194–1250), another Holy Roman emperor was one of the most brilliant of all early kings. He spoke nine languages and wrote in seven. During his crusade, the Saracen commander al-Kamil, was so astonished to find a European who understood Arabic and was familiar with Arabic literature, science and philosophy, he made a favorable peace. Frederick was also interested in zoological, mathematical and anatomy subjects and founded the University of Naples in 1224.

When the Emperor Frederick II married his third wife, the English princess, Isabella, she arrived with her own company of musicians. A document relative to the purchase of a sackbut for her ensemble is one of the earliest references to that instrument.[42]

The Emperor Frederick II returned from his Crusade with a number of Arabic slaves, including some young trumpet players who performed at meal times.

---

36 'Li estoires de chiaus qui conquisent Coustantinoble' (1216), quoted in Edward Stone, trans., *Three Old French Chronicles of the Crusades* (Seattle: The University of Washington Press, 1939), 179.

37 M. Balthasar Saldoni, *Diccionario biografio-bibliografico de Efemerides de musicos españoles*, I, 334, and Hillgarth, *The Spanish Kingdoms* (Oxford, 1976), I, 54.

38 Hillgarth, Ibid., I, 54.

39 Higino Angles, 'Die Instrumentalmusik bis zum 16. Jahrhundert in Spanien,' in *Natalicia Musicologica* (Oslo, 1962), 148.

40 Hillgarth, *The Spanish Kingdoms*, I, 179.

41 Pietro da Eboli, *Liber ad Honorem Augusti* (Berne, Burgerbibliothek, Mss. Del Cod. Di Berna 120).

42 Georgina Masson, *Frederick II of Hohenstaufen* (New York, 1973), 270. This document was lost in World War II.

> He selected Negro boys between sixteen and twenty to form a musical corps; they were magnificently clad and taught to blow large and small silver trumpets. We may assume that the duty of this imperial band was to play at meal times, since the courts of Anjoy and Aragon, whom Frederick copied in every way, indulged this custom.[43]

Matthew Paris describes the visit of the English Earl Richard to Frederick II in 1241. The English visitor was welcomed,

> with the greatest joy and honor, the citizens and their ladies coming to meet him with music and singing, bearing branches of trees and flowers, dressed in holiday garments and ornaments.

Frederick himself entertained the visitor with the performance of two Saracen girls, whom he had brought back with him from his Crusade.

> Two Saracen girls of handsome form, mounted upon four round balls placed upon the floor, namely, one of the two on two balls, and the other on the other two. They walked backwards and forwards, clapping their hands, moving at pleasure on these revolving globes, gesticulating with their arms, singing various tunes, and twisting their bodies according to the tune, beating cymbals or castanets together with their hands.[44]

Richard was shown 'various kinds of musical instruments' by the emperor, again most likely instruments he had brought back from the crusade.[45] When Richard departed, after a four-month visit, Frederick II arranged that his travel through Italy would be greeted officially in each city.

> By the emperor's command, he was met on his route by the inhabitants of the cities, mounted on noble horses, richly equipped, dressed in silk and other costly garments, attended by vocal and instrumental musicians, with elegant devices; but I shall here, omitting all the others, make particular mention of the rejoicings at one place. On his approaching Cremona, the Cremonese came joyfully to meet him with the emperor's elephant in advance of them, handsomely decorated, and bearing a wooden sort of tower, in which the masters of the animal sat, playing on trumpets, and exultingly clapping their hands together.[46]

---

[43] Ernst Kantorowicz, *Frederick the Second*, trans. E. O. Lorimer (New York, 1957), 312.

[44] Matthew Paris, *English History*, trans. J. A. Giles (London: Bohn, 1852), I, 369ff.

[45] Ibid., I, 370.

[46] Ibid., I, 385ff.

On Medieval Civic Music

AFTER THE FALL OF THE ROMAN EMPIRE and the retraction of its protecting armies, and the subsequent pillages by the migrant hordes, many towns in Western Europe built great encircling walls for security.[1] As night approached, even with the gates closed, security remained a primary concern for now in a town without lights there was fear of individual predators, rouges and especially fire—which could destroy the entire town.

It was for these concerns that the towers were built on and within the walls and with them came the first important civic musician, the civic watchman. By the thirteenth century Milan had one hundred and twenty and Frankfurt one hundred and forty of these towers.[2] Kastner believed the origin of these towers could be found earlier in the Middle Ages in portable towers which could be moved with armies for lookout purposes.[3] At first these towers had bells which could be used for warning purposes, but by the late Middle Ages towns began to hire trumpet-type players for this purpose, for the trumpet player could give a more precise signal. In a famous incident in Cracow, a tower musician blew a warning on his trumpet on the approach of the Tartar hordes in 1241. In the middle of his fanfare a Tartar arrow pierced his throat and the fanfare was left unfinished.[4] This tower function gradually expanded to include serving as a surrogate clock (at night when the civic clock could not be seen).

An interesting account of civic music in Italy dates from the occupation of Milan by the Franconian King, Conrad II, in 1037. The Archbishop of Milan, Aribert, seeking a means of organizing the resistance of the town's people, created a civic symbol called the *carroccio*. This was a large wagon which contained an altar, the civic flag, and at the rear eight trumpeters who played a fanfare to assemble the people. The priests, also on the wagon, read a field mass and gave the last rites for those killed in the resistance. An Italian scholar describes it as,

> a curious emblem of superstition and faith, of popular poetry and military discipline, of fantastic images of religion and the nation; a wagon of victory and later of peace around which you would fight with energy and die with enthusiasm.[5]

---

[1] An excellent example which can still be seen is the wall around Lucca, in Italy.
[2] Edmund A. Bowles, 'Tower Musicians in the Middle Ages,' in *Brass Quarterly* (V), 91.
[3] Georges Kastner, *Manuel General de Musique Militaire* (Paris, 1848), 80ff.
[4] This fanfare is reproduced in S. Mizawa, *Nicholas Copernicus* (New York, 1943), 73.
[5] R. Bonfadini, 'Le origini del Comune di Milano,' in *Albori della Vita Italiana* (Milano, 1897).

In peace time the *carroccio* was used for important civic celebrations. One saw it, for example, when the Queen of Sicily visited Milan on 7 October 1268. On this occasion the civic band of Milan, consisting of tamburi, shawms and trumpets performed seated upon it.[6] Venice and Florence also had these movable civic wagons.[7]

In general references to individual civic bands are still rare during the Middle Ages, but there is a record of civic 'trombe e I corni' in 1121 in Milan[8] and a visitor to Genoa in 1180 reported hearing 'jogleurs, chanteors e troubadours' in residence.[9] A notarized document from 1213 converts the service of twenty-four musicians from the court of Monferrato to municipal duty.[10]

We have somewhat more information from Florence, including a civic document dated 8 February 1232, stating that the band should have both summer and winter uniforms in order that they can represent the city in an honorable manner.[11] From 1291 we have an extant contract for the engagement of six trumpets for the city.[12] It was also during the thirteenth century that the first civic musicians guild was founded in Florence, the 'La Filarmonica dei Laudesi.'[13]

In Siena the civic band can be dated from 1262 when they were to accompany the city fathers when they left the city hall and were to perform for all civic celebrations. The players were given clothing, housing and a monthly salary based on the amount of performance. The purchase and care of the instruments were the responsibility of the players.[14]

In England, the same need for watchmen was evident, as we see in an order by King Henry III:

> ... but for a full remedy of enormities in the night ... in the yeare of Christ 1253 Henrie the third commanded Watches in Cities, and Borough Towners to be kept, for the better observing of peace and quietnesse amongst his people.[15]

One London document of 1296 suggests that it was the responsibility of the person who lived nearest the watch point to maintain the watchman, who now is called a 'wait.'

---

[6] Bernardino Corio, *L'Historia di Milano volgarmente scritta* (Padoa, 1646), 251.

[7] Bonanni, *Gabinetto armonico* (Rome, 1722).

[8] Corio, *L'Historia di Milano volgarmente scritta*, 57.

[9] George Grove, *The New Grove Dictionary of Music and Musicians* (London: Macmillan, 1980), VII, 204.

[10] Ibid.

[11] Giuseppe Zippel, *I Suonatori della Signoria di Firenze* (Trento, 1892).

[12] Alessandro Vessella, *La Banda* (Milan, 1935), 37.

[13] Zippel, *I Suonatori della Signoria di Firenze*.

[14] Vellella, *La Banda*, 39.

[15] J. Stowe, *Survey of London* (London, 1618), 158.

[Each gate of the city is to be] shut by the servant dwelling there, and that he shall have a wayt at his own expense.[16]

These thirteenth-century English watch musicians had an extraordinary advantage of being eligible for the use of land in exchange for wait service. During the period of Henry III (1216–1272) there is a record of 'Simon le Wayte' who held a virgate of land at Rockingham during his tenure as 'castle-wayte.' A similar musician, 'Gilbert the Wayte,' was paid in the same fashion during the reign of Edward I (1272–1307). Examples of this form of payment continued for four hundred years.[17]

One of the traditional duties for the London Waits was appearing in the annual Lord Mayor's Procession, which dated from 1215. All the civic guilds, called 'companies' or 'corporations,' participated in this event and eventually they would all each have their own independent musicians.

In France we find a reference to civic musicians in Paris in a tax roll of 1295.[18] In the German-speaking countries the medieval information regarding official civic music is fragmentary, but an extant civic statue from Mulhouse (then German-speaking) of the twelfth century limits the number of wind players which can be used for private weddings at six.[19] An early account of the music at a typical wedding reads,

> Then there is a jesting song, the cook shouts, the meal is spread out, the hall swarms with cheering people and melodious dances; there is a procession with wedding songs preceding and following.[20]

Hamburg and Breslau both had four-men civic wind bands during the thirteenth century.[21] Civic musician guilds were also founded in Germany during the thirteenth century, in particular the *Marienbruderschaft der Musicanten und Spielleute zu St. Catherinen* of Lübeck and the *Nicolai-Brüderschaft* of Vienna, founded in 1288.[22]

As we near the end of the Middle Ages we begin to find literature which provides more interesting detail regarding the activities of the civic musicians. First, a tale in the *Gesta Romanorum* speaks of an unnamed king's custom of announcing to a condemned man that he was going to be put to death forthwith by arranging a predawn serenade with songs and trumpets at his house.[23]

---

[16] Alan Warwick, *A Noise of Music* (London: Queen Anne Press), 33.
[17] Lyndesay G. Langwill, *The Waits* (Hinrichsen, 1952), 171.
[18] Grove, II, 326; VII, 205.
[19] M.B. Bernhard, *Notice sur la Confrerie des Jouers d'Instruments d'Alsace* (Paris, 1844), 5, fn. 2.
 Zu der kockzyd sal man nicht mer habn danne sechs spylmann dy tencze und reygin machin.
[20] *Scorn for the World: Bernard of Cluny's De Contemptu Mundi*, trans. Ronald Pepin (East Lansing: Colleagues Press, 1991), III.
[21] Walter Salmen, *Der Fahrende Musiker im Europäischen Mittelalter* (Kassel, 1960), 89.
[22] Wilhelm Ehmann, *Tibilustrium* (Kassel, 1950), 28, quotes some of the original charter.
[23] *Gesta Romanorum*, trans. Charles Swan (London: C. and J. Rivington, 1824), II, 213ff.

Another interesting passage deals with the watchman in the tower. Most medieval accounts of this person refer only to rather simple musical signals. In the 'Romance of the Rose,' however, we find a watchman performing a number of sophisticated instruments and even singing from the tower.

> Each evening he would mount the battlements
> And play his bagpipe, trumpet, horn, or shalms.
> At one time he would sing descants and lays
> And all the latest songs, to Cornish pipes;
> Another time, accompanied with a flute,
> Dispraising ladies, he would sing like this:
>
> > *There is no maid who will not smile*
> > *When she hears tales of lechery.*
> > *The whores will paint, men to beguile;*
> > *For all are full of treachery.*
> > *If the fool's not talking all the while,*
> > *She's mistress of the ogling style.*
> > *There is no maid who will not smile*
> > *When she hears tales of lechery.*[24]

We have mentioned that the watchman-musician in the tower, during the night, served as a surrogate clock. It was a custom to play a special melodic signal, called the *Aubade*, just before dawn, to warn lovers to run back to their own houses before first light. One song which refers to this practice is by the famous Wolfram von Eschenbach:

> At daybreak you have always sung
> the dirge of secret love,
> the bitterness following on the sweet.
> No matter what you urged upon them
> when the morning star was rising,
> those who received love and woman's favor
> in such a way
> that they had to part,
> Watchman, be quiet,
> sing of that no more![25]

Two thirteenth-century writers have contributed particularly interesting accounts of processions as they include string players riding on horses! Ulrich von Liechtenstein gives the entire order of such a procession:

---

[24] Guillaume de Lorris and Jean de Meun, 'The Romance of the Rose,' trans. Harry Robbins (New York: Dutton, 1962), XIX, 63. The work of de Meun begins with Chapter XX.

[25] 'Der helnden minne ir klage,' in Wolfram von Eschenbach, *Titurel and the Songs*, trans. Marion Gibbs and Sidney Johnson (New York: Garland Publishing, 1988), 83.

> A flutist was the next to come
> who beat with skill upon a drum.
> Four squires were riding after him
> in uniforms of modish trim
> and each had brought three spears along,
> well-made and large, which with thong
> were bound together. One could praise
> these bearers for their courtly ways.
>
> Two maidens rode behind the squires
> and every bit of their attires
> was gleaming white from head to toe.
> The both looked very pretty so.
> A fiddler rode behind each maid;
> my heart was happy when they played,
> and when the two would fiddle high
> a marching tune most pleased was I.[26]

Wolfram von Eschenbach provides the details of a similar procession.

> After these rode trumpeters, who are still required today, and a drummer kept hitting his drum and swinging it high in the air. The master would not have thought much of the lot if flute players had not been riding along with the rest, and three good fiddlers.[27]

A type of civic music we have not yet mentioned is occupational music. There are numerous references in the literature of the first three centuries of the Christian Era to various kinds of occupational music. The most familiar, as in older literature, is that of the shepherd. In the second-century poem, 'Daphnis and Chloe,' we read of the shepherd's use of the three kinds of instruments still found today, the transverse flute, the panpipe and the reed-pipe.[28] This same poet describes the construction of the panpipe.

> Daphnis, after cutting some slender reeds, piercing them at the joints, and fastening them together with soft wax, would practice playing the panpipe until it was dark.[29]

We read here also of a more 'modern' panpipe construction, 'nine reeds fastened together with bronze instead of wax.'[30] This same poem also mentions the singing of seamen[31] and the agricultural songs of reapers, of a 'rustic nature.'[32]

---

[26] Ulrich von Liechtenstein, *In Service of Ladies*, trans. J. W. Thomas (Chapel Hill: The University of North Carolina Press, 1969), lines 485ffr. The first musician mentioned here is the 'one-man band' known as the pipe and tabor player.

[27] Wolfram von Eschenbach, *Parzival*, trans. Helen Mustard and Charles Passage (New York: Vintage Books, 1961), 12.

[28] Longus, 'Daphnis & Chloe,' trans. Paul Turner (London: Penguin Books, 1956), I, 4.

[29] Ibid., I, 10.

[30] Ibid., I, 15.

[31] Ibid., III, 21.

[32] Ibid., IV, 38.

A poem of Callimachus, mentions the music of the laborers who draw water from wells.

> ... many a drawer of water is singing the Song of the Well ...[33]

St. John Chrysostom gives a broad sampling of professions using music for the purpose of relieving the burden of toil.

> Travelers also, driving at noon the yoked animals, sing as they do, lightening by their songs the hardships of the journey. And not only travelers, but also peasants often sing as they tread the grapes in the wine press, gather the vintage, tend the vine, and perform their other tasks. Sailors do likewise, pulling at the oars. Women, too, weaving and parting the tangled threads with the shuttle, often sing a certain single melody, sometimes individually and to themselves, sometimes altogether in concert. This they do, the women, travelers, peasants, and sailors, striving to lighten with a song the labor endured in working, for the mind suffers hardships and difficulties more easily when it hears songs and chants.[34]

To this list, Paulinus of Nola adds the sailors joyfully singing their usual rowing-songs[35] and Capella the trumpets which 'sharpen the keen edge of wrestlers and other competitors in public games.'[36]

The first medieval music treatise which gives significant attention to the world of civic music was the *De Musica* (ca. 1300 AD) by Johannes de Grocheo. First, he departs from the long-held concept of organizing music by the three categories of celestial, vocal and instrumental. Grocheo instead proposes to bring music down from the heavenly spheres and instead will use the practical classifications practiced by 'the men in Paris,' for it is there that the principles of all liberal arts are 'sought out diligently.' For this reason he presents his new classification system:

1. Civic or simple music, which they call vulgar [*vulgus*: of the masses] music,
2. Composed or regular music by rule, which they call measured music.
3. Ecclesiastic music, designed for praising the Creator, made from the first two and to which these two are best adapted.[37]

It is for his subsequent elaboration of specific forms of secular and sacred music that Grocheo's treatise is best known, and indeed it is a discussion of secular forms which will not be equaled until the *Syntagma Musica* of Praetorius in 1619. He begins with vocal civic, or popular, music and the *cantus gestual*, the epic song of former great leaders and their deeds.

---

33 *Callimachus*, trans. C. A. Trypanis (Cambridge: Harvard University Press, 1975), 197.

34 St. John Chrysostom, 'Exposition of Psalm XLI,' quoted in Oliver Strunk, *Source Readings in Music History* (New York: Norton, 1950), 68.

35 *The Poems of St. Paulinus of Nola*, trans. P. G. Walsh (New York: Newman Press, 1975), Poem 17, 101.

36 *Martianus Capella and the Seven Liberal Arts*, trans. William Harris Stahl and Richard Johnson (New York: Columbia University Press, 1977), II, 358.

37 Johannes de Garlandia, *De Mensurabili Musica*, trans. Stanley Birnbaum (Colorado Springs: Colorado College Music Press, 1978), 11.

> This kind of song ought to be provided for old men, working citizens and for average people when they rest from their accustomed labor, so that, having heard the miseries and calamities of others, they might more easily bear up under their own, and so that their own tasks be more gladly approached. Thus, this kind of song is a support for the whole state.[38]

Next he discusses the *coronate cantus*, a song of quality, accompanied on instruments 'by masters and students,' which deals with 'delightful and serious material, as about friendship and charity.'

> This is normally composed by kings and nobles and performed before the kings and princes of the earth so that it may move their souls to audacity and bravery, to magnanimity and liberality, which lead all things to a good order.[39]

The *versiculate* is similar to the *coronate cantus*, but not of such high quality, and is appropriate for the young, 'lest they fall completely into idleness.'[40]

He next turns his attention to three types of songs associated with young men and women. Of the round, or *rotundellus*, he notes only that it is slow, and performed by young people in festivals. The *stantipes*, is characterized by 'diversity' in both text and melody.

> This kind of song causes the souls of young men and girls to concentrate because of its difficulty and turns them from improper thinking.[41]

Similarly, the *ductia* is a rapid, light song, sung in chorus.

> This influences the hearts of girls and young men and keeps them from vanity and is said to have force against that passion which is called love or Eros.[42]

Grocheo begins his discussion of instrumental music by giving new aesthetic preference to the string family, because they are capable of 'a subtler and better difference of sound.'[43] Of these, he prefers the vielle as the principal melodic instrument most suitable to all kinds of music.

> As some instruments by their sound may move the souls of men more than others, for example, the drum and trumpet in war games and tournaments, on the vielle, however, all musical forms are understood more thoroughly.[44]

---

[38] Ibid., 15.

[39] Ibid., 16.

[40] Ibid.

[41] Ibid., 17.

[42] Ibid.

[43] Ibid., 19. The strings he mentions are the psalter, cithara, lyre, Saracen guitar, and vielle.

[44] Ibid., 19.

The instrumental *ductia* is accompanied by percussion instruments, which 'measure' it and the movement of the performer,

> and excite the soul of man to moving ornately according to that art they call dancing, and they measure its movement in ductiae and in choral dance.[45]

The instrumental *stantipes* is not accompanied by percussion and is characterized by 'a complicated succession of concords.' The latter,

> makes the soul of the performer and also the soul of the listener pay close attention and frequently turns aside the souls of the wealthy from depraved thinking.[46]

It was for these instrumental forms, which lack the syllables of the text to identify the groupings of the notes intended by the composer, that Grocheo says the custom of using ligatures was adopted.[47] This is a very interesting statement in view of the fact that today the question of ligatures in early music is generally taught as being simply a form of short-hand by scribes. Grocheo's definition, on the contrary, seems a more logical explanation, particularly in view of the recommendation by Praetorius that ligatures should be replaced by slurs.

---

[45] Ibid.
[46] Ibid., 20.
[47] Ibid., 24.

On the Medieval Chorus

IN THE THIRD-CENTURY POETRY OF CALLIMACHUS, we find the suggestion that the ancient Greek tradition of accompanying choral music with instruments was still being practiced.

> Apollo is in the choir; I hear the lyre.[1]

In another work by this poet there is a clue to the style of this choral repertoire, where we read of a chorus singing 'a sweet ode.'[2]

There is also some evidence that the ancient Greek tradition of the chorus with dance was still in evidence at this time, and a passing reference to those who are 'unmusical at dances,' by Clement of Alexandria may be a reference to these.[3]

An extant poem by the first-century poet, Lucilius, suggest that in banquets of the wealthy it was still possible to hear choral ensembles.

> I never knew, Epicrates, that you were a tragedian or a choral aulos player or any other sort of person whose business it is to have a chorus with them. But I invited you alone; you, however, came bringing with you from home a chorus of dancing slaves, to whom you hand all the dishes over your shoulder as a gift. If this is to be so, make the slaves sit down at the table and we will come and stand at their feet to serve.[4]

According to a Roman historian contemporary to these times, Ammianus Marcellinus (330–391 AD), the productions of the theater were extraordinary and employed enormous numbers of musicians, including choirs.

> The vast and magnificent theaters of Rome were filled by three thousand female dancers, and by three thousand singers, with the masters of the respective choruses. Such was the popular favor which they enjoyed, that, in a time of scarcity...the merit of contributing to the public pleasures exempted them from a law, which was strictly executed against the professors of the liberal arts.[5]

---

[1] *Callimachus*, trans. C. A. Trypanis (Cambridge: Harvard University Press, 1975), 163.

[2] Ibid., 239. A very intriguing fragment by this poet reads, in entirety, '... who ... invented the Italian scale.'

[3] Clement of Alexandria, 'The Miscellanies,' trans. Alexander Roberts, in *Ante-Nicene Christian Library* (Edinburgh: T. & T. Clark, 1869), XII, Book V, iv.

[4] *The Greek Anthology,* IV, 10, 11.

[5] Quoted in Edward Gibbon, *The History of the Decline and Fall of the Roman Empire* (Philadelphia: Coates), III, 32.

Sidonius, a French born writer of the fifth century makes a passing reference to choirs in the ancient Greek model when he criticizes those choirs who, through good singing, make bad compositions appear good.[6] We wish he had told us more about the choral tradition of the Goths, and their conductors, which he only mentions in a reference to the dinner music of Theodoric, the King of the Goths.

> Withal there is no noise of hydraulic organ, or choir with its conductor intoning a set piece; you will hear no players of lyre or flute, no master of the music, no girls with cithara or tabor; the king cares for no strains but those which no less charm the mind with virtue than the ear with melody.[7]

A passing mention of secular choral performance by St. Gregory Nazianzus (325–389 AD) is particularly interesting in its details which throws light on the role of the conductor and the placement of the singers.

> I thought, in my vain imaginings, that once I had control of this throne (outward show carries great weight) I could act like a chorus leader between two choruses. Putting the two groups chorus-fashion, one on this side of me, the other on that, I could blend them with myself and thus weld into a unity what had been so badly divided.[8]

This and similar passages suggest that performances by choral ensembles were still given in public music festivals in the fourth century. This, in spite of the fact that the early Church was very hostile toward secular festivals. St. John Chrysostom (347–407 AD) finds a passage in the Old Testament where, he warns us, God did not like festivals of any kind—not to mention instrumental music!

> But do their festivals have something solemn and great about them? They have shown that these, too, are impure. Listen to the prophets; rather, listen to God, and with how strong a statement he turns his back on them. 'I have found your festivals hateful, I have thrust them away from myself.'[9]
>
> Does God hate their festivals and do you share in them? He did not say this or that festival, but all of them together. Do you wish to see that God hates the worship paid with percussion, lyres, harps and other instruments? God said: 'Take away from me the sound of your songs and I will not hear the canticle of your harps.'[10] If God said: 'Take them away from me,' do you run to listen to their trumpets?[11]

---

[6] *Sidonius Poems and Letters*, trans. W. B. Anderson (Cambridge: Harvard University Press, 1965), II, 445.

[7] Ibid., I, 6.

[8] Saint Gregory of Nazianzus, 'Concerning his own Life,' trans. Denis Meehan (Washington, D.C.: The Catholic University of America Press), 119.

[9] Amos 5:21. The *Revised Standard Version* reads, 'I hate, I despise your feasts, and I take no delight in your solemn assemblies.'

[10] Amos 5:23. The *Revised Standard Version* reads, 'Take away from me the noise of your songs; to the melody of your harps I will not listen.'

[11] St. John Chrysostom, 'Discourses Against Judaizing Christians,' trans. Paul W. Harkins (Washington, D.C.: The Catholic University of American Press), 26.

The fact is that in the older cities, such as Athens, Alexandria and Rome the ancient pagan religious-cults continued until the end of the fourth century, with more than seven hundred pagan temples still standing in Rome alone by the end of that century.[12] The emperor Julian (331–363 AD) desired to reestablish some of these old cults, especially that of Cybele and the worship of the Sun, for which he composed a hymn. Gibbon also discusses a brief revival of the festival of the Lupercalia, a festival of arts and agriculture, but there is no mention of music.[13]

The most frequently mentioned form of music in the new Church is the singing of hymns, although musically we know little about these early forms. Undoubtedly they were sung in unison, as indeed St. Gregory Nazianzus implies, 'while they harmonize many mouths into a single voice.'[14] This would make plausible the resultant effect described by St. Paulinus of Nola (354–431 AD) when he speaks of the congregation of the faithful engaging in 'lusty rendering of holy hymns.'[15]

It has long been recognized that some of the Psalms seems to indicate antiphonal or responsorial form of singing, and St. Basil (329–379 AD) mentions such two-part antiphonal singing in the fourth century. This account is unusually interesting in suggesting that some of the original musical traditions may have come from older religious practice, the Church's protestations against the 'pagans' notwithstanding.

> As to the charge regarding psalmody, by which especially our slanderers terrify the more simple, I have this to say, that the customs now prevalent are in accord and harmony with those of all the churches of God. Among us the people come early after nightfall to the house of prayer, and in labor and affliction and continual tears confess to God. Finally, rising up from their prayers, they begin the chanting of psalms. And now, divided into two parts, they chant antiphonally, becoming master of the text of the Scriptural passages, and at the same time directing their attention and the recollectedness of their hearts. Then, again, leaving it to one to intone the melody, the rest chant in response; thus, having spent the night in a variety of psalmody and intervening prayers, when day at length begins to dawn, all in common, as with one voice and one heart, offer up the psalm of confession to the Lord, each one making His own the words of repentance. If, then, you shun us on this account, you will shun the Egyptians, and also those of both Libyas, the Thebans, Palestinians, Arabians, Phoenicians, Syrians, and those dwelling beside the Euphrates—in one word, all those among whom night watches and prayers and psalmody in common have been held in esteem.[16]

In another place, St. Basil describes at greater length the style of the fourth-century psalms. It is not entirely clear, however, whether the special attributes he recognizes here are due to the style of the music or the text.

---

[12] Will Durant, *The Age of Faith* (New York: Simon and Schuster, 1950), 33.

[13] Edward Gibbon, *The History of the Decline and Fall of the Roman Empire*, III, 239ff.

[14] Saint Gregory of Nazianzus, 'Concerning his own Affairs,' 34.

[15] *The Poems of St. Paulinus of Nola*, trans. P. G. Walsh (New York: Newman Press, 1975), Poem 27, 542ff.

[16] St. Basil, 'Letter to the Clergy of Neo-Caesarea,' in *Letters of Saint Basil*, trans. Sister Agnes Way (New York: Fathers of the Church, 1955), II, 83.

> A psalm implies serenity of soul; it is the author of peace, which calms bewildering and seething thoughts. For, it softens the wrath of the soul, and what is unbridled it chastens. A psalm forms friendships, unites those separated, conciliates those at enmity … So that psalmody, bringing about choral singing, a bond, as it were, toward unity, and joining the people into a harmonious union of one choir, produces also the greatest of blessings, charity.[17]

The chief value of singing psalms, according to Basil, is 'to calm and soften the wicked spirits which trouble souls.'[18] But he makes a curious distinction here, which again reminds us of the 'pagan' ancient Greek philosophers, in saying that a 'bad' person cannot properly sing the psalms.

> Not if someone utters the words of the psalm with his mouth, does that one sing to the Lord; but, all who send up the psalmody from a clean heart, and who are holy, maintaining righteousness toward God, these are able to sing to God, harmoniously guided by the spiritual rhythms. How many stand there, coming from fornication? How many from theft? How many concealing in their hearts deceit? How many lying? They think they are singing, although in truth they are not singing. For, the Scripture invites the saint to the singing of psalms. 'A bad tree cannot bear good fruit,' nor a bad heart utter words of life.[19]

The 'Dark Ages,' which are dated from the sixth century, take this name primarily from the general disappearance in Western Europe of secular letters, in particular philosophy, history and science. As Cassiodorus observed already at the beginning of the sixth century,

> Arithmetic, Theoretical Geometry, Astronomy, and Music are discoursed upon to listless audiences, sometimes to empty benches.[20]

In another place, Cassiodorus mentions that teachers' salaries were being cut back and argues that instead they should be increased. Here, in making an analogy, he mentions choirs singing in harmony, something you will not read about in standard music texts.

> Therefore, since it is clear that rewards feed the arts, I have judged it abominable that anything should be stolen from the teachers of youth; they should instead be incited to their noble studies by an increase in their fees.
> For the school of grammar has primacy: it is the fairest foundation of learning, the glorious mother of eloquence, which has learnt to aim at praise, to speak without fault. As good morals view an alien crime, so it views a dissonant error in the course of declamation. For, as the musician creates the sweetest song from a choir in harmony, so, by well ordered modulations of sound, the grammarian can recite in meter.

---

[17] St. Basil, 'Homily 14,' in *Exegetic Homilies*, trans. Sister Agnes Way (Washington, D.C.: The Catholic University of America Press), 213.

[18] Ibid., 214. In Homily 21, Ibid., 341, Basil says the purpose of psalm singing is to 'correct the passions of the soul.' He then quotes, without comment, references to many musical instruments in Psalm 61.

[19] Ibid., 217.

[20] Letter to 'the Illustrious Consularis,' III, lii, in *Variae*, trans. Thomas Hodgkin (London: Frowde, 1886).

A poem of the sixth century by the famous Gregory the Great (540–604 AD) remembers a deceased choir member.

> O founts of ears, O knees, O hands of Carterius, that appeased Christ by most pure sacrifices. How like all mortals has he ceased to be. The choir there in heaven required a hymn singer.[21]

While another poet of this time adds that on the Day of Judgment all the humans will join in a great choir!

> And righteous souls shall raise a song,
> and the pure and chosen shall praise their Sovereign's majesty;
> strain on strain shall mount to glory,
> sweetly perfumed with their goodly deeds.[22]

An eye-witness description of music heard at a banquet at the court of Charlemagne (742–814 AD) suggests that even on such occasions this court heard a high level of aesthetic choral music.

> The bishop ordered skilled choristers to advance: they were accompanied by every musical instrument one could think of, and by the sound of their singing they could have softened the hardest hearts.[23]

There is a lovely anecdote regarding Charlemagne and the choral singing he heard while traveling. The poor singer was lucky to have encountered Charlemagne on a day when he was in a forgiving mood!

> One day when Charlemagne was on a journey he came to a great cathedral. A certain wandering monk, who was unaware of the Emperor's attention to small detail, came into the choir and, since he had never learned to do anything of the sort himself, stood silent and confused in the middle of those who were chanting. Thereupon the choir-master raised his baton and threatened to hit him, if he did not sing. The monk, not knowing what to do or where to turn, and not daring to go out, twisted and contorted his throat, opened his mouth wide, moved his bottom jaw up and down, and did all that he could to imitate the appearance of someone singing. The others present had not the self-control to stop laughing. Our valiant Emperor, who was not to be moved from his serenity by even the greatest events, sat solemnly waiting until the end of the Mass, just as if he had not noticed this pretense at singing. When it was all over, he called the poor wretch to him and, taking pity on his struggles and the strain he had gone through, consoled with these words: 'My good monk, thank you very much for your singing and your efforts.' Then he ordered him to be given a pound of silver to relieve his poverty.[24]

---

[21] *The Greek Anthology*, II, viii, 144. A poem by Gregory, in Ibid., 22, speaks of the panpipe in a metaphorical sense.

[22] 'The Phoenix,' Ibid., I, iv, 540ff.

[23] Einhard and Notker the Stammerer, *Two Lives of Charlemagne*, trans. Lewis Thorpe (Harmondsworth: Penguin Books, 1981), 112.

[24] Ibid., 100ff.

In another case where we wish the writer had given us much more detail, the philosopher, Psellus, makes an interesting reference to choral music during the reign of the empress, Theodora of Constantinople, in 1042 AD.

> Some made thanks-offerings to God for their deliverance, others acclaimed the new empress, while the common folk and the loungers in the market joined in dancing. The revolution was dramatized and they composed choral songs inspired by the events that had taken place before their eyes.[25]

Gibbon describes the music heard in a procession honoring a tenth-century emperor in Constantinople.

> From either side they echoed in a responsive melody the praises of the emperor; their poets and musicians directed the choir, and long life and victory were the burden of every song.[26]

By the thirteenth century, a period more in character with the coming Renaissance than the end of the Middle Ages, references to church choirs begin to include the accompanying instruments, which were for so long not allowed by the Church, and language which suggests more musical performances. Descriptions of church music in this French literature are rare, one of the more interesting being found in Wace's *Roman de Brut*.

> Now within the church Mass was commenced with due pomp and observance. The noise of the organ filled the church, and the clerks sang tunably in the choir. Their voices swelled or failed, according as the chant mounted to the roof, or died away in supplication. The knights passed from one church to the other.[27]

The English text upon which this passage is based seems even more complimentary of the quality of the musical performance.

> Afterwards, when the procession was over, so much organ music was played in the two churches and the choirs sang so sweetly that, because of the high standard of the music offered, the knights who were there hardly knew which of the churches to enter first. They flocked in crowds, first to this one, then to the other, so that if the whole day had been spent in celebration they would not have been bored. Finally, high mass was celebrated in both churches.[28]

After the organ was accepted into the church, gradually the rest of the instruments, for which the organ was only a surrogate, began to appear. A charming reference to the use of string instruments in the service in the thirteenth century is found in the works of Gautier de Coinci (ca. 1218–1236 AD).

---

25 Michael Psellus, *Chronographia*, trans. E. R. A. Sewter (Baltimore: Penguin Books, 1966), V, 39.
26 Gibbon, *The History of the Decline and Fall of the Roman Empire*, IV, 569.
27 Robert Wace, *Roman de Brut*, trans. Gwyn Jones (London: Dent, 1962), 67.
28 *Geoffrey of Monmouth's The History of the Kings of Britain*, trans. Lewis Thorpe, (Baltimore: Penguin Books, 1966), 228.

> When the mouth is working hard the heart should so strive, and so press upon the strings of its viele, and so tune them up, that with the first word the bright sound ascends without delay to Paradise. Then their singing is pleasing to God. But there are many [church singers] who have such a viele that will go out of tune all the time unless it is tuned up with strong wine.[29]

In the *De Musica* (ca. 1300 AD) by Johannes de Grocheo we get the first discussion of choral forms which provides rare subjective and musical descriptions and not mere theoretical ones. The *ductia*, he writes, is a rapid, light song, sung in chorus.

> This influences the hearts of girls and young men and keeps them from vanity and is said to have force against that passion which is called love or Eros.[30]

One of his remarks suggests that the ancient Choral dance is still present. The instrumental *ductia* is accompanied by percussion instruments, which 'measure' it and the movement of the performer,

> and excite the soul of man to moving ornately according to that art they call dancing, and they measure its movement in ductiae and in choral dance.[31]

Now Grocheo turns to church music, beginning with the famous thirteenth-century *motet*.

> This kind of song ought not to be propagated among the vulgar, since they do not understand its subtlety nor do they delight in its hearing, but it should be performed for the learned and those who seek after the subtleties of the arts.[32]

What he refers to here, but does not exactly say, is that the thirteenth-century motet had become a multi-lingual choral work featuring baudy songs.

Organum is ecclesiastical music, sung for the praise of God. Music in the same style which is sung at 'parties and feasts given by the learned and the rich,' is called *conductus*. Commonly, he says, both are called *organum*.

Hocket is 'a cut-up song,' composed in two or more voices, 'pleasing to the hot-tempered and to young men because of its mobility and speed.'[33]

The *Hymn* is 'an ornate song, having many verses,' sung for the faithful, that 'it may excite their hearts and souls to devotion,' before the readings and psalms. It is sung again afterward to 'reawake them and reinvigorate them' for the reading of the evangelical psalms.[34]

---

[29] V. R. Koenig, ed., *Les Miracles de Nostre Dame par Gautier de Coinci* (Geneva, 1955–1970), IV, 184.

[30] Johannes de Garlandia, *De Mensurabili Musica*, trans. Stanley Birnbaum (Colorado Springs: Colorado College Music Press, 1978),

[31] Ibid.

[32] Ibid., 25.

[33] Ibid., 26.

[34] Ibid., 35.

Finally, Grocheo discusses the intended influence on the listener of the various parts of the Mass. The *Kyrie Eleyson* is intended to 'move the hearts of those hearing it to devout praying and to listening devoutly to the Oration.' He adds to this description a curious footnote.

> It is performed in the Greek language, either because the Latins seem to have gotten the foundations of all the arts from the Greeks, or because Greek words are more weighty than others or more exact in designation, or because of some mystery which we do not wish to express at the present time.[35]

The *Responsory* and *Alleluia* are sung 'in the manner of *stantipes* or *coronate cantus*, so that they may impose devotion and humility in the hearts of their audience.' But the *Sequence* is sung,

> in the manner of *ductia*, so that it may make them joyful and lead them to receive correctly the words of the New Testament.[36]

The *Preface*, he calls a simple song intended to make the faithful devout and prepared for the *Sanctus*. The latter he calls 'a sign of the earthly and militant Church,' and is sung 'ornately and slowly, to move Christians to fervent charity and delight in God.'[37] In this case, and in the Hymn, where Grocheo uses the expression '*sung ornately*,' we have to wonder if this is a reference to the improvisation which is well documented in early Church music.

The *Agnus Dei*, Grocheo suggests, is to create in the listener a feeling of 'peace and concord.'[38]

In a letter to an old university friend, Petrarch (1304–1374) mentions that in Bologna music was experiencing a decline in the arts in general. We are not sure what he was talking about, unless he was a closet member of the *musica antique*, but we are drawn to his comment for his reference to choral dance performances, which one would judge had at long last come to an end. He mentions that songs have been replaced with laments and 'girls dancing in chorus' by gangs of bandits.[39]

We conclude with a comment by Girolamo Cardano (1501–1576), whose education began under his father, a lawyer in Milan, who taught him arithmetic, geometry[40] and astrology. Music lessons were made possible, secretly, through the aid of his mother.

Cardano observed, 'In antiquity dancing was called a sixth part of music.'[41] A more accurate representation of the view of the ancient Greeks would be to say that they believed dance to be the part of music you could see. This viewpoint must be understood in their constant reference to the fact that music is the only art which one cannot see. Our interest is in Car-

---

35 Ibid., 38.
36 Ibid., 40.
37 Ibid., 41.
38 Ibid.
39 Letter to Guido Sette, in *Letters from Petrarch*, trans. Morris Bishop (Bloomington: Indiana University Press, 1966), 266.
40 The father was consulted several times on geometry by Leonardo da Vinci.
41 Clement Miller, *Hieronymus Cardanus, Writings on Music* (American Institute of Musicology, 1973), 117.

dano's following observation on the relationship of ancient dance and music, one we have not found in extant ancient literature. Whether he read a book which no longer exists, or had a conversation with a choral member who possessed important passed down information we do not know. But it is most interesting that he claims that the movements of Greek choral performances were patterned on even earlier statues.

> Dancing and gesticulation express the ample movements that were left from antique statues, and the movements were then transferred from the figures to choral dances, and from choral dances to wrestling schools.[42]

---

[42] Ibid., 119.

Bibliography

CHAPTER 1 ON SECULAR MUSIC IN ANCIENT SOCIETIES

Athanassakis, Apostolos N. *The Homeric Hymns*. Baltimore: Johns Hopkins University Press, 1976.
Athenaeus. *Deipnosophistae*.
Chamberlin, Henry H. *Last Flowers*. Cambridge: Harvard University Press, 1937.
Davenport, Guy. *Archilochos, Sappho, Alkman*. Berkeley: University of California Press, 1980.
Homer. *Iliad*.
Livy. *A History of Rome*.
Longus. *Daphnis & Chloe*. Translated by Paul Turner. London: Penguin Books, 1956.
Ovid. *Metamorphoses*.
Ovid. *Tristia*.
Plutarch. *Concerning Music*.
Plutarch. *Customs of the Lacedaemonians*.
Propertius. *The Poems*.
Quintilian. *The Education of an Orator*.
Sendrey, Alfred. *Music in the Social and Religious Life of Antiquity*. Rutherford: Fairleigh Dickinson University Press, 1974.
Seneca. *Apocolocyntosis*.
Suetonius. *The Twelve Caesars*. New York: Penguin, 1989.
Tacitus. *Annals*.
Tibullus. *The Poems*.
Virgil. *Georgics*.

CHAPTER 2 ON THE SECULAR FESTIVALS OF ANCIENT GREECE AND ROME

Athenaeus. *Deipnosophistae*.
Calpurnius Siculus. *Eclogue I*.
Demosthenes. 'Against Leptines' Translated by J. H. Vince. Cambridge: Harvard University Press, 1954.
Demosthenes. 'The First Philippic.'
Horace. *Odes*.
Jebb, Richard C. *Bacchylides*. Hildesheim, Georg Olms Verlagsbuchhandlung, 1967.
Juvenal. *Satire VI*.
Nagy, Gregory. *Pindar's Homer*. Baltimore: Johns Hopkins University Press, 1982.
Ovid. *Metamorphoses*.
Ovid. *Amores*.

Plato. *Laws*.
Pliny the Elder. *Natural History*.
Propertius, *Poems*.
Saint Justin Martyr. *Saint Justin Martyr*. New York: Christian Heritage.
St. John Chrysostom. 'Discourses Against Judaizing Christians.' Translated by Paul W. Harkins. Washington, D.C.: The Catholic University of American Press.
Seneca, *Trojan Women*.
Strabo. *The Geography of Strabo*. Translated by Horace L. Jones. Cambridge: Harvard University Press, 1960
Tibullus. *Poems*.
Virgil. *Georgics*.
Virgil. *The Aeneid*

Chapter 3 On Ancient concert Halls

Aristophanes. *Clouds*.
Aristotle. *Metaphysica*.
Athenaeus. *Deipnosophistae*.
Carter, Tim. 'The North Italian Courts,' in *The Early Baroque Era*. Englewood Cliffs: Prentice Hall, 1994.
Cavalieri, Emilio de. *Rappresentazione di Anima, et di Corpo*, Preface. Quoted in Carol MacClintock. *Readings in the History of Music in Performance*. Bloomington: Indiana University Press, 1979.
Conway, Geoffrey S. *The Odes of Pindar*. London: Dent, 1972.
Juvenal. *Satires*.
Lang, Paul Henry. *Music in Western Civilization*. New York, 1941.
Nagy, Gregory. *Pindar's Homer*. Baltimore: Johns Hopkins University Press, 1982.
Plutarch. *Lives*.
Sendrey, Alfred. *Music in the Social and Religious Life of Antiquity*. Rutherford: Fairleigh Dickinson University Press, 1974.
Seneca. *Epistolae*.
Siculus, Calpurnius. *Eclogues*.

Chapter 4 Memories of Ancient Concerts

Anonymous. *Il Novellino*. Translated by Edward Storer. London: Routledge.
Aretino, Pietro. *Dialogues*. Translated by Raymond Rosenthal. New York: Marsilio, 1971.
Aristophanes. *The Clouds*.
Beer, Johann. *Musicalische Diskurse* (Nürnberg, 1710.
Benoit, Marcelle. In 'Paris, 1661–87: the Age of Lully.' In *The Early Baroque Era*. Englewood Cliffs: Prentice Hall, 1994.

Burney, Charles. *Memoirs of the Life and Writings of the Abate Metastasio*. New York: Da Capo Press, 1971.]
Calmo, Andrea. *Lettere*. Edited by V. Rosso. Turin, 1888.
Cellesi, L. 'Documenti per la storia musicale di Firenze.' In *Rivista Musicale Italiana* (1927).
Chaucer. *Canterbury Tales*.
D'Amico, John. *Renaissance Humanism in Papal Rome*. Baltimore: Johns Hopkins University Press, 1983.
David, Hans T. and Arthur Mendel. *The Bach Reader*. New York: Norton, 1966.
Devillers, Leopold. *Essai sur l'historie de la musique a Mons*. Mons, 1868.
Gilliodts-Van Severen, Louis, 'Les menestrels de Bruges.' In *Essais d'Arceologie Brugeoise*. Bruges, 1912.
Grosse, H. and H. R. Jung, eds. *Georg Philipp Telemann Briefwechsel*. Leipzig, 1972.
Heinichen, Johann David. *General-Bass Treatise* [1711]. Quoted in George Buelow. *Thorough-Bass Accompaniment according to Johann David Heinichen*. Ann Arbor: UMI Research Press, 1986.
Juvenal. *Satires*.
Kelly, Michael. *Reminiscences*. London, 1826.
Larner, John. *Culture and Society in Italy, 1290–1420*. New York: Scribner's, 1971.
Marino, Giambattista. *L'Adone* [1623]. Translated by Harold Priest. Ithaca: Cornell University Press, 1967.
Mattheson, Johann. *Der vollkommene Capellmeister* (1739). Translated by Ernest Harriss. Ann Arbor: UMI Research Press, 1981.
Motta, E. *Musici alla Corte degli Sforza: ricerche e documenti milanesi*. Milano, 1887.
Murray, John. *Antwerp in the Age of Platin and Brueghel*. Norman: University of Oklahoma Press, 1970.
North, Roger. *Memoirs of Music*. Edited by Edward Rimbault. London: Bell, 1846.
Pirrotta, Nino and Elena Povoledo. *Music and Theatre from Poliziano to Monteverdi*. Cambridge: Cambridge University Press, 1982.
Pirrotta, Nino. *Music and Culture in Italy from the Middle Ages to the Baroque*. Cambridge: Harvard University Press, 1984.
Plato. *Ion*.
Polk, Keith. *Ensemble Instrumental Music in Flanders: 1450–1550* [Unpublished].
Reese, Gustave. *Music in the Renaissance*. New York: Norton, 1959.
Smithers, Don L. *The Music and History of the Baroque Trumpet*. London: Dent.
Strunk, Oliver. *Source Readings in Music History*. New York: Norton, 1950.
Symonds, John Addington, trans. *The Life of Benvenuto Cellini*. New York: Scribner's, 1914.
Symonds, John Addington. *Renaissance in Italy*. New York: Capricorn Books, 1964.
Van Aerde, Raymond. *Menestrels Communaux ... a Malines, de 1312 a 1790*. Mechelen, 1911.
Vesce, Thomas E., trans. *The Knight of the Parrot*. New York: Garland, 1986.
Vessella, Alessandro. *La Banda* (Milan, 1935).

Wangermee, Robert. *Flemish Music and Society in the Fifteenth and Sixteenth Centuries*. New York, 1968.
Wilson, John. *Roger North on Music*. London: Novello, 1959.
Wytsman. *Anciens airs et chansons populaires de Termonde*. Quoted in Edmond Vander Straeten. *La Musique aux Pays Bas avant le XIXe Siècle*. New York, 1959.

Chapter 5 On the Ancient Greek Chorus

Aristophanes. *The Themophoriazusae*.
Athenaeus. *Deipnosophistae*.
Conway, Geoffrey S. *The Odes of Pindar*. London: Dent, 1972.
Davenport, Guy. *Archilochos, Sappho, Alkman*. Berkeley: University of California Press, 1980.
Demosthenes. *Against Leptines*. Translated by J. H. Vince. Cambridge: Harvard University Press, 1954.
Farmer, Henry G. 'The Music of Ancient Mesopotamia.' In *The New Oxford History of Music*. London: Oxford University Press, 1966.
Herodotus. *Histories*.
Nagy, Gregory. *Pindar's Homer*. Baltimore: Johns Hopkins University Press, 1982.
Oates, Whitney J., ed. *The Complete Greek Drama*. New York: Random House, 1938.
Plato. *Hippias Minor*.
Plato. *Laws*.
Plutarch. *Customs of the Lacedaemonians*.
Plutarch. *Laconic Apophthegms*.
Polybius. *The Histories*. Translated by W. R. Paton. Cambridge: Harvard University Press, 1954.
Sendrey, Alfred. *Music in the Social and Religious Life of Antiquity*. Rutherford: Fairleigh Dickinson University Press, 1974.
Sprague, Rosamond Kent. *The Older Sophists*. Columbia: University of South Carolina Press, 1972.

Chapter 6 On the Ancient Roman Chorus

Gibbon, Edward. *The History of the Decline and Fall of the Roman Empire*. Philadelphia: Coates.
Horace. *Odes*.
Juvenal. *Satires*.
Livy. *The Early History of Rome*.
Lucian. *Icaromenippus*.
Pliny the Elder. *Natural History*.
Pliny the Younger. *The Letters of the Younger Pliny*. New York: Penguin, 1969.
Saint Gregory of Nazianzus. 'Concerning his own Life.' Translated by Denis Meehan. Washington, D.C.: The Catholic University of America Press.

Sendrey, Alfred. *Music in the Social and Religious Life of Antiquity*. Rutherford: Fairleigh Dickinson University Press, 1974.
Seneca. *Epistolae*.
Seneca. *The Trojan Women*.
Sheldon, Winthrop D. In *A Second Century Satirist*. Philadelphia: Drexel Biddle, 1901.
Suetonius. *The Twelve Caesars*. New York: Penguin, 1989.
Tacitus. *Annals*.
The Greek Anthology. Translated by W. R. Paton. Cambridge: Harvard University Press, 1939.

Chapter 7 On Music of Ancient Courts

Ammianus Marcellinus. *Constantius et Gallus*. Translated by John C. Rolfe. London: Heinemann, 1935.
Arrian. *The Campaigns of Alexander*.
Athenaeus. *Deipnosophistae*.
Cicero, *De Finibus*
Farmer, Henry G. 'The Music of Ancient Mesopotamia.' In *The New Oxford History of Music*. London: Oxford University Press, 1966.
Giovanni da Prato. *Paradiso degli Alberti*. (1389).
Herodotus. *Histories*.
Homer. *The Homeric Hymns*. Translated by Apostolos N. Athanassakis. Baltimore: Johns Hopkins University Press, 1976.
Homer. *The Odyssey*. Translated by A. T. Murray. London: Heinemann, 1960.
Ovid. *Amores*.
Pliny the Elder. *Natural History*,
Plutarch. *Lives*.
Polybius. *The Rise of the Roman Empire*.
Sachs, Curt. *The History of Musical Instruments*. New York, 1940.
Sendrey, Alfred. *Music in the Social and Religious Life of Antiquity*. Rutherford: Fairleigh Dickinson University Press, 1974.
Suetonius. *Lives of the Caesars*.
Suetonius. *The Twelve Caesars*. New York: Penguin, 1989.
The Scriptores Historiae Augustae. Translated by David Magie. London: Heinemann, 1924.

Chapter 8 Theater Music in the Ancient World

Aelius Donatus. 'On Comedy and Tragedy.' In Barrett H. Clark. *European Theories of the Drama*. New York: Crown, 1918.
Aeschylus. *The Seven Against Thebes*.
Aristophanes. *Peace*.
Aristophanes. *The Acharnians*.

Aristophanes. *The Clouds*.
Aristophanes. *The Ecclesiazusae*.
Aristophanes. *The Frogs*.
Aristophanes. *The Knights*.
Aristophanes. *The Thesmophoriazusae*.
Aristotle. *Poetics*.
Athenaeus. *Deipnosophistae*.
Calpurnius Siculus. *Eclogue VII*.
Cassiodorus. *Variae*. Translated by Thomas Hodgkin. London: Frowde, 1886.
Cicero. *Academica*.
Cicero. *De Finibus*.
Cicero. *Paradoxa Stoicorum*.
Euripides. *Alcestis*.
Euripides. *Electra*.
Euripides. *Helen*.
Euripides. *Iphigenia in Aulis*.
Euripides. *The Bacchae*.
Euripides. *The Heracleidae*.
Euripides. *The Phoenissae*.
Euripides. *The Suppliants*.
Euripides. *The Trojan Women*.
Gibbon, Edward. *The History of the Decline and Fall of the Roman Empire*. Philadelphia: Coates.
Gregory the Great. 'Pastoral Care.' Translated by Henry Davis. New York: Newman Press, 1978.
Homer. *The Iliad*.
Horace. *The Art of Poetry*.
Hrotswitha. *The Plays of Hrotswitha of Gandersheim*. Larissa Bonfante. New York: New York University Press, 1979.
Julian, 'Letter to a Priest,' in *The Works of the Emperor Julian*. Translated by Wilmer Wright (London: Heinemann, 1913), II, 335.
Lactantius. *The Divine Institutes*. Translated by William Fletcher in *The Works of Lactantius*. Edinburgh: T. & T. Clark, 1886.
Novatian. *The Spectacles*. Translated by Russell J. DeSimone. In *Fathers of the Church*. Washington, D.C.: The Catholic University of America Press.
Oliver Strunk. *Source Readings in Music History*. New York: Norton, 1950.
Plautus. *The Rope*.
Plautus. *The Twin Menaechmi*.
Pliny the Younger. *The Letters of the Younger Pliny*. New York: Penguin, 1985.
Polybius. *Histories*.
Procopius. *The Secret History*. Harmondsworth: Penguin Books, 1981.

Quintilian. *The Education of an Orator*.
Reale, Giovanni. *A History of Ancient Philosophy*. Albany: State University of New York Press, 1987.
Sendrey, Alfred. *Music in the Social and Religious Life of Antiquity*. Rutherford: Fairleigh Dickinson University Press, 1974.
Sophocles. *Ajax*.
Sophocles. *Philoctetes*.
St. Augustine. *The City of God*. Translated by Gerald G. Walsh. In *Fathers of the Church*. New York, 1954.
Suetonius, *The Twelve Caesars*. New York: Penguin, 1989.
Tacitus. *The Annals*.
Tertullian. 'Spectacles.' Translated by Rudolph Arbesmann in *Disciplinary, Moral and Ascetical Works*. New York: Fathers of the Church, 1959.
Tertullianus. *The Writings of Tertullianus*. Edinburgh: T. & T. Clark, 1895.
The Life of Saint Mary Magdalene and of her Sister Saint Martha. Translated by David Mycoff. Kalamazoo: Cistercian Publications, 1989.

CHAPTER 9 ON MUSIC COMPETITION IN THE ANCIENT WORLD

Aristotle. *Politica*.
Athenaeus. *Deipnosophistae*.
Brownson, Carleton L., trans. *Anabasis*. Cambridge: Harvard University Press, 1947.
Cervantes, Miguel de. *Don Quijote,*. Translated by Burton Raffel. New York: Norton, 1995.
Chappell, W. *The History of Music*. London: Chappell.
Conway, Geoffrey S. *The Odes of Pindar*. London: Dent, 1972.
Davenport, Guy, trans. *Archilochos, Sappho, Alkman*. Berkeley: University of California Press, 1980.
Jebb, Richard C. *Bacchylides*. Hildesheim, Georg Olms Verlagsbuchhandlung, 1967.
Lang, A. *Theocritus, Bion and Moschus*. London: Macmillan, 1920.
London Gazette (March 21, 1699).
Marchant, E. C. *Scripta Minora*. Cambridge: Harvard University Press, 1956.
Miller, Walter, trans. *Cyropaedia*. Cambridge: Harvard University Press, 1960.
North, Roger. *Memoirs of Music*. Edited by Edward Rimbault. London: Bell, 1846.
Ovid. *Metamorphoses*.
Plato. *Laws*.
Plutarch. *Concerning Music*.
Plutarch. *Lives*.
Polybius. *The Histories*. Translated by W. R. Paton. Cambridge: Harvard University Press, 1954.
Quintilian. *The Education of an Orator*.

Sendrey, Alfred. *Music in the Social and Religious Life of Antiquity*. Rutherford: Fairleigh Dickinson University Press, 1974.

Sprague, Rosamond Kent. *The Older Sophists*. Columbia: University of South Carolina Press, 1972.

Strabo. *The Geography of Strabo*. Translated by Horace L. Jones. Cambridge: Harvard University Press, 1960.

Suetonius. *Lives of the Caesars*.

Vives, Juan. *Vives: On Education*. Translated by Foster Watson. Cambridge: University Press, 1913.

Xenophon. *Oeconomicus*. In E. C. Marchant. *Memorabilia and Oeconomicus*. Cambridge: Harvard University Press, 1953.

CHAPTER 10 ENTERTAINMENT MUSIC IN THE ANCIENT WORLD

Athenaeus. *Deipnosophistae*.

Bell, Clair, trans. *Peasant Life in Old German Epics*. New York: Octagon Books, 1965.

Bloomfield, S. T. *The History of Thucydides*. London: Longman, Rees, Orme, Brown, and Green, 1829.

Cassiodorus. *Variae*. Translated by Thomas Hodgkin. London: Frowde.

Cicero. *De Finibus*.

Cicero. *De Officiis*.

Cicero. *In Defense of Murena*.

Dickinson, John. *The Stateman's Book of John of Salisbury*. New York: Russell & Russell, 1963.

Duke Ernst. Translated by J. W. Thomas and Carolyn Dussere, in *Medieval Tales*. New York: Continuum, 1983.

Galen. *On the Natural Faculties*. Translated by Arthur John Brock. Cambridge: Harvard University Press, 1979.

Gibbon, Edward. *The History of the Decline and Fall of the Roman Empire*. Philadelphia: Coates.

Juvenal. *Satire*.

Oliver Strunk. *Source Readings in Music History*. New York: Norton, 1950.

Paris, Matthew. *English History*. Translated by J. A. Giles. London: Bohn, 1852.

Peter Green, trans. *Roman Poets of the Early Empire*. London: Penguin Group, 1991.

Plato, *Laws*.

Plato. *Gorgias*.

Plato. *Republic*.

Pliny the Elder. *Natural History*.

Salvian. *On the Government of God*. Translated by Eva Sanford. New York: Columbia University Press, 1930.

St. Basil. 'Letter to Glycerius.' In *Letters of Saint Basil*. Translated by Sister Agnes Way. New York: Fathers of the Church, 1951.

St. Bernard. *The Letters of St. Bernard of Clairvaux*. Translated by Bruno James. Chicago: Regnery, 1953.
St. John Chrysostom. *Baptismal Instructions*. Translated by Paul W. Harkins. Westminster, MD: The Newman Press, 1963.
Strassburg, Gottfried von. *Tristan*. Translated by Arthus Hatto. Harmondsworth: Penguin Books, 1960.
Suetonius. *Lives of the Caesars*.
Tacitus. *Annals*.
The Scriptores Historiae Augustae. Translated by David Magie. London: Heinemann, 1924.
Thomas, J. W. *The Best Novellas of Medieval Germany*. Columbia, S.C.: Camden House, 1984.
Thomas, J. W., trans. *Tannhauser: Poet and Legend*. Chapel Hill: University of North Carolina.
Valerius Martial. *Epigrams*.

Chapter 11 Banquet Music in the Ancient World

Ammianus Marcellinus. *Constantius et Gallus*. Translated by John C. Rolfe. London: Heinemann, 1935.
Athenaeus. *Deipnosophistae*.
Cicero. *De Officiis*.
Clement of Alexandria. 'The Instructor.' Translated by William Wilson. Edinburgh: T. & T. Clark, 1884.
Epicurus. Translated by Cyril Bailey. Oxford: Clarendon Press, 1926.
Farmer, Henry G. 'The Music of Ancient Egypt.' *New Oxford History of Music*. London: Oxford University Press, 1966.
Gibbon, Edward. *The History of the Decline and Fall of the Roman Empire*. Philadelphia: Coates.
Homer. *The Iliad*.
Homer. *The Odyssey*. Translated by A. T. Murray. London: Heinemann, 1960.
Laurin. Translated by J. W. Thomas. In *The Best Novellas of Medieval Germany*. Columbia, S.C.: Camden House, 1984
Manniche, Lise. *Music and Musicians in Ancient Egypt*. London: British Museum Press, 1991.
Plato. *Symposium*.
Quintilian. *The Education of an Orator*.
Sendrey, Alfred. *Music in the Social and Religious Life of Antiquity*. Rutherford: Fairleigh Dickinson University Press, 1974.
Sharpe, Samuel. *Egyptian Antiquities in the British Museum*. London, 1862.
Sidonius. *Sidonius Poems and Letters*. Translated by W. B. Anderson. Cambridge: Harvard University Press, 1965.
Strunk, Oliver. *Source Readings in Music History*. New York: Norton, 1950.
Suetonius. *Lives of the Caesars*.
Tacitus. *Annals*.

Venerable Bede. *Ecclesiastical History of England*. Translated by J. A. Giles. London: Bohn, 1849.
Wolfram von Eschenbach. *Parzival*. Translated by Helen Mustard and Charles Passage. New York: Vintage Books, 1961.

Chapter 12 Wedding Music in the Ancient World

Athanassakis, Apostolos N., trans. *Theogony, Works and Days, Shield*. Baltimore: Johns Hopkins University Press, 1983.
Athenaeus. *The Deipnosophists*. Translated by Charles Burton Gulick. Cambridge: Harvard University Press, 1951.
Ausionius. *Ausonius*. Translated by Hugh G. Evelyn White. London: Heinemann, 1961.
Chamberlin, Henry H. *Last Flowers*. Cambridge: Harvard University Press, 1937.
Duke Ernst. Translated by J. W. Thomas and Carolyn Dussere. In *Medieval Tales*. New York: Continuum, 1983.
Durant, Will. *Caesar and Christ*. New York: Simon and Schuster, 1944.
Euripides. *Heracles*.
Euripides. *Iphigenia in Aulis*.
Euripides. *The Trojan Women*.
Gibbon, Edward. *The History of the Decline and Fall of the Roman Empire*. Philadelphia: Coates.
Hartmann von Aue. *Erec*. Translated by Thomas Keller. New York: Garland, 1987.
Homer. *Iliad* and *Odyssey*.
Martianus Capella. *Martianus Capella and the Seven Liberal Arts*. Translated by William Harris Stahl and Richard Johnson. New York: Columbia University Press, 1977.
Medieval Lore. Translated by Robert Steele .London: Stock, 1893.
Menander. *The Girl from Samos*.
Miller, Norma, trans. *Menander Plays and Fragments*. London: Penguin Books, 1987.
Musaeus. 'Hero and Leander.' Translated by Cedric Whitman. Cambridge: Harvard University Press, 1975.
Plato. *Laws*.
Psellus, Michael. *Chronographia*. Translated by E. R. A. Sewter. Baltimore: Penguin Books, 1966.
St. John Chrysostom, 'Homilies on Genesis 46–67.' Translated by Robert C. Hill. Washington, D.C.: The Catholic University of America Press.
Staines, David. *The Complete Romances of Chretien de Troyes*. Bloomington: Indiana University Press, 1993.

Chapter 13 Funeral Music in the Ancient World

Aeschylus. *The Supplices*.
Athenaeus. *The Deipnosophists*. Translated by Charles Burton Gulick. Cambridge: Harvard University Press, 1951.

Carpenter, Nan Cooke. *Music in the Medieval and Renaissance Universities*. Norman: University of Oklahoma Press, 1958.
Euripides. *Helen*.
Euripides. *Iphigenia in Tauris*.
Euripides. *The Suppliants*.
Gregory the Great. 'Dialogue Four.' Translated by Odo Zimmerman. New York: Fathers of the Church, 1959.
Grove, George. *The New Grove Dictionary of Music and Musicians*. Edited by Stanley Sadie. London: Macmillan, 1980.
Life of Columba. Translated by Alan Anderson and Marjorie Anderson. London: Nelson, 1961.
Ovid. *Fasti*.
Sendrey, Alfred. *Music in the Social and Religious Life of Antiquity*. Rutherford: Fairleigh Dickinson University Press, 1974.
Songs from the Elder Edda, Volume 49. *The Harvard Classics*. New York: Collier, 1910.
Varro. *On the Latin Language*.

CHAPTER 14 ON MUSIC OF THE ANCIENT MILITARY

Aristides Quintilianus. *De Musica*. Quoted in Andrew Barker. *Greek Musical Writings*. Cambridge: Cambridge University Press, 1989.
Arrian. *The Campaigns of Alexander*. New York: Penguin, 1978.
Athenaeus. *Deipnosophistae*.
Cicero. *Tusculan Disputations*.
Euripides. *The Trojan Women*.
Herodotus. *The Histories*. New York: Penguin, 1977.
Josephus. *The Jewish Wars*.
Kastner, Georges. *Manuel General de Musique Militaire*. Paris, 1848.
Livy. *A History of Rome*.
Livy. *The War with Hannibal*. New York: Penguin classics, 1980.
Plutarch. *Lives*.
Polybius. *The Histories*. Translated by W. R. Paton. Cambridge: Harvard University Press, 1954.
Polybius. *The Rise of the Roman Empire*. New York: Penguin, 1981.
Sallust. *The Jugurthine War*.
Sendrey, Alfred. *Music in the Social and Religious Life of Antiquity*. Rutherford: Fairleigh Dickinson University Press, 1974.
Seneca. *Thyestes*.
Suetonius. *Lives of the Caesars*.
Tacitus. *Annals*.
Tacitus. *The Complete Works of Tacitus*. New York: Modern Library, 1942.

The Anabasis of Cyrus. Translated by Carleton L. Brownson. In *Anabasis*. Cambridge: Harvard University Press, 1947.

Thucydides. *The Peloponnesian War*. New York: Modern Library, 1951.

Valerius Flaccus. *Argonautica*.

Virgil. *Aenei*.

Wilmanns, G., ed. *Corpus inscriptionum latinarum*. Berlin, 1881.

Chapter 15 On Medieval Military Music

'The Destruction of Da Derga's Hostel.' Translated by Whitley Stokes. In *Epic and Saga*, Volume 49, *The Harvard Classics*. New York: Collier, 1910.

'The Lay of Hamdir.' In *Songs from the Elder Edda*, Volume 49, *The Harvard Classics*. New York: Collier, 1910.

'The Story of the Volsungs and Niblungs.' Translated by Eir'kr Magnœsson and William Morris in *Epic and Saga*, Volume 49, *The Harvard Classics*. New York: Collier, 1910.

Ammianus Marcellinus. *Constantius et Gallus*. Translated by John C. Rolfe. London: Heinemann, 1935.

Cassiodorus. *Variae*. Translated by Thomas Hodgkin. London: Frowde, 1886.

Farmer, Henry G. *The Rise and Development of Military Music*. London, 1912.

Gibbon, Edward. *The History of the Decline and Fall of the Roman Empire*. Philadelphia: Coates.

Gregory of Tours. *The History of the Franks*. Translated by Lewis Thorpe. Harmondsworth: Penguin Books, 1974.

Harrison, Robert, trans. *Of the Digby 23 mss in the Bodleian Library, Oxford*. New York: New American Library, 1970.

Wolfram von Eschenbach. *Parzival*. Translated by Helen Mustard and Charles Passage. New York: Vintage Books, 1961.

Wolfram von Eschenbach. *Willehalm*. Translated by Charles Passage. New York: Ungar, 1977.

Chapter 16 On Music of the medieval Courts

'Li estoires de chiaus qui conquisent Coustantinoble' [1216]. Quoted in Edward Stone, trans., *Three Old French Chronicles of the Crusades*. Seattle: The University of Washington Press, 1939.

Ammianus Marcellinus. *Constantius et Gallus*. Translated by John C. Rolfe. London: Heinemann, 1935.

Bowles, Edmund. 'Haut and Bas: The Grouping of Musical Instruments in the Middle Ages.' In *Musica Disciplina* (1954).

Cancellieri, Francesco. *Storia di solenni possessi de' Sommi Pontefici*. Rome, 1802.

Carpenter, Nan Cooke. *Music in the Medieval and Renaissance Universities*. Norman: University of Oklahoma Press, 1958.

Davis, H. W. C. *Medieval England*. Oxford, 1928.

Der mittelenglische Versroman über Richard Löwenherz. Edited by K. Bruner. Vienna and Leipzig, 1913.
Durant, Will. *The Age of Faith*. New York: Simon and Schuster, 1950.
Eboli, Pietro da. *Liber ad Honorem Augusti*. Berne, Burgerbibliothek, Mss. Del Cod. Di Berna 120.
Einhard and Notker the Stammerer. *Two Lives of Charlemagne*. Translated by Lewis Thorpe. Harmondsworth: Penguin Books, 1981.
Gibbon, Edward. *The History of the Decline and Fall of the Roman Empire*. Philadelphia: Coates.
Gregory of Tours. *The History of the Franks*. Translated by Lewis Thorpe. Harmondsworth: Penguin Books, 1974.
Hazlitt, W. C. *The Venetian Republic*. New York, 1915.
Higino Angles, Higino. 'Die Instrumentalmusik bis zum 16. Jahrhundert in Spanien.' In *Natalicia Musicologica*. Oslo, 1962.
Hillgarth. *The Spanish Kingdoms*. Oxford, 1976.
Kantorowicz, Ernst. *Frederick the Second*. Translated by E. O. Lorimer. New York, 1957.
Lull, Ramon. *Libre de Meravelles*.
Masson, Georgina. *Frederick II of Hohenstaufen*. New York, 1973.
Page, Christopher. *Voices and Instruments of the Middle Ages*. London: Dent, 1987.
Paris, Matthew. *English History*. Translated by J. A. Giles. London: Bohn, 1852.
Richard of Ely. 'The Life of Hereward the Wake.' In *Three Lives of the Last Englishmen*. Michael Swanton. New York: Garland Publishing, 1984.
Saldoni, M. Balthasar. *Diccionario biografio-bibliografico de Efemerides de musicos españoles*.
Sidonius. *The Letters of Sidonius*. Translated by O. M. Dalton. Oxford: Clarendon Press, 1915.
Songs from the Elder Edda, Volume 49, *The Harvard Classics*. New York: Collier, 1910.
The Greek Anthology. London: Heinemann, 1925.
The Scriptores Historiae Augustae. Translated by David Magie. London: Heinemann, 1924.
Veit, Gottfried. *Die Blasmusik*. Innsbruck, 1972.
Vessella, Alessandro. *La Banda*. Milan, 1935.

CHAPTER 17 ON MEDIEVAL CIVIC MUSIC

Bernard of Cluny. *Scorn for the World: Bernard of Cluny's De Contemptu Mundi*. Translated by Ronald Pepin. East Lansing: Colleagues Press, 1991.
Bernhard, M. B. *Notice sur la Confrerie des Jouers d'Instruments d'Alsace*. Paris, 1844.
Bonanni. *Gabinetto armonico*. Rome, 1722.
Bonfadini, R. 'Le origini del Comune di Milano.' In *Albori della Vita Italiana*. Milano, 1897.
Bowles, Edmund A. 'Tower Musicians in the Middle Ages.' In *Brass Quarterly* (V).
Corio, Bernardino. *L'Historia di Milano volgarmente scritta*. Padoa, 1646.
Ehmann, Wilhelm. *Tibilustrium*. Kassel, 1950.
Gesta Romanorum. Translated by Charles Swan. London: C. and J. Rivington, 1824.

Johannes de Garlandia. *De Mensurabili Musica*. Translated by Stanley Birnbaum. Colorado Springs: Colorado College Music Press, 1978.
Kastner, Georges. *Manuel General de Musique Militaire*. Paris, 1848.
Langwill, Lyndesay G. *The Waits*. Hinrichsen, 1952.
Longus. *Daphnis & Chloe*. Translated by Paul Turner. London: Penguin Books, 1956.
Lorris, Guillaumne and Jean de Meun, 'The Romance of the Rose.' Translated by Harry Robbins. New York: Dutton, 1962.
Martianus Capella. *Martianus Capella and the Seven Liberal Arts*. William Harris Stahl and Richard Johnson. New York: Columbia University Press, 1977.
Mizawa, S. *Nicholas Copernicus*. New York, 1943.
Salmen, Walter. *Der Fahrende Musiker im Europaischen Mittelalter*. Kassel, 1960.
St. John Chrysostom. 'Exposition of Psalm XLI.' Quoted in Oliver Strunk. *Source Readings in Music History*. New York: Norton, 1950.
St. Paulinus of Nola. *The Poems of St. Paulinus of Nola*. Translated by P. G. Walsh. New York: Newman Press, 1975.
Stowe, J. *Survey of London*. London, 1618.
Ulrich von Liechtenstein. *In Service of Ladies*. Translated by J. W. Thomas. Chapel Hill: The University of North Carolina Press, 1969.
Vessella, Alessandro. *La Banda*. Milan, 1935.
Warwick, Alan. *A Noise of Music*. London: Queen Anne Press.
Wolfram von Eschenbach. *Wolfram von Eschenbach, Titurel and the Songs*. Translated by Marion Gibbs and Sidney Johnson. New York: Garland Publishing, 1988.
Wolfram von Eschenbach. *Parzival*. Helen Mustard and Charles Passage. New York: Vintage Books, 1961.
Zippel, Giuseppe. *I Suonatori della Signoria di Firenze*. Trento, 1892.

CHAPTER 18 ON THE MEDIEVAL CHORUS

Callimachus. *Callimachus*. Translated by C. A. Trypanis. Cambridge: Harvard University Press, 1975.
Cassiodorus. *Variae*. Translated by Thomas Hodgkin. London: Frowde, 1886.
Clement of Alexandria. 'The Miscellanies.' Translated by Alexander Roberts, in *Ante-Nicene Christian Library*. Edinburgh: T. & T. Clark, 1869.
Durant, Will. *The Age of Faith*. New York: Simon and Schuster, 1950.
Einhard and Notker the Stammerer. *Two Lives of Charlemagne*. Translated by Lewis Thorpe. Harmondsworth: Penguin Books, 1981.
Geoffrey of Monmouth. *The History of the Kings of Britain*. Translated by Lewis Thorpe. Baltimore: Penguin Books, 1966.
Gibbon, Edward. *The History of the Decline and Fall of the Roman Empire*. Philadelphia: Coates.

Johannes de Garlandia. *De Mensurabili Musica*. Translated by Stanley Birnbaum. Colorado Springs: Colorado College Music Press, 1978.

Koenig, V. R., ed. *Les Miracles de Nostre Dame par Gautier de Coinci*. Geneva, 1955–1970.

Miller, Clement. *Hieronymus Cardanus, Writings on Music*. American Institute of Musicology, 1973.

Petrarch. *Letters from Petrarch*. Translated by Morris Bishop. Bloomington: Indiana University Press, 1966.

Psellus, Michael. *Chronographia*. Translated by E. R. A. Sewter. Baltimore: Penguin Books, 1966.

Saint Gregory of Nazianzus. *Concerning his own Life*. Translated by Denis Meehan. Washington, D.C.: The Catholic University of America Press.

Sidonius. *Sidonius Poems and Letters*. Translated by W. B. Anderson. Cambridge: Harvard University Press, 1965.

St. Basil. 'Letter to the Clergy of Neo-Caesarea.' In *Letters of Saint Basil*. Translated by Sister Agnes Way. New York: Fathers of the Church, 1955.

St. Basil. 'Homily 14.' In *Exegetic Homilies*. Translated by Sister Agnes Way. Washington, D.C.: The Catholic University of America Press.

St. John Chrysostom. *Discourses Against Judaizing Christians*. Translated by Paul W. Harkins. Washington, D.C.: The Catholic University of American Press.

St. Paulinus of Nola. *The Poems of St. Paulinus of Nola*. Translated by P. G. Walsh. New York: Newman Press, 1975.

Wace, Robert. *Roman de Brut*. Translated by Gwyn Jones. London: Dent, 1962.

About the Author

Dr. David Whitwell is a graduate ('with distinction') of the University of Michigan and the Catholic University of America, Washington DC (PhD, Musicology, Distinguished Alumni Award, 2000) and has studied conducting with Eugene Ormandy and at the Akademie für Musik, Vienna. Prior to coming to Northridge, Dr. Whitwell participated in concerts throughout the United States and Asia as Associate First Horn in the USAF Band and Orchestra in Washington DC, and in recitals throughout South America in cooperation with the United States State Department.

At the California State University, Northridge, which is in Los Angeles, Dr. Whitwell developed the CSUN Wind Ensemble into an ensemble of international reputation, with international tours to Europe in 1981 and 1989 and to Japan in 1984. The CSUN Wind Ensemble has made professional studio recordings for BBC (London), the Köln Westdeutscher Rundfunk (Germany), NOS National Radio (The Netherlands), Zürich Radio (Switzerland), the Television Broadcasting System (Japan) as well as for the United States State Department for broadcast on its 'Voice of America' program. The CSUN Wind Ensemble's recording with the Mirecourt Trio in 1982 was named the 'Record of the Year' by The Village Voice. Composers who have guest conducted Whitwell's ensembles include Aaron Copland, Ernest Krenek, Alan Hovhaness, Morton Gould, Karel Husa, Frank Erickson and Vaclav Nelhybel.

Dr. Whitwell has been a guest professor in 100 different universities and conservatories throughout the United States and in 23 foreign countries (most recently in China, in an elite school housed in the Forbidden City). Guest conducting experiences have included the Philadelphia Orchestra, Seattle Symphony Orchestra, the Czech Radio Orchestras of Brno and Bratislava, The National Youth Orchestra of Israel, as well as resident wind ensembles in Russia, Israel, Austria, Switzerland, Germany, England, Wales, The Netherlands, Portugal, Peru, Korea, Japan, Taiwan, Canada and the United States.

He is a past president of the College Band Directors National Association, a member of the Prasidium of the International Society for the Promotion of Band Music, and was a member of the founding board of directors of the World Association for Symphonic Bands and Ensembles (WASBE). In 1964 he was made an honorary life member of Kappa Kappa Psi, a national professional music fraternity. In September, 2001, he was a delegate to the UNESCO Conference on Global Music in Tokyo. He has been knighted by sovereign organizations in France, Portugal and Scotland and has been awarded the gold medal of Kerkrade, The Netherlands, and the silver medal of Wangen, Germany, the highest honor given wind conductors in the United States, the medal of the Academy of Wind and Percussion Arts (National Band Association) and the highest honor given wind conductors in Austria, the gold medal of the Austrian Band Association. He is a member of the Hall of Fame of the California Music Educators Association.

Dr. Whitwell's publications include more than 127 articles on wind literature including publications in Music and Letters (London), the London Musical Times, the Mozart-Jahrbuch (Salzburg), and 52 books, among which is his 13-volume *History and Literature of the Wind Band and Wind Ensemble* and an 8-volume series on *Aesthetics in Music*. In addition to numerous modern editions of early wind band music his original compositions include 5 symphonies.

David Whitwell was named as one of six men who have determined the course of American bands during the second half of the 20th century, in the definitive history, *The Twentieth Century American Wind Band* (Meredith Music).

A doctoral dissertation by German Gonzales (2007, Arizona State University) is dedicated to the life and conducting career of David Whitwell through the year 1977. David Whitwell is one of nine men described by Paula A. Crider in *The Conductor's Legacy* (Chicago: GIA, 2010) as 'the legendary conductors' of the 20th century.

'I can't imagine the 2nd half of the 20th century—without David Whitwell and what he has given to all of the rest of us.' Frederick Fennell (1993)

About the Editor

CRAIG DABELSTEIN began studying the piano at age seven and took up the saxophone at age twelve. Mr Dabelstein has Bachelor of Arts (Music) and Bachelor of Music degrees from the Queensland Conservatorium of Music, where he majored in the performance of classical saxophone repertoire. He also has a Graduate Diploma of Learning and Teaching and a Graduate Certificate in Editing and Publishing from the University of Southern Queensland.

He has held the principal alto and tenor saxophone chairs in the Australian Wind Orchestra and has been an augmenting member of the Queensland Philharmonic Orchestra, the Queensland Symphony Orchestra, and the Queensland Pops Orchestra. For many years he was also a member of the Queensland Saxophone Quartet.

He has been a casual conductor of the Young Conservatorium Symphonic Winds, and has previously been a saxophone teacher at the Queensland Conservatorium of Music. He is a regular conductor of the Queensland Wind Orchestra, having served as their artistic director and chief conductor from 2004 to 2009.

Craig Dabelstein is a research associate for the *Teaching Music Through Performance in Band* series of books, contributing analyses to volumes 7, 8, 1 (rev. edn), and the *Solos with Wind Band Accompaniment* volume. He served as the copyeditor and layout designer of the *Australian Clarinet and Saxophone Magazine* from 2007 to 2009 and he has written many CD and book reviews for *Music Forum* magazine. He is the editor of the second editions of the books by Dr. David Whitwell including *A Concise History of the Wind Band*, *Foundations of Music Education*, *Music Education of the Future*, *The Sousa Oral History Project*, *Wagner on Bands*, *Berlioz on Bands*, *The Art of Musical Conducting*, and the *Aesthetics of Music* series (8 volumes) and *The History and Literature of the Wind Band and Wind Ensemble* series (13 volumes). From 1994 to 2012 he was a staff member at Brisbane Girls Grammar School. He now teaches woodwinds and conducts bands at St. Joseph's College, Gregory Terrace, Brisbane, Australia.

www.ingramcontent.com/pod-product-compliance
Lightning Source LLC
Chambersburg PA
CBHW081350230426
43667CB00017B/2776